The Structure of Human Memory

A Series of Books in Psychology

Editors:
Richard C. Atkinson
Jonathan Freedman
Gardner Lindzey
Richard F. Thompson

The Structure of Human Memory

Edited by

Charles N. Cofer

THE PENNSYLVANIA STATE UNIVERSITY

W. H. Freeman and Company
San Francisco

Library of Congress Cataloging in Publication Data

Symposium on the Structure of Human Memory, New York, 1975.
    The structure of human memory.

    Includes bibliographies and index.
    1. Memory—Congresses.   I. Cofer, Charles Norval.
II. Title.   [DNLM: 1. Memory—Congresses.   BF371
S9895s 1975]
BF371.S96 1975   153.1'2   76–2581
ISBN 0–7167–0705–5
ISBN 0–7167–0715–2 pbk.

9 8 7 6 5 4 3 2 1

Contents

Contributors

Daniel G. Bobrow
Xerox Corporation
Palo Alto Research Center
3333 Coyote Hill Road
Palo Alto, California 94304

John P. Brockway
Fachbereich Psychologie
Universitat Konstanz
D-775 Konstanz
Fed. Rep. Germany

Donna L. Chmielewski
Department of Psyschology
North Carolina State University
Raleigh, North Carolina 27607

Charles N. Cofer
Department of Psychology
The Pennsylvania State University
University Park, Pennsylvania 16802

William K. Estes
Department of Psychology
The Rockefeller University
New York, New York 10021

Kevin J. Gilmartin
American Institute for Research
1791 Arastradero Road
(P.O. Box 1113)
Palo Alto, California 94302

Walter Kintsch
Department of Psychology
University of Colorado
Boulder, Colorado 80302

David E. Meyer
Bell Laboratories
Murray Hill, New Jersey 07974

Allen Newell
Department of Psychology
Carnegie-Mellon University
Pittsburgh, Pennsylvania 15213

Donald A. Norman
Department of Psychology
University of California, San Diego
La Jolla, California 92037

Roger C. Schank
Department of Computer Science
Yale University
New Haven, Connecticut 06520

Roger W. Schvaneveldt
Department of Psychology
State University of New York
Stony Brook, New York 11790

Herbert A. Simon
Department of Psychology
Carnegie-Mellon University
Pittsburgh, Pennsylvania 15213

Terry Winograd
Artificial Intelligence Laboratory
Department of Computer Science
Stanford University
Stanford, California 94305

The Structure of Human Memory

1

An Historical Perspective

Charles N. Cofer

The study of memory by psychologists has a long history of experimental work, dating from the publication in 1885 of Hermann Ebbinghaus' monograph, *Memory*. However, consideration of memory has not been solely the province of psychologists. Memory has been a topic of interest to philosophy as early as the time of Plato and Aristotle; to psychiatry and neurology as part of the diagnostic examination; to psychoanalysis as represented in Freud's theory of forgetting as a consequence of repression; to literature as seen in Proust's *Remembrance of Things Past*; and, recently, to computer scientists and students of artificial intelligence, who must provide a "memory" or storage of facts, principles, and operations in order to write programs for complex processing by computer.

It is beyond the scope of this book to deal with memory as it concerns psychiatry, psychoanalysis, and literature. Philosophy does not enter directly either, although the thoughtful reader will discern in these pages a number of philosophical issues, largely in the form of implicit assumptions about memory and the ways in which human beings deal with and represent experience. Representations that endure after an actual experience has ended are, of course, the essence of memory. Memory is the name we give to our ability,

good or poor, to hold in mind both recent experiences and those which consti-
tute our pasts. We remember what we learned in school, what we have read,
what people have said, where we live and work, what we did yesterday and
what we must do today or tomorrow. Of course, a common complaint is that
we do not remember things well; this is one of the reasons for our interest
in memory. Were our memories perfect, never failing us in time of need, we
should probably not concern ourselves with memory at all.

The contributions to this book rest on the assumption that memorial processes can be studied. This assumption has underlain all experimental work
on memory since it was initiated by Ebbinghaus in the years 1879–1880 (see
Ebbinghaus, 1885, p. 33). Yet, in the last quarter century, the problems to
which experimentation has been directed have shifted from those that concerned Ebbinghaus. While his emphasis on careful laboratory procedures and
quantitive methods remains, recent investigators have identified new problems
and devised new techniques for their study. The chapters in this book represent
some of these conceptual and methodological developments. It will be instructive to discuss, in summary form, the concerns of students of memory throughout the history of its experimental study, the methods they have used in
experimentation, and how both those concerns and those methods have altered
as the decades have passed.

The Ebbinghaus Tradition

Ebbinghaus, in the introduction to his monograph (pp. 1–2), referred to certain
effects of memory, which presumably spurred him to study memory. He
pointed out three effects of memory: (a) we can "by an exertion of the will"
recover lost states (i.e., reproduce them); (b) prior states can occur to us
involuntarily (i.e., spontaneously); (c) even without the reproduction of "lost
states," the states continue to have influence—they may govern "a certain
range of thought" and they represent "the boundless domain of the effect of
accumulated experiences. . . ." Ebbinghaus also spoke of the conditions on
which memory depends, referring to differences among individuals and to differences in the contents to be regained. He suggested roles for attentiveness
and interest, as well as for repetition, as conditions of memory. He pointed
out how little was known about memory, and he saw a value in applying the
methods of natural science to its study. Yet, he realized the difficulties. How,
he asked, can we keep "constant the bewildering mass of causal conditions
which, insofar as they are of mental nature, almost completely elude our
control, and which, moreover, are subject to endless and incessant change?"
Further, how can we "measure numerically the mental processes which flit
by so quickly and which on introspection are so hard to analyze?" (pp. 7–8).

Ebbinghaus solved these methodological difficulties by setting up laboratory studies of memory on himself. He standardized conditions, invented materials to be studied, devised a procedure of investigation, and found ways of measuring his results in quantitative form.

The study of memory, as Ebbinghaus realized, is difficult, and he thought to circumvent these difficulties by the means just listed. It is not clear whether he felt that his studies contributed to the solution of the problems he raised in his introductory chapter. At any rate, he did not discuss his findings in relation to those problems.

How did he solve the problems of method he had set forth? Basically, he solved them by studying the retention of associations he acquired under strictly controlled conditions. First, he invented the nonsense syllable, a unit composed of a vowel surrounded by two consonants which was not a three-letter word. He made up over 2300 of these syllables and, for an experiment, assembled some of the syllables into a list to be learned in order from beginning to end. He used lists of varying lengths (e.g., 8 items or 32 items), read through each list a number of times, tested his ability to recite the items in order from memory, and concluded his study of a list when he could recite the items in order without error either once or twice.

As a measure of performance, Ebbinghaus simply counted the number of repetitions it took him to be able to recite the list without error; he also measured the time in seconds required for him to learn lists to this criterion of mastery. With this measure he could compare for difficulty lists of different lengths and could measure their retention over time. To assess retention, he relearned lists; if after a time interval he could relearn a list in fewer repetitions or in less time than had been required for original learning then there was a saving. He used the savings method to study retention or forgetting as well as to examine certain other problems (e.g., the formation of remote associations).

The methods introduced by Ebbinghaus dominated the study of memory (called verbal learning by Meumann as early as 1913) for 65 to 70 years. A basic feature of his methods is that material is presented *de novo* to a person who is to learn or remember it. As Meyer and Schvaneveldt point out in their chapter of this volume, some recent investigations of memory omit this step and use procedures to gain access to what a person already knows. However, before the developments to which Meyer and Schvaneveldt refer occurred, even investigators not sympathetic to the use of nonsense syllables, rote memory, or repetition in studies of memory (such as Bartlett, 1932) presented the to-be-remembered material to their subjects.

We cannot review here all of the work that was conducted in the Ebbinghaus tradition (see McGeoch and Irion, 1952). But the bulk of it was concerned with five main problems: (a) the conditions governing economy in learning; (b) the differences in acquisition and retention occasioned by different sorts of materials, for example poems versus lists of nonsense syllables; (c) differences among people in learning and retention; (d) the conditions and the theory of forgetting; (e) the transfer of training, that is, the extent to which and the conditions under which learning one thing (e.g., one language) affects the learning of another thing (e.g., another language) either positively or negatively. Numerous variations in methods, procedures, and materials were introduced in the course of these various studies but their general tenor remained close to that of Ebbinghaus' work.

The Bartlett Tradition

In 1932 Frederick C. Bartlett reported experiments that deviated in several ways from those of the Ebbinghaus tradition. He did present a passage—a story —but usually only once. He tested for recall of the passage over substantial time intervals. Bartlett opposed the use of repetition and meaningless materials, although his famous story, "The War of the Ghosts," was a version of an Eskimo folk tale and contained a number of unfamiliar elements, such as unusual sequences, supernatural ideas, and actions (e.g., hunting for seals) not common in the experience of his experimental subjects, who were British. He published some of the "recalls" he obtained, and they displayed a great deal of error when compared with the original. They were abbreviated for one thing, but, more dramatically, they contained normalizations of the original content in the direction of making that content more compatible with the subject's knowledge and cultural experience. From these recalls, Bartlett concluded that memory is a schematic process—people remember a general impression of a passage they have read and a few details; out of these components they construct or reconstruct a version which they believe is a fair representation of the original.

Bartlett's findings have received a good deal of citation, but until recently they were not followed up very much by further studies or by theoretical analysis. Most of the work reported in this book is, however, more in his tradition than in the tradition of Ebbinghaus.

Structural Analyses of Memory

That memory may be viewed as a system of interrelated components is a structural idea. It is not an entirely new idea, as William James (1890, 1, pp. 643–648) distinguished between *primary memory*, one that endured for a very brief period of time, and *secondary memory*, "the knowledge of a former state of mind after it has already once dropped from consciousnesss . . ."

(p. 648). Meumann (1913, p. 317) made a similar distinction. Further, there have long been tests of an individual's *memory span*, that is, of the maximum number of digits, letters, isolated words, or words in sentences one can report in order after a single presentation. James' distinction, however, was essentially a phenomenal one, and the concept of memory span has been used mainly to test intelligence, compare the abilities of people of different ages, and study psychological and neurological disorders.

The recent development of structural models of memory was foreshadowed in Miller's (1956) paper. Miller used data from memory-span experiments to show that normal, adult, educated people can repeat back in order an average of only seven digits, letters, or words, despite the different informational loads that these kinds of material carry. He recognized, of course, that we are capable of much better memorial performances than this, and he suggested that the capacity of memory is augmented by coding or recoding devices. For example, we can perhaps remember 25 words rather than 7 if, say, the 25 words include 5 words from each of 5 categories, such as animals, weapons, articles of clothing, names of countries, and names of cities. As we listen to or read the list of words we can recode this input into the category names and, at recall, remembering the category names, produce the instances to which they are related.

In his paper Miller developed the notion of the organism as an information-processing device, with a limited capacity for handling information but with procedures for overcoming, at least to some extent, this limited capacity. Broadbent (1958) introduced an information-processing approach that contained explicitly a short-term memory (STM) of limited capacity. While information resided in this memory, it could be rehearsed and transferred to a more permanent store; alternatively, without rehearsal, it would be lost.

At about this time, Brown (1958), Peterson and Peterson (1959), and Sperling (1960) reported investigations of short-term memory. Peterson and Peterson showed that under certain conditions there is rapid forgetting of subspan items (like nonsense syllables), and Sperling suggested that after very brief visual presentation the information in the visual image is lost very rapidly. It seemed obvious to various writers that these observations required that there be not one but several memories in the human system, a very short-term memory as suggested by Sperling's findings, a short-term memory according to the Brown-Peterson experiments, and a long-term memory (LTM) to accommodate the obvious fact that all of us can and do retain enormous amounts of information over very long time intervals. Models of this kind are represented in Figure 2.1 (p. 18) of the chapter by Gilmartin, Newell, and Simon and in Figure 6.1 (p. 117) of the chapter by Norman and Bobrow.

Short-term memory has received much study over the years since it was first described in the late 1950s, and there has been a great deal of controversy over whether a multiple-component structure of memory is necessary or whether a unitary model of memory is sufficient. This controversy revolves around the question of whether different processes must be postulated for short-term and long-term memories (almost everyone seems to accept the very short-term memory or sensory memory). The issue is complex and the experiments numerous; a full discussion is beyond the scope of this introduction. An alternative to the concept of different processes has been provided by Craik and Lockhart (1972) who analyze different depths of processing.

A major contribution of the work on short-term memory has been the study of the retention of single items (words or syllables) so that the list-learning technique introduced by Ebbinghaus is not necessary. On the other hand, the experimental study of short-term memory has been complex, typically involving the repeated testing of the same individual on different items in an experimental session. Many writers feel that this procedure introduces numerous complications, including interference effects from prior items and strategies employed by the research participants in their efforts to cope with the task. In their chapter, Gilmartin, Newell, and Simon consider explicitly the notion of strategies in the use of short-term memory. We can now summarize their chapter.

As can be seen in Figure 2.1 (p. 18), short-term memory (STM) is intermediate to the sensory stores (iconic, echoic, and the corresponding imagery stores) and long-term memory (LTM). Rather unusual in this model (compare Figure 6.1, p. 117, in Norman and Bobrow's chapter) is the explicit link provided between the imagery stores and LTM; this link provides for recognition of the information in the imagery store and the transfer of an appropriate symbol from LTM into STM. This linkage indicates the importance of LTM to the recognition and identification of items in STM experiments, usually ignored or implicitly assumed in other models. STM is conceived as a limited capacity store, and when new items enter it, the older items are bumped out unless rehearsal has reintroduced them at the front of STM. A grouping process can be employed in rehearsal and a group can be composed of items that are not adjacent in STM.

The components used in strategies are listed on page 22, and a strategy is outlined in Figure 2.4 (see p. 25; see also p. 24). Perhaps the most significant component of this strategy is the decision to rehearse the first two groups. Alternative decisions would have different consequences. Indeed, in the simulations (pp. 27–28), the effects of different decisions with respect to the size of the rehearsal groups can easily be seen.

It appears that Gilmartin et al. have assumed a particular structure for STM but have allowed through strategies various ways in which the processes in STM can be controlled, with varying effects. They propose structural arrangements to represent memory, but, through strategies, they permit a good deal of flexibility. The correspondence between the results of their simulations and the data obtained in experiments with human individuals is striking.

Structural models of memory represent a departure from simple associative models of memory. The latter, seemingly present in the works of such writers as Hobbes, Locke, Hume, and Ebbinghaus, represent the memorial process as a system of paths or chains of association that lead us from a question or some other cue to the answer or fact which memory contains. In his chapter, Estes indicates some of the difficulties that relatively recent research has provided for models stressing chains of associations. He points to the finding of backward associations and to the fact that the grouping of items in different ways (without changing their order or sequence) during the presentation of materials in a learning task makes their acquisition almost impossible.

Perhaps more significant than these findings, according to Estes, were the studies of free recall. This technique, in which a list of items (such as words) is presented one by one, has the essential feature that the subject can recall the items in any order in which they occur to him. Bousfield (1953) showed that if a set of words, each belonging to one of several mutually exclusive categories, is presented in random order, subjects tend to recall them, not in the order of presentation, but in groups or clusters of categorically related items. It is as if the instances are coded or recoded into category representations. One can think of these representations as occupying a level in a hierarchy higher than the instances themselves (as might be seen in a two-level tree structure, for example). The findings with the free-recall method accorded well with Miller's (1956) analysis of recoding, which, as he said, could occur at several levels. Mandler (1967, 1968) verified the plausibility of this sort of analysis in his empirical studies of free recall (see, also, Tulving, 1968).

Estes has tried to specify in his chapter (see, also, Estes, 1972) a reformulation of association theory that can account for some of these phenomena. His central idea is that when two events are experienced together they become associated with a *control element*. Further, control elements themselves can be associated with other control elements, so that a hierarchical structure can be built. Thus, in the presentation of a string of 12 letters segmented into groups of 3, we might have a structure like the following (Estes, 1972, p. 185):

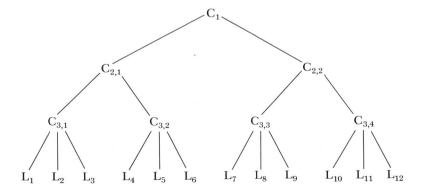

In this diagram, L stands for a letter and C stands for control elements; the representation of the grouping is obvious. For reasons given in his chapter, and elsewhere, Estes believes that, within a general associative framework, his model can deal with grouping (or chunking), memory for the frequencies with which events occur, and information about the temporal order in which events occur. Explanations for some of these memorial capacities are not obvious in other theories. However, Estes does not propose that his hierarchical association model can handle everything, and he suggests that there may be levels of memory theory corresponding to different phenomena.

Structural accounts of memory can be more complex than those we have considered so far. For example, it may be desirable to subdivide the long-term-memory component already mentioned. Tulving (1972) made such a suggestion, pointing out that in our long-term memories we have available to us knowledge of the episodes in our pasts as well as knowledge of rules, facts, principles, and the like which have an existence independent of our own personal pasts. He suggested the terms *episodic memory* and *semantic memory* for these two classes of knowledge. One might distinguish them in the following way. My knowledge of how to take the square root of a number is representative of knowledge that is independent of me as an individual; it is part of arithmetic, a system of rules which anyone can learn. However, my memory or knowledge of having learned this skill—where and by whom it was taught to me or in what book I studied it—is more or less unique; it is a memory of an event or events that occurred in a time or place in my past. The rules for finding a square root are part of semantic memory; the remembrance of where, when, and how I learned those rules is part of episodic memory.

Tulving stressed differences between these two sorts of memories. One difference is that semantic memory is productive or generative, whereas episodic memory is not. Thus, I can apply the rules for taking a square root to any number, or my knowledge of the rules for alphabetizing words to any words. Memory for episodes does not have this character. There are, no doubt, parts of semantic memory which are not productive or generative either, like knowledge I may have of the succession of Presidents of the United States or of the sequence of the Kings and Queens of England. But much knowledge in semantic memory is potentially generative. This feature of semantic memory is elaborated to a large extent in the chapters summarized in the next section.

The chapter by Meyer and Schvaneveldt, however, represents another way of looking at semantic memory. These authors have measured reaction times for the verification of the truth or falsity of certain kinds of sentences and for the recognition or identification of words in various contexts. Performance in tasks like these is highly accurate, but consistent reaction-time differences do appear. Meyer and Schvaneveldt follow a view of the structural organization of semantic memory introduced by Quillian (1968; see Collins and

Quillian, 1969). The basic idea is that words are organized in memory some-what as in a thesaurus, with words of similar meaning located near one another and with a hierarchical principle encompassing levels of abstractness or generality.

The data seem to support the notions of loci of storage and hierarchical organization (but see Conrad, 1972). However, the effects of preceding context on word-recognition latency indicate that word encoding and access as well as comprehension of relations are affected by the organization of the meaningful relations among the items. The model diagrammed in Figure 4.9 (p. 73) provides an integration of Meyer and Schvaneveldt's findings.

Memory in Complex Functions

Most of what has been said so far has concerned short- or long-term memory for individual items and lists of items, although, as noted, the chapter by Meyer and Schvaneveldt deviates from the dominant research methods of the prior sections, and Bartlett's work was carried out with stories. The remaining chapters of this volume are concerned with complex processes. Kintsch's studies were conducted with meaningful passages as were those reported by Cofer, Chmielewski, and Brockway. Winograd and Schank are concerned with memory in the processing of language. Norman and Bobrow discuss a model for complex processes and use the idea of the schema, the concept introduced to the study of memory by Bartlett. It is probably fair to say that the chapters discussed in this section are closer to Bartlett's tradition than to that of Ebbinghaus and that structural matters, while not ignored, are less salient than they are to the chapters discussed in the preceding section.

Perhaps the simplest way to introduce this section is to say that the authors of chapters 5 through 9 examine the knowledge that people have with which an input, such as a story, factual passage, or conversation, interacts. Further, there is a recognition that the person who is asked to perform in a memorial situation is an active participant in it; he or she judges what the demands of the situation are and develops strategies and marshals resources to deal with those demands.

Ebbinghaus attempted to exclude past knowledge from his experiments by using nonsense syllables. Bartlett stressed the role of knowledge and of the effort after meaning, using passages that deviated from ordinary knowledge so that normalizing processes could be observed. However, Bartlett gave few specifications with respect to the knowledge engaged by a passage, contenting himself with the notion of the schema.

Since the mid 1960s, however, a growing body of literature has begun to articulate and to expand a view of memory compatible with Bartlett's views. A major impetus to this formulation came from the Chomskian revolution in linguistics, with its important distinction between the surface structures or appearances of sentences and their underlying structures. While Chomsky's (1957, 1965) emphasis on syntax and transformational rules was important, it is clear that what we remember after a single reading or hearing of material tends rather to be its sense, its gist, what it is about. Thus Sachs (1967) was able to show that memory for the form of sentences does not persist very long, whereas memory for semantic relations persists longer (see, also, Jarvella, 1971). Further, in certain situations, people make errors in their memorial performances, these errors being systematic in kind. Pompi and Lachman (1967) found that recognition errors were consistent with the themes of the material that had been studied. Bransford and Franks (1971) showed that subjects would judge an integrative sentence as actually having been presented when, in fact, only its component ideas had been read to the subjects. A set of references pertinent to this work on memory is given in the chapter by Cofer et al., and Kintsch's chapter also provides several examples.

Observations such as these can indicate that meaningful input engages a portion of a person's knowledge and initiates activities or processes which (a) integrate that input with existing knowledge, (b) fill in gaps or information missing from the input, and (c) provide contexts in terms of which the information taken in can be remembered. A fully developed theory along these lines is not yet available, but the remaining papers in this book contribute information and ideas pertinent to such a theory.

Kintsch represents the meaning of a passage or text by means of text bases, that is, lists of propositions. He clearly calls upon knowledge of the world for the rules employed in forming propositions, and the reader of a passage employed in one of Kintsch's experiments must have a good deal of knowledge in order to comprehend it and perform as requested. In his chapter, however, Kintsch does not explore or assess the nature of the knowledge necessary. His interests lie elsewhere. How well is reproductive memory correlated with characteristics of texts as represented in text bases? How much and under what conditions do subjects add to a text from their general knowledge at recall or during the initial reading of the passage? Do they infer and add events to a pictorial representation of events as well as to a verbal text? What is the overall character (the macrostructure or the schema) of a narrative? Does this macrostructure serve the reader in her or his recall? Is it useful in writing abstracts of the communication? Kintsch's chapter presents empirical answers to all of these questions. Memory is related to the text-base representation, but subjects do add material from general knowledge under some conditions. They make inferences with respect to both verbal and pictorial presentations of materials. Macrostructures for narratives can be described, and they do serve the person in memorial and abstract-writing tasks.

Norman and Bobrow provide a structural description of cognitive processing, including of course, memory, and their model is designed to integrate the phenomena of attention, perception, memory, and cognition. In working toward this goal, they reject the linear processing models (illustrated in Figure 6.1, p. 117) which have been prominent in information-processing models. Rather, they wish to provide for a much more unified or integrated system (as do Gilmartin et al., to some extent). Thus, for example, Norman and Bobrow maintain that attentional and perceptual operations can be driven by schemata (a top-down analysis) as well as being activated by sensory input itself (bottom-up analysis). They give examples of both directions of processing in the case of the identification of a face and its components, showing, among other things, that to the extent that the prevailing schema is one for a face and that the contextual information is suggestive of a face, the identification of the component parts requires little detail or can be achieved even when the components have the form of other objects. They consider processing principles and means of gaining access to schemata through the proposal of context-dependent descriptions. They apply their ideas to the notion of depth of processing and to the phenomenon of autonomous or subconscious problem solving.

Memory is an important component of computer systems because programs must be able to store information for use as needed in performing the many tasks researchers undertake with computers. In his chapter, Winograd describes some notions about memory that people who work with computers and computer programs have developed. He considers memorial elements, how they are accessed, and how they provide recall, giving examples for recall from relatively simple organizations of memory. However, complex arrangements, including hierarchies, are possible. Winograd does not suggest that existing structures for handling memory in computer systems can simulate all human memorial functions; rather, he suggests that thinking about human memory can benefit from the experience and suggestions of those who must provide arrangements for memory in computer systems.

Schank is concerned with the processing and understanding of language, and his chapter is divided, essentially, into two parts. In the first, he analyzes examples to demonstrate that a sentence cannot be understood unless one knows what it is about as well as some rules of inference for determining what has been left out. The use of inference, Schank says, is required because the overt expression of a sentence seldom, if ever, includes all the information necessary to its understanding. Schank lists a set of inference classes.

In the second part of his chapter, Schank discusses memory in relation to sentence processing, having demonstrated that memory is essential to that activity. He suggests that memorial representations are formed according to his conceptual-dependency analysis in which the role of action is central (a list of primitive actions is provided), and he regards the memory of events as being composed of linked chains of such conceptualizations, rejecting the structure of semantic memory central to the work of Meyer and Schvaneveldt.

Schank says that memory is "a morass of episodes" (p. 180); however, episodes can become generalized. Then they are inferences. In addition, in memory there are "scripts;" a script is "a giant causal chain of conceptualizations that have been known to occur in that order many times before" (p. 180). Scripts set up expectations as to what will happen. Further, there are "plans," which are like scripts except that they are used frequently because they are attached to goals. All of these concepts are used to represent knowledge in memory, the central problem, as Schank sees it, in understanding language.

The chapter by Cofer et al. is also concerned with knowledge. However, their purpose is to describe the knowledge with which a prose passage makes contact, and they have developed a method that they think bypasses the accuracy constraint under which people tend to operate when they attempt to recall something from memory. In using their generated-statements procedure, their underlying purpose is to attempt to resolve the conflict in the literature that has arisen between abstractive views of reproductive memory and constructive accounts of memory. It is their belief that many prose passages used in memory experiments do activate substantial amounts of related knowledge and that whether the resulting recall will be accurate or inaccurate will depend upon a number of conditions (see Brockway, Chmielewski, and Cofer, 1974, pp. 195–196 and 207–208). Among these conditions are the *operations* that a person may use with respect to the knowledge activated to generate an indefinitely large number of pertinent statements. Since these statements are potential (their number perhaps depending on the size of the knowledge set activated by a passage), accurate recall depends on a person's ability to differentiate between his pertinent knowledge and that which was actually in the input.

Summary

It is clear that the studies presented in this book do not respect the tradition of Ebbinghaus and that most of them do accord in a general way with Bartlett's views. The authors have focused their research on knowledge (or long-term memory or semantic memory) and have emphasized a more integrated memorial system than has often been envisaged in structural models of memory. They are concerned, by and large, with the use of existing knowledge in memorial tasks or with the interaction between that knowledge and those tasks. They have not dealt to any great extent with the acquisition of knowledge or with its development over the life span. The Ebbinghaus tradition was concerned with the acquisition of knowledge, albeit with adults in limited laboratory conditions and with impoverished materials. How knowledge is acquired in the child and in the adult, and how that acquisition is affected by and in turn affects the existing knowledge structures are problems of supreme importance that require further investigation.

With respect to questions concerning the structure of memory, most of the authors of the papers in this book seem to accept structural arrangements. However, structure is not regarded as "something given, something fixed, erected inside the brain in all its complexity, like a Gothic cathedral sitting in a town square" (Kintsch, 1974, p. 23). Rather, there is provision for inter-action of parts, for nonlinear orders of processing, and for restructuring in the light of task demands and contextual conditions. The structural idea is a convenient metaphor, perhaps more congenial to the thought processes of the investigator (influenced as she or he may be by analogies with libraries, ency-clopedias, the thesaurus, and dictionaries) than descriptive of actual memorial functioning in the individual.

REFERENCES

Bartlett, F. C. *Remembering*. Cambridge: Cambridge University Press, 1932.
Bousfield, W. A. The occurrence of clustering the recall of randomly arranged asso-ciates. *Journal of General Psychology*, 1953, *49*, 229–240.
Bransford, J. D., and Franks, J. J. The abstraction of linguistic ideas. *Cognitive Psy-chology*, 1971, *2*, 331–350.
Broadbent, D. E. *Perception and communication*. London: Pergamon, 1958.
Brockway, J., Chmielewski, D., and Cofer, C. N. Remembering prose: Productivity and accuracy constraints in recognition memory. *Journal of Verbal Learning and Verbal Behavior*, 1974, *13*, 194–208.
Brown, J. Some tests of the decay theory of immediate memory. *Quarterly Journal of Experimental Psychology*, 1958, *10*, 12–21.
Chomsky, N. *Syntactic structures*. The Hague: Mouton, 1957.
Chomsky, N. *Aspects of the theory of syntax*. Cambridge, Mass.: M.I.T. Press, 1965.
Collins, A. M., and Quillian, M. R. Retrieval time from semantic memory. *Journal of Verbal Learning and Verbal Behavior*, 1969, *8*, 240–247.
Conrad, C. Cognitive economy in semantic memory. *Journal of Experimental Psy-chology*, 1972, *92*, 149–154.
Craik, F. I. M., and Lockhart, R. S. Levels of processing: A framework for memory research. *Journal of Verbal Learning and Verbal Behavior*, 1972, *11*, 671–684.
Ebbinghaus, H. *Memory* (H. A. Ruger and C. E. Bussenius, trans.). New York: Teachers College, 1913. Reprint. New York: Dover, 1964. (Originally published in 1885.)
Estes, W. K. An associative basis for coding and organization in memory. In A. W. Melton and E. Martin (Eds.), *Coding processes in human memory*. Washington, D.C.: Winston, 1972.
James, W. *The principles of psychology* (2 vols.). New York: Henry Holt, 1890.
Jarvella, R. J. Syntactic processing of connected speech. *Journal of Verbal Learning and Verbal Behavior*, 1971, *10*, 409–416.

Kintsch, W. *The representation of meaning in memory*. Hillsdale, N.J.: Erlbaum, 1974.

Mandler, G. Organization and memory. In K. W. Spence and J. T. Spence (Eds.), *The psychology of learning and motivation*, (Vol. 1). New York: Academic Press, 1967.

Mandler, G. Association and organization: Facts, fancies, and theories. In T. R. Dixon and D. L. Horton (Eds.), *Verbal behavior and general behavior theory*. Englewood Cliffs, N.J.: Prentice-Hall, 1968.

McGeoch, J. A., and Irion, A. L. *The psychology of human learning*. New York: Longmans, Green, 1952.

Meumann, E. [*The psychology of learning: An experimental investigation of the economy and technique of learning*] (J. W. Baird, trans.) New York: D. Appleton, 1913. (Originally published in 1912.)

Miller, G. A. The magical number seven, plus or minus two: Some limits on our capacity for processing information. *Psychological Review*, 1956, *63*, 81–97.

Peterson, L. R., and Peterson, M. J. Short-term retention of individual items. *Journal of Experimental Psychology*, 1959, *58*, 193–198.

Pompi, K. E., and Lachman, R. Surrogate processes in the short-term retention of connected discourse. *Journal of Experimental Psychology*, 1967, *75*, 143–150.

Quillian, M. R. Semantic memory. In M. Minsky (Ed.), *Semantic information processing*. Cambridge, Mass.: M.I.T. Press, 1968.

Sachs, J. Recognition memory for syntactic and semantic aspects of connected discourse. *Perception and Psychophysics*, 1967, *2*, 437–442.

Sperling, G. The information available in brief visual presentations. *Psychological Monographs*, 1960, *74*, No. 11.

Tulving, E. Theoretical issues in free recall. In T. R. Dixon and D. L. Horton (Eds.), *Verbal behavior and general behavior theory*. Englewood Cliffs, N.J.: Prentice-Hall, 1968.

Tulving, E. Episodic and semantic memory. In E. Tulving and W. Donaldson (Eds.), *Organization of memory*. New York: Academic Press, 1972.

2

A Program Modeling
Short-Term Memory
Under Strategy Control

Kevin J. Gilmartin, Allen Newell,
and Herbert A. Simon

The model described in this paper is an information-processing model of human memory that derives its flexibility of performance from strategies controlling the use of its memory stores and processing time. More generally, this discussion is concerned with the strategy of using strategies as intervening variables between task environments and performance.

Role of Strategies

We hold as a basic assumption that the behaviors humans will show in a task environment depend on the strategies they use. The qualitative and quantitative differences in performance between subjects are due in part to differences in their strategies for processing the information available to them;

Research reported in this chapter was supported in part by Research Grant MH-07722 from the National Institute of Mental Health and in part by the Advanced Research Projects Agency of the Office of the Secretary of Defense (F-44620-73-C-0074) which is monitored by the Air Force Office of Scientific Research.

the changes in a particular subject's performance as he becomes experienced at a task are largely due to progressive changes in his strategies. In fact, what psychologists refer to as an "experienced subject" is someone who has explored the effects of using various strategies in a particular task environment and who has discovered and acquired strategies that lead to effective performance.

If a model of memory derives flexibility from using strategies for accomplishing its basic processes of encoding, storage, and retrieval, then we can try to apply that model to explain the effects on behavior of changes in task instructions as well as to explain how a subject is able to act upon a suggestion for performing the task better. By viewing changes in performance as reflecting changes in strategy, we can ask how and why the strategy changes as the task environment changes. In this way we can explore the correspondence between the processing demands of a task and the strategies for its optimal performance.

A body of knowledge about this correspondence between tasks and optimal strategies for humans could, in turn, serve as the groundwork for two related projects: first, it could provide the basis for classifying tasks in terms of the types of information processing used by experienced subjects while performing them (as opposed to a classification in terms of the types of stimuli presented and the types of responses required); and second, it could enable researchers to develop the ability to decompose a task into a number of basic information-processing requirements and, from that analysis, to predict the strategies that would allow best task performance. This latter ability, if sufficiently developed, would make it possible to suggest how new equipment should be designed to best fit the information-processing limitations of humans and how operators should be trained to perform new tasks (i.e., in what strategies they should be trained to increase efficiency and decrease errors).

To summarize, we believe that there are certain advantages to making the source of flexibility in models of human performance more like what we assume to be the source of flexibility in humans. In particular, we postulate flexibility in strategies, within relatively fixed constraints of a memory model, as opposed to postulating variation from task to task in the size of short-term memory, the basic write-time of long-term memory, and other structural parameters.

Background

The approach we describe here is not a new one, but it is a relatively neglected one in investigations of short-term memory. Much of the research on memory using standard paradigms is done without even postulating what processes subjects use to perform the tasks assigned. To find the antecedents of our approach one must generally look at the studies of more active cognitive tasks.

Bruner, Goodnow, and Austin (1956) developed in some depth the concept of strategies for performing a task. In their classic book on concept attainment, they explored the effects that various strategies would have on the utilization of information, the memory load, and the probability of failing to identify a concept. Bruner et al., defined a strategy as being a regularity in decision making: "The phrase 'strategies of decision making' is not meant in a meta-phorical sense. A strategy refers to a pattern of decisions in the acquisition, retention, and utilization of information that serves to meet certain objectives, i.e., to insure certain forms of outcome and to insure against certain others" (p. 54).

Atkinson and Shiffrin (1968) discussed various types of strategies used by subjects while performing a memory task, including control processes in the sensory registers, in short-term memory, and in long-term memory. They defined a control process as a process that is not a permanent feature of memory but is instead a transient phenomenon under the control of the subject. Atkinson and Shiffrin suggested that it might be fruitful to classify experiments in terms of the control processes the subjects would be led to use. However, in their work, the concept of control process was used simply to let the scientist formulate and fit separate models for separate situations.

Recently we (Newell and Simon, 1972) made a comprehensive examination of the methods subjects use to solve various types of problems. By analyzing thinking-aloud protocols, we were able to describe a subject's strategy for performing a task as being composed of a fixed set of elementary information processes that are evoked by both aspects of the external environment and the internal representation of the problem. The problems that we asked our subjects to perform were much more complex than the typical task in a short-term memory experiment, and consequently, the "elementary" processes that we isolated during our 1972 investigation are at a higher level than the primitive processing components in the model to be described here. Never-theless, the methods used to solve problems in that examination are similar to the strategies in this model of short-term memory: both are major inter-vening variables between task environments and behavior.

The Model SHORT

Our particular model of short-term memory (STM) is a computer program written in SNOBOL, which has been named SHORT. It represents a theory of how humans use STM, and, to a lesser extent, how they use long-term memory (LTM) and the sensory-related buffers during common STM tasks.

SHORT is not simply a theory of how STM tasks are performed; it is able to perform several of those tasks itself and can be tested under various experimental conditions as though it were a subject. The SHORT model is entirely deterministic, with no probability functions built into any of its processes. Only the generation of stimuli and the subsequent presentation of these stimuli to the model during a simulation can be at all random.

The structure that SHORT assumes is shown in Figure 2.1. The memory stores are LTM, STM, and two buffers in series for each sensory modality (a sensory store and an imagery store). When an item is presented auditorily or visually to SHORT, it is automatically registered in the appropriate sensory store: echoic memory or iconic memory. The literature indicates that humans rapidly lose information from the sensory stores as a function of time: information in the visual sensory store persists for a total duration of 250 msec (Averbach and Coriell, 1961) to 500 msec or more (Sperling, 1960), while information in the auditory sensory store lasts for at least 3 or 4 seconds, even with interference (Glucksberg and Cowen, 1970; Darwin, Turvey, and Crowder, 1972). SHORT is constructed so that when a stimulus is terminated, that stimulus persists for 250 msec in the visual sensory store and for 3 seconds in the auditory sensory store. When SHORT accesses a sensory store, part or all of the information in that store is copied into the imagery store in the same

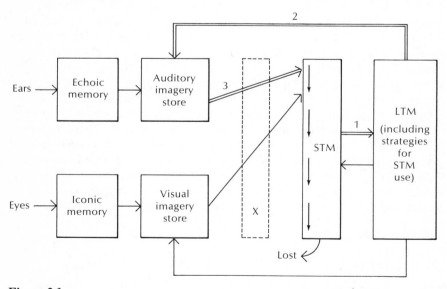

Figure 2.1

The memory stores and the flow of information between them in SHORT. Arrows 1, 2, and 3 represent the flow of information during implicit auditory rehearsal; X represents the process of recognition or perception which has access to information in LTM.

modality. The contents of an imagery store are assumed to be closely related to the encoding of the physical characteristics of the stimulus. The process of perception (recognition) consists of a search for a match between the patterns of information in an imagery store and the patterns previously stored in LTM. If a match is found, a symbol denoting the corresponding entry in LTM is placed in STM. Figure 2.2 represents the contents of STM (a) immediately before, and (b) immediately after a pattern is recognized; the contents of LTM are unchanged by the operation, and therefore LTM is not represented in Figure 2.2b. In Figures 2.2 and 2.3, an asterisk is the first character of the symbols in STM. This convention is used to indicate that theoretically there is no relation between the structure of a symbol in STM and the physical characteristics of the pattern it denotes. The symbols in STM are the internal names of entries in LTM.

In our model, STM is a linear array of 8 cells, each of which can hold a single symbol, or chunk. The size of STM was set at 8 cells because that value produced a span of STM, in the immediate-recall paradigm, of 5–6 chunks, the normal span for adults. The rest of the capacity of STM is occupied by various kinds of control information—place keepers or symbols that indicate the status of some part of the system. Relatively few types of such control symbols are used in SHORT.

SHORT incorporates a first-in-first-out displacement theory of STM. That is, whenever a new symbol is placed in STM, it causes the oldest symbol in STM to be lost. Symbols entered at one end of STM move to adjacent cells down the length of STM and are finally bumped out of, and lost from, the back end of STM as newer items displace them.

Items can be retained indefinitely in STM only by rehearsal, that is, by inserting a new copy of the item at the front of STM. Items in STM can be grouped for rehearsal; the grouping scheme is part of the system's strategy for performing a particular task. Items that are assigned to the same rehearsal group are not contiguously grouped together in adjacent cells, but rather each one has an associated label that specifies that it is a member of a particular group. In Figure 2.2, some of the symbols in STM are tagged with the digit 1 or 2 to indicate membership in the first or second rehearsal group. An item can be assigned to one of three groups: although some subjects report dividing strings of items into more than three groups in STM (Anders, 1971), most do not, and hence SHORT has been limited to three rehearsal groups in STM. Of course, an item may not be assigned to any rehearsal group, but in that case it will not be rehearsed and will eventually be lost. All searching, or scanning, in STM is from back to front; the basic operation, called NEXT CHUNK, moves attention to the next symbol toward the front of STM (see Figure 2.2). There is evidence (Anders, 1971, 1973) that for short sequences of items humans search STM from the oldest items toward the newest items in this way. As part of its strategy for performing the task, SHORT can rehearse

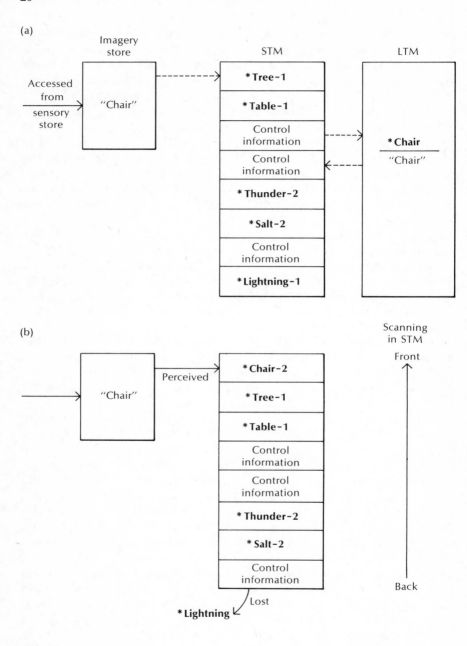

Figure 2.2
The structure of STM in SHORT (a) before and (b) after a new item has been perceived. **Asterisks** indicate internal names of entries in LTM; digits are rehearsal group tags.

a particular group of items, or it can start at the back of STM, search for the first occurrence of any symbol associated with a group, and then rehearse that group. Rehearsal is a three-step process. (The flow of information during implicit auditory rehearsal is indicated in Figure 2.1 by the numbered double arrows.) First, a symbol in STM is used to access the corresponding entry in LTM (so the symbols designating entries in LTM may be thought of as addresses or pointers). Second, stored at that entry in LTM is information about the chunk, its relations to other chunks, and so on. There may also be stored at that entry small programs for saying and writing the chunk if it has an external name and for imaging the chunk visually or auditorily. The program for imaging places into an imagery store a pattern of information identical to the information that would be in that imagery store if the item had just been entered from the external environment. That is, the act of imaging sets up symbol patterns in an imagery store that are related to the physical characteristics of the item as a stimulus. Third, this pattern in the imagery store can be reperceived, and a new symbol denoting it can be placed in the front of STM, completing the process of rehearsal. Thus, as is indicated in Figure 2.3, rehearsal involves (1) accessing an entry in LTM, (2) imaging the pattern designated, and (3) reperception.

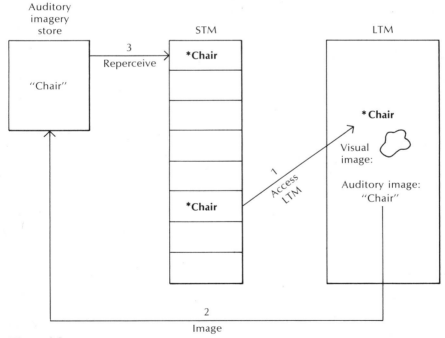

Figure 2.3
Three-step rehearsal in SHORT. An **asterisk** indicates the internal name of an entry in LTM.

All of the major processes in the model (accessing the contents of a sensory store, perception or recognition, accessing LTM, imaging, outputting an item) are charged time on a simulated clock. This accounting for time limits SHORT to roughly the same amount of processing per second as a human is able to do: SHORT can rehearse 4.0 single-syllable items, or 2.9 two-syllable items, in a second.

Construction of Strategies

The behavior of SHORT on a particular task depends on its strategy for performing that task. A strategy comprises knowledge in LTM of the task requirements and a set of decision processes for managing the information in STM. Some of the decision processes that might be specified in a strategy are: the way that items will be grouped for rehearsal, which groups to rehearse when, whether to ignore some of the items as they are presented or to process them all, how to search STM and LTM when it is time to respond.

The following is a list of the major processes used in SHORT's strategies.

1. Access a sensory store
2. Perceive the contents of an imagery store
3. Assign an item to a rehearsal group
4. Rehearse an item
5. Rehearse a group of items
6. Rehearse the oldest group of items
7. Search STM for a control symbol
8. Access an entry in LTM
9. Search LTM
10. Image a pattern
11. Output an item
12. Output a group of items

There are also a few more specialized processes that would not be used in every task; one example is the process of recoding digits into a number and vice versa. New strategies are constructed from these basic components. The possible strategies for SHORT are limited to the various ways that the processes can be combined.

When we use SHORT to simulate performance on a particular task, we assume that the subject being simulated employs a strategy that would perform the task as well as possible. That is, the simulation assumes adaptive behavior in the subject and, hence, does not take the strategy as a free parameter to be fitted to the observed behavior. This gives us a certain advantage over many other models of STM. Most models are adjusted on each task to mimic human performance as closely as possible, thus serving mainly a descriptive role.

Often the constraints built into a model are not sufficient to prevent it from outperforming humans or performing qualitatively differently from humans. On the other hand, with SHORT we have searched for those strategies that perform a task best, and then we have compared SHORT's behavior using those strategies to human behavior. This allows us to note those cases where the proper constraints have not been built into the model, where it is possible for the model to outperform humans, or where the optimal strategies lead to behavior qualitatively different from human behavior. SHORT is vulnerable to being disproved. When SHORT outperforms humans at some task, either the subjects could be taught to improve their performances by using SHORT's strategy for performing the task, or else the model is, at least partially, wrong.

LTM is represented in SHORT in a rudimentary way, consisting for the most part of only unlabeled associations. Two chunks that are being rehearsed together may be consolidated as a new entry in LTM. As soon as one act of consolidation is complete, the next two chunks to be rehearsed consecutively will be used for the next consolidation. Consolidation continues to completion even if the pair of chunks is lost from STM during the consolidation period. The process of consolidation occurs over a period of time, but it does not reduce the system's processing capacity; it is assumed that consolidation is performed concurrently with the other ongoing processes.

We have looked at a number of studies where, for various reasons, it can be assumed that recall is from LTM, not STM, and we have calculated from the subjects' performance the average time needed to consolidate a new entry in LTM. Almost all estimates are in the range of 7–10 seconds per consolidation, and most estimates are in the range of 8–9 seconds. SHORT has therefore been set to require 8 seconds to consolidate a new entry in LTM.

Experimental Tests of SHORT

SHORT, as a model, predicts a wide range of experimental findings and has been run formally in a number of simulations. The tasks that have been simulated are the STM-span paradigm, forward serial recall of supraspan lists, backward serial recall, single presentation of short lists of paired associates, and the Peterson and Peterson paradigm with a distractor task (Gilmartin, 1975). These simulations have included variations in the presentation rate, the stimulus material, the modality of presentation, the delay of the respond signal, as well as in the strategy used to perform a particular task.

SHORT does very well simulating most of these tasks. However, it may be instructive to discuss some simulations where discrepancies between model and data (as well as matches between the two) were visible. In the experiment in question we analyzed simulations of forward serial recall of words presented visually and auditorily with variations in the strategy for performing the task.

SHORT's performance was qualitatively different from the human data in some respects, raising questions about the model and about the limitations in human performance. During forward serial recall, a supraspan sequence of items is presented once, after which the subject is asked to recall the items in the order in which they were presented. In our experimental simulations, the sequences were composed of 9 words from SHORT's repertoire, presented at the rate of 1/sec with a duration of .5 seconds for each item. In the first set of simulations, presentation was visual, the response signal following the offset of the last item by .5 seconds.

The strategy SHORT used to perform the forward serial recall task with visual presentation is listed below (translated from SNOBOL into English), and the same strategy is represented as a flow diagram in Figure 2.4.

1. Wait until the first item is presented, testing for the presence of a stimulus every 100 msec.
2. Access the sensory store and perceive the stimulus, entering the item in STM.
3. Is this the signal to respond? If so, output the first two rehearsal groups; output the last group, indicating that it is at the end of the list, and stop.
4. Rehearse whichever of the first two rehearsal groups has a member nearest the back of STM.
5. Has a new item been presented? If so, go to 2, if not, go to 4.

The number of items assigned to each of the rehearsal groups can affect the shape of the serial position curve. The serial position curve is the proportion of items recalled at each of the nine positions in the presented sequences. Since only the first two groups are being rehearsed in this strategy, it is the size of those groups that affects performance. The visually presented forward serial recall task was simulated three times, with the number of items in each of the first two rehearsal groups specified to be 2-2, 3-2, and 2-3, respectively. Each simulation consisted of 50 trials. The resulting serial position curves are presented in Figure 2.5. Trials were scored as free recall even though SHORT was "told" that recall had to be in serial order. The mean number of words recalled in the three simulations was 4.56, 5.26, and 5.02, respectively. Jahnke (1965), who scored forward serial recall in the same manner, reported for human subjects means of 4.6 words recalled for lists of both 6 and 10 words.

It can be seen that the 2-2 grouping of the first two rehearsal groups leads to poorer performance than the 3-2 grouping or the 2-3 grouping. This is because a strategy to rehearse only four items underestimates the capacity of STM; when an attempt is made to rehearse five items, an average of at least .5 item more is recalled from the first two groups.

We have found that, on the average, SHORT's performance is just a little better than the reported human performance. The greatest discrepancy between SHORT's performance and human performance on this task occurs at

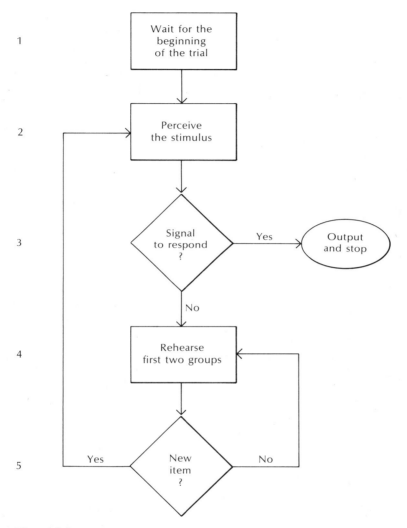

Figure 2.4
The strategy used by SHORT to perform forward serial recall.

the last serial position. As is evident in Figure 2.6, humans show little or no recency effect during forward serial recall of visually presented lists (e.g., Jahnke, 1965; Conrad and Hull, 1968; Craik, 1969); SHORT can always report the last item in a list by perceiving the later items in the list without rehearsing them. An alternative strategy is to ignore the later items in the list. Although this increases recall at the early serial positions somewhat, total

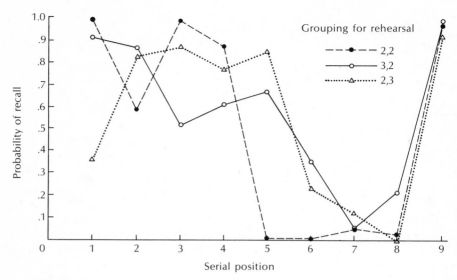

Figure 2.5
Simulation of forward serial recall of words presented visually at 1/sec.

recall is lower. It is curious that humans do not report one of the last items presented in each list; possibly if they were taught to do so it would improve their overall performance. In any case, this is an instance where the class of strategies that lead to the best performance of the task by SHORT causes the program to perform in a qualitatively different manner than an average human subject.

The next two simulations involve forward serial recall after auditory, instead of visual, presentation of items. The sequence length and the rate and duration of item presentation are unchanged. The strategy for recall with auditory presentation is slightly different from the strategy for recall following visual presentation, the change in strategy having the effect of accessing the auditory sensory store during recall before the information in it decays. When the response signal is perceived and the first group is output, leaving some space in STM where additional items can be stored, the contents of the auditory sensory store are accessed and perceived before the second and third groups are output from STM.

In Figure 2.7, the results from two simulations after auditory presentation are compared to the results following visual presentation. The grouping scheme for rehearsal, 3 items in the first group and 2 in the second, was the same in all three cases.

The first "auditory" simulation was equivalent to the "visual" simulation, with the response signal being presented .5 seconds after the termination of the last item. The resulting serial position curve shows a modality effect, that is, better recall of the final items on the list following auditory presentation. While there is a discrepancy between SHORT's performance and human performance at the last serial position following visual presentation, their levels of performance are similar following auditory presentation (see Figure 2.6).

One usual difference between auditory and visual presentation, other than the modality, is that the response signal follows the last item in visual presentation, but is often simultaneous with the last item in auditory presentation (the experimenter's voice drops on the last item). This earlier response signal should allow more of the contents of the auditory sensory store to be accessed before decaying, producing a larger modality effect. In the second auditory simulation, the response signal was presented simultaneously with the last item. As predicted, this produced an even larger recency effect. However, it was not foreseen that this increase would be at the expense of the middle serial positions. When the last item and the response signal are both entered into STM at the same time, there is a higher probability of an item being

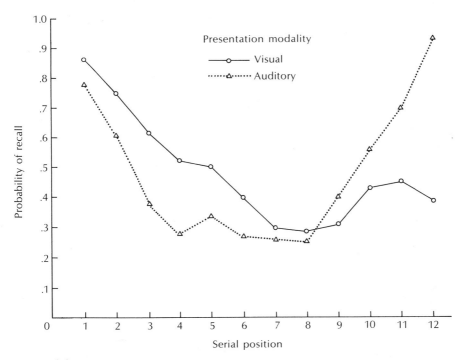

Figure 2.6
Forward serial recall of words presented at 1/sec, after Craik (1969) Exp. I.

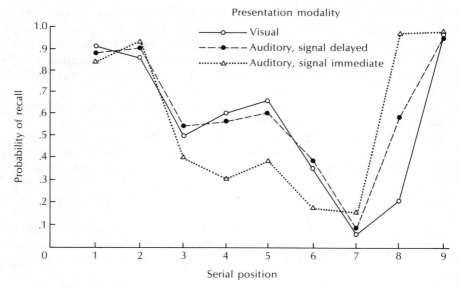

Figure 2.7
Simulation of forward serial recall of words presented at 1/sec.

lost from STM than when the last item is entered into STM, followed by a period of rehearsal, and then the response signal is entered into STM. It is interesting to note that in some studies that compare recall by humans after visual and auditory presentation, recall is slightly better over the first half of the list following visual presentation, while the recency effect is much larger following auditory presentation (Murdock, 1966; Craik, 1969).

Conclusion

We would like to summarize what we believe to be some of the advantages of postulating strategies as genuine variables that intervene between task environments and performance:

1. Strategies can be specified in psychologically meaningful terms, that is, in terms of processes that we believe humans use, such as perceiving, rehearsing, and searching through STM and LTM.

2. We should be able to train subjects to use several strategies for performing a task and then compare their performance using those strategies to a model's performance using the same strategies. This would allow fine tuning of a model.

3. If constraints are built into a model such that it cannot outperform humans, we can search for a strategy that performs a particular task best, rather than a strategy that mimics human performance. In that case, when we compare the model's performance to human performance, we will be testing the validity of the initial constraints. A model that has constraints built into it such that it cannot perform in a manner impossible for humans can be used to predict human performance on entirely new tasks within its domain.

This point can be restated in another way. One method of modeling the variation in human performance from task to task is to adjust parameters until the model shows the same level of performance as human subjects. The best-fitting parameter values characterize or describe the human performance of each task. But this approach provides no basis for setting the parameter values to predict human performance in a new task.

In our modeling we have tried to incorporate psychologically motivated, fixed constraints into the model so that it cannot outperform humans. The constraints impose ceilings on the model's performance so that in situations where humans perform well, the model will be able to perform well also, but in situations where humans have difficulty in performing the task, the model will be unable to perform any better than humans. With this type of model, we can predict human performance on a new task by discovering the best performance of the task that the model can exhibit. If the constraints have been specified correctly, the best performance of the model will be close to the best performance of humans in the same task.

Viewing strategies as major intervening variables between task environments and behavior also opens up some challenging research questions:

    a. What is happening as a subject gets better at a task over the first few blocks of trials? What, explicitly, is he doing differently?

    b. How does a subject choose between alternative methods of performing a task?

    c. How does a person create new and better strategies from previous ones?

REFERENCES

Anders, T. R. Retrospective reports of retrieval from short-term memory. *Journal of Experimental Psychology*, 1971, *90*, 251–257.

Anders, T. R. A high-speed, self-terminating search of short-term memory. *Journal of Experimental Psychology*, 1973, *97*, 34–40.

Atkinson, R. C., and Shiffrin, R. M. Human memory: A proposed system and its control processes. In Spence, K. W., and Spence, J. T. (Eds.), *The psychology of learning and motivation* (Vol. 2). New York: Academic Press, 1968.

Averbach, E., and Coriell, A. S. Short-term memory in vision. *Bell System Technical Journal*, 1961, *40*, 309–328.

Bruner, J. S., Goodnow, J. J., and Austin, G. A. *A study of thinking.* New York: Wiley, 1956.

Conrad, R., and Hull, A. J. Input modality and the serial position curve in short-term memory. *Psychonomic Science*, 1968, *10*, 135–136.

Craik, F. I. M. Modality effects in short-term storage. *Journal of Verbal Learning and Verbal Behavior*, 1969, *8*, 658–664.

Darwin, C. J., Turvey, M. T., and Crowder, R. G. An auditory analogue of the Sperling partial report procedure: Evidence for brief auditory storage. *Cognitive Psychology*, 1972, *3*, 255–267.

Gilmartin, K. J. *An information-processing model of short-term memory.* Doctoral dissertation, Carnegie-Mellon University. Ann Arbor, Michigan: University Microfilms No. 75-09-082, 1975.

Glucksberg, S., and Cowen, G. N., Jr. Memory for nonattended auditory material. *Cognitive Psychology*, 1970, *1*, 149–156.

Jahnke, J. C. Primacy and recency effects in serial-position curves of immediate recall. *Journal of Experimental Psychology*, 1965, *70*, 130–132.

Murdock, B. B., Jr. Visual and auditory stores in short-term memory. *Quarterly Journal of Experimental Psychology*, 1966, *18*, 206–211.

Newell, A., and Simon, H. A. *Human problem solving.* Englewood Cliffs, N.J.: Prentice-Hall, 1972.

Sperling, G. The information available in brief visual presentations. *Psychological Monographs*, 1960, *74*, (11, Whole No. 498).

3

Structural Aspects of Associative Models for Memory

William K. Estes

The Concept of Structure

What do we mean by the structure of memory? If the terms are taken literally, the answer may be nothing at all. Often we speak of memory as though it were a warehouse in which things to be remembered are kept in some arrangement like goods on stockroom shelves. But we know that memory actually is not such an entity, in fact, not an entity at all, but rather an aspect of the functioning of a complex information-processing system (Reitman, 1965). This aspect is somewhat analogous to the functioning of libraries or warehouses. Items of information—words, numbers, propositions—are fed into the system and, in a sense, are later retrieved. However, we have no reason to think that between input and output the words, numbers, or propositions are stored in specific locations somewhere in the head. What is inside the head is a fabulous conglomeration of interconnected nerve cells. One property important to the functioning of the system is that the input of a message, say a printed word, generates a change in the state of excitability of some portion

Preparation of this paper was supported in part by Grant MH23878 from the National Institute of Mental Health.

of the ensemble of cells with the result that the system responds differently to later input of the same or related messages.

To clarify what we mean when we speak of the structure of memory, we need first of all to understand that we refer actually to the structure of a theory or model within whose framework we are trying to interpret how memory functions. We may try to express our ideas concerning some aspects of memory function in an analogy, for example, by pointing to the similarities of input-output relations between an individual's performance and the functioning of a library. If in this context we ask whether the individual's memory is hierarchically organized, we mean to ask whether the best-fitting model (the closest analogy) is a library in which the classification of volumes follows a hierarchical scheme. But we may try instead to comprehend the individual's performance by assuming that it reflects the operation of a network of logical elements, like the switches and connectors in a telephone system or computer. Then our remark about hierarchical structure refers to the arrangement of logical elements that must be assumed in order to explain performance.

In either case, successful predictions lend support to the assumptions of a model but cannot be taken to mean that the structure of the organism's memory is like that of the pictorialization. Many properties of the transmission of impulses through the nervous system can be nicely illustrated in terms of the well-known, iron-wire analogy (Lillie, 1925), but one would not care to go on to infer that the structure of a nerve fiber resembles that of a corroded segment of iron wire.

Even though a model describes a system up to a point, the model may be grossly misleading if taken too literally. We need to allow for the possibility that the concept of structure as applied to memory in computers is inappropriate when applied to the memory of a living organism. Even with computers, we find at least two senses of structure. The most literal meaning of structure in the case of computers refers to the hardware, that is, to the components such as magnetic cores that have a fixed capacity in terms of the number of words of information they can store, or to the registers that are permanently connected by means of cables to other registers or devices. This meaning of structure seems to be the one intended in the "stores" of certain current memory models.

However, a computer programmer need not know the details of the hardware structure of his machine. In writing his programs he deals with logical blocks of memory locations, logical pages, and logical devices, and when running the programs he creates a file structure for the information that must be held in memory. He generally creates and runs his programs with no direct reference at all to the hardware of the machine. It is the logical structure generated by programs that the user of the system has to understand. Structure in this second sense refers to the way in which the information entered in the system is organized relative to the procedures available for operating on it.

When concepts of structure are carried over from computers to human memory, one often sees an almost overpowering tendency to construct diagrams resembling those that picture the hardware components of a computer and to speak as though human memory had a preexisting structure into which items of information can be placed. I think it is fair to say that structural concepts of the hardware variety have served on occasion as useful devices to aid in the communication of general ideas about memory (for a good current illustration, see the "conveyer-belt" model of Murdock, 1974, chapter 10), but their usefulness is being challenged by recent theoretical developments. In the Atkinson-Shiffrin (1968) system, for example, the short-term buffer becomes, not a stack of locations into which items can be entered, but rather a component of the memory system by virtue of which representations of recently presented items are kept in a highly available state through repeated rehearsal. Further, there are clear symptoms in the current literature of a growing disenchantment with the whole conception of fixed memory stores (see, for example, Craik and Lockhart, 1972). Thus in the remainder of the present article I shall confine attention to the concept of logical structure, the structure that takes form as incoming information is transformed and organized under the rules of operation of the memory system.

The first point to emphasize about logical structure is that it need not, and in general does not, correspond in any direct way to the structure portrayed in the block diagrams or flow diagrams that are used to illustrate the general workings of the memory system within any particular theory. Structure takes form as information is processed and therefore cannot be discussed in relation to any specific theory until the flow diagrams have been implemented in terms of a model that actually processes and organizes information. One type of implementation is a computer program that simulates the behavior of an individual whose memory operates in accord with the premises of a given theory. By actually running a program one can ascertain the structural properties that the system imposes on the information it deals with. Perhaps the best example of this procedure that has yet been proposed in theoretical treatments of memory is Feigenbaum's elementary-perceiver-and-memorizer (EPAM) model for verbal learning and retention, within which structure takes the form of a network of images and test nodes, or comparators (Feigenbaum, 1963). Another route to implementing diagrams is by way of the formulation of a mathematical model that defines states of information with regard to prior inputs of event sequences and postulates rules for transition among states (Bower and Theios, 1964; Greeno, 1974). A third route is by way of a model formulated in more primitive terms, that is, in terms referring not to information or information processing but rather to abstract elements and the logical relations among them. This last route is epitomized in association theory, older and newer versions of which will be the main focus of attention in later sections of this chapter.

Being clear about what we mean when we use terms like structure of memory has quite material implications for the way we do research. For one thing we can save much fruitless effort in trying to answer unanswerable questions. A most important class of these in current cognitive psychology considers the relative merits of the two principal theoretical approaches to memory—information-processing theory and learning theory. We shall see that these theories derive from different levels of analysis of the phenomena of memory; it is thus better to regard them as complementary rather than competitive.

What are Information-Processing Models?

It is hard to define information-processing models constructively, but it is easy to do so by complementation, for the information-processing approach arose in psychology primarily as a reaction against the behavioristic framework of learning theory and especially as a reaction against stimulus-response association theory. Viewed apart from any philosophical commitments, the study of learning is the study of the ways in which organisms' behavioral dispositions change as a function of experience. I think that nearly all who have thought about the matter deeply would agree that, in principle, all laws of learning could be expressed in stimulus-response terminology. The question is whether they should be. The hazard in confining ourselves to a stimulus-response terminology is not the possibility of being proved wrong, but rather the danger of being too particularistic and thus unable to arrive at principles general enough to be useful in solving problems or interpreting new situations.

Beginning in the early 1950s a number of investigators, including Attneave (1954), Hovland (1952), and Miller (1953), noted that if an individual's response tendencies change with experience then observations of his behavior yield information as to what experiences he has had. Thus we can objectively speak of information being stored in an individual's brain and retrieved by way of tests of memory. This view has had a number of fruitful consequences in research. First of all, an approach oriented in terms of informational concepts allows an investigator to escape from the confines of stimulus-response descriptions and encourages attempts to arrive at a more abstract characterization of the information stored and retrieved (formally, the task of information theory). Further, this approach suggests the value of analyzing the detailed sequence of both the observable and the inferred operations performed by an individual engaged in a cognitive task, that is, engaged in the process of taking in, storing, transforming, and retrieving information. Finally, the task of carrying out these analyses is facilitated by methods developed in connection with information-processing systems oriented around digital computers rather than human brains.

This kind of information-processing theory has some obvious advantages. It necessitates close attention to the information-processing requirements of a task and thus is often useful in uncovering constraints on the learner that would not otherwise be apparent. Further, one can embody the theoretical notions in a program and thus ensure that the implications claimed for the ideas actually follow—the proof being obtained by running the program.

As presented in the current literature, information-processing models often have a very different look from, say, the mathematical models of stochastic learning theories. Rather than equations and matrices, we see block diagrams picturing sequences of memory stores and devices such as comparators that operate on the information as it passes through the sequence. It is tempting, but probably incorrect, to infer that the structure of these diagrams portrays the structure of memory.

To clarify our thinking, we might note that the constituents of the information flow diagrams, like those of mathematical models, are merely symbols used to express assumptions as to how the cognitive system works. To verify the implications of an information-processing model with regard to memory structure, one must implement the flow diagram in terms of a computer program or an appropriate alternative logical or mathematical formalization. Then one can discover by simulation or derivation how items of information that are input to the system become organized in memory.

The essence of the information-processing approach is that the component processes and mechanisms of the system operate on items of information, not on stimuli or responses. Consequently, in this type of model, the structural properties of material stored in memory are independent of the mode of input. In contrast, if one treats problems of memory within the framework of learning theory, one views the organism, not as operating directly on items of information, but rather as responding to stimulus situations that carry information. As a result, concepts that are taken for granted (treated as primitives) in an information-processing model must be derived from more elementary assumptions in a learning model. The task of relating concepts of stimulus and response to concepts of information has fallen to the lot of association theory.

What is Association Theory?

Association theory originated in the concept that experiences are represented in an individual's memory as separate units which become linked so that reactivation of one unit leads more or less automatically to reactivation of those with which it is associated. But precisely what becomes associated? In various versions of association theory the answer ranges from ideas to stimuli and responses to abstract linguistic entities.

In the writings of the British associationists (e.g., in David Hartley, 1749; James Mill, 1829) it was presumed that the laws of association operate on ideas, entities that are accessible to objective scientific investigation through introspection and not through any other means. The concept of association made its way into experimental psychology through two routes. One of these led through the first experimental research on human memory, the other through the conditioning laboratory.

Ebbinghaus and his successors in the investigation of simple laboratory phenomena of memory, and later, the American "functional psychologists" left little room in their work for niceties of definition, but they all tacitly assumed that the elements of association are direct representations in memory of the items (such as nonsense syllables and adjectives) presented to a subject as part of the experimental task. The earliest experiments on memory (Ebbinghaus, 1885), and indeed most of those performed for many subsequent decades, involved extremely simple materials. A typical experiment required the memorization of a list of unrelated words or nonsense syllables, the task being taken to represent in its essentials the kind of learning that goes on in the memorization of vocabulary items or the like. To explain how memorization occurs, early investigators postulated that traces of the individual items of a list must be laid down in some form in the brain; these traces, or *engrams* as they were termed, would originally be unrelated, but connections or associations would form among them as a consequence of repeated experience with the items of the list. Then on later occasions, activation of one member of a pair of associated engrams would lead to activation of the other and thus provide a basis for recall of the corresponding item.

Experiments on conditioning were quite different in form from those on list-learning, but they posed a similar conceptual problem. A stimulus that originally does not evoke a given response comes to do so after the stimulus and response have been experienced together. The standard interpretation, following Pavlov (1927) and Thorndike (1931), was that an association or connection is formed between representations of the stimulus and the response. This concept of stimulus-response association was basic to the learning theories of Guthrie (1935), Hull (1943), and Skinner (1938). It seemed to solve the problem of the testability of the theories by virtue of the close correspondence between associations and observed stimulus-response relationships.

Only in quite recent times have researchers come to appreciate that rigorous testability of a theory does not depend on conceptual elements being mapped in a one-to-one fashion onto observable events. Thus, in the statistical theory of learning proposed by the writer (Estes, 1950, 1959), the units of association are abstract elements whose function is solely to enable one to derive testable propositions regarding relations between behavioral events.

Clearly, what is common to association theories is not their choice of units but rather their logical form. Any specific association theory comprises a definition of units and relations and a set of assumptions regarding the conditions under which the relations hold. In classical association models only one relation is assumed, that of a one-to-one connection between elements, although these connections might vary in strength. The interpretation of learning in terms of these associative connections is accomplished almost entirely by means of a single logical relation, the exclusive OR. Thus in the case of the conditioned reflex, an original stimulus evokes (is connected to) either its original response or the to-be-conditioned response; strengthening of one connection implies weakening of the other. Or, in paired-associate learning, the result of an effective training trial is to establish, or strengthen, a connection between the stimulus and response members of an item. Consequently, the structure of memory in association models takes the form of an ensemble of pairwise connections between stimuli and responses, representations of items, or homogeneous abstract elements.

This theoretical structure seemed too conceptually meager to offer any promise of interpreting the complex organizational aspects of human memory. Consequently, although during the first five or six decades of this century researchers continually refined association models to predict details of performance in a limited number of laboratory tasks, concurrently, they were setting the stage for the exuberant response of psychologists during the seventies to new approaches that seemed better equipped to cope with problems of structure and organization in memory (Miller, Galanter, and Pribram, 1960; Tulving and Donaldson, 1972).

These new approaches, well represented in other chapters of this volume, have had salutary effects on research, and their orientation in terms of information-processing concepts and computer analogies has encouraged psychologists to attack problems of memory that are much more complex than those that appeared tractable within the conceptual framework of stimulus-response associations.

Nonetheless, it is important to distinguish the intrinsic from the connotative properties of models. From the standpoint of a logical analysis, there are no limits on the complexity of information-processing structures constructed on the basis of associative concepts. Further, it is worth keeping in mind that association theory has guided the greater part of the research that has been done on human learning and memory, and thus is the type of theory that we are best equipped by experience to work with effectively. We need not be surprised to see that association theory is responding with its usual resilience to new challenges and in the process is generating new models quite different in appearance from those identified with connectionism.

In one current line of development, the elements of association are redefined in terms of linguistic concepts (Anderson and Bower, 1973). Another strategy is to maintain a close correspondence between the elementary units and the independently observable behavioral events while at the same time augmenting the very limited set of logical relations among elements that is utilized in classical theories (Estes, 1972, 1973). In the remainder of this chapter, I shall briefly review some of the specific shortcomings of earlier association theories that prompted researchers to develop new theoretical bases for investigation, and I shall outline a reformulation of association theory that combines classical concepts with currently influential ideas concerning the role of coding in memory.

Revising Association Theory: From Chains to Hierarchies

While it is obvious that new theoretical ideas have been needed to deal with the comprehension and retention of meaningful verbal material, it is also true, though less obvious, that new theoretical developments have been just as much needed to provide adequate interpretations of simpler experimental phenomena.

For several decades, much of the research conducted under the mantle of association theory (in this country, at least) was concerned either with paired-associate learning, the experimental analogy of the acquisition of vocabulary items, or with the learning of lists or other items in serial order. The interpretation of the learning of a vocabulary item (for example, of the acquisition of the ability to give a foreign word as a response to a corresponding English word as a stimulus) was simply that a directional association forms in the memory system leading from the representation of the stimulus to the representation of the response. By direct extension, researchers interpreted the memorization of a list of items, as for example the digits of a telephone number, in terms of directional associations between the successive items in the list. They maintained that once these associations are established, seeing or hearing any one item as a stimulus causes a person to give the name of the next item as a response. To account for the fact that memory for a list does not disintegrate entirely if one item is omitted during recall, these early theorists had to assume that remote associations exist between nonadjacent items.

This version of association theory, which we call the chain-association model, is descriptive of simple experimental phenomena up to a certain point, but even within its original sphere of applicability, it ultimately ran into difficulties. Even in the simplest case of a paired-associate item, an interpretation in terms of a single association proved inadequate. Findings concerning backward recall, that is an individual's ability to recall the stimulus member of an item when given the response member as a cue, produced the addition of the concept of *backward associations*. Furthermore, continued testing of the implications of the chain-association model for the learning of lists resulted in several observations that challenged the validity of the model. For example, one might have expected that preliminary training on pairs of items in a list (on A-B, C-D, and E-F in the list ABCDEF) would, by establishing a portion of the required associations, result in a substantially accelerated speed of learning of the list as a whole—a prediction that has by no means been uniformly borne out in practice (Murdock, 1974). Even the idea that successive repetitions of a list cause the automatic strengthening of interitem associations ran afoul of the finding that such repetitions produce no increase in recall if the items are grouped differently on successive presentations (for example, AB, pause, CD, pause, EF on the first repetition, but ABC, pause, DEF, on the second) (Bower and Winzenz, 1969).

But perhaps the greatest single source of dissatisfaction with the chain-association model arose as a result of the flourishing of studies of free recall. In the typical free-recall experiment a subject is presented with a list of items, most often unrelated words, and then asked to recall them in any order. As illustrated in the top section of Figure 3.1, the classical association model could account for recall on the assumption that successive items of the list become connected by learned associations. Thus, if the list presented comprised the sequence of words *hat, star, dog, . . .* , the starting signal would become associated with *hat, hat* with *star*, and so on. The signal to start recall would lead to reactivation of these associations in the same order.

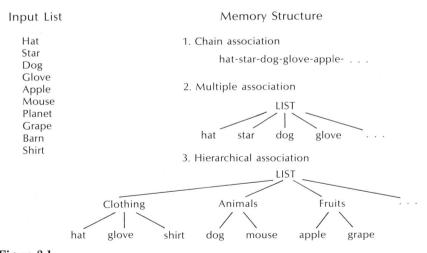

Figure 3.1
Three alternative association models for the memory structure mediating free recall of a list of words.

An immediate problem for the model is that in the typical experiment the items are presented in a different order on every repetition of a list and this variation in order produces no obvious difficulty for subjects, whereas according to the chain association model it should raise prohibitive difficulties.

One could revise the model by assuming that each of the list words becomes independently associated with a common cue that serves as a label for the list, as illustrated in the center section of Figure 3.1. Now a signal to start recall would activate all of the associations simultaneously. Variations in the order of presentation of the list words from trial to trial would raise no difficulty for this version of the model. However, consideration of the properties characteristic of recall protocols in free-recall experiments brings forth a new problem. Typically, subjects do not recall words in random order but rather tend to produce groups or clusters of semantically related words in their response protocols, a phenomenon termed *secondary organization* or *categorical clustering* by Tulving (1968).

These and other aspects of recall data suggest that the memory structure responsible for free recall takes the form neither of chain associations between individual items nor of independent multiple associations, but rather of a hierarchical structure in which related items are associated with a common category label and the category names are associated with a common cue for the list, as illustrated in the bottom section of Figure 3.1.

In order to handle the numerous facts indicating that free recall reflects a hierarchical organization of material, we clearly require a richer model than can be supplied by classical association theory. The problem is how to arrive at the type of model required. A direct approach, and the one most often exemplified in the contemporary literature, is simply to formulate a new model embodying the assumption that the basic structure of memory is such as to impose a hierarchical organization on remembered material, just as the wooden forms used by a builder dictate the form that the building under construction will take on once the poured concrete has hardened. Thus a number of currently influential models, for example, those of Collins and Quillian (1969) and of Mandler (1968) begin with the presumption that the memory system is organized in a tree structure of interconnected nodes and that incoming, to-be-remembered, material is assimilated into this pre-existing structure.

However, this direct postulational approach is not in the spirit of association theory. From the associationist viewpoint, a major aspect of our task should be to find more primitive assumptions from which we can derive predictions that a particular organization of recall behavior will emerge under particular conditions. Our first step must be to reexamine the basic units and operations of association theory to see if we can modify the basic assumptions though an independent rationale that will enable us to derive the organizational properties of recall.

In classical association theory the predominant strategy is to seek units, for example stimuli and responses or elementary ideas, that do not vary from one individual to another and to represent the information an individual gains as a result of his experiences by means of the associative relations or connections established between units. Various specific association theories generally recognize one basic relation, the associative connection, and only one or at most only a few basic units. Thus, in classical conditioning theory, the result of an effective learning experience is represented in terms of an S-R association or a chain of such associations; in the connectionism of Ebbinghaus and Thorndike, an individual's memory for an experience is represented in terms of a chain or network of associations between ideas, and so on. We can divide recent attempts to elaborate and extend association theory to deal with the more complex phenomena of semantic memory into two principal categories, one which I shall term *psycholinguistic association theory* and another which I shall term *associative coding theory*.

Psycholinguistic Association Theory

In their extremely influential book, *Human Associative Memory*, Anderson and Bower (1973) present a thoroughgoing revision and extension of association theory that retains the idea of simple and general units but introduces a variety of associative relations between units. In order to permit accounts of semantic memory and sentence comprehension, Anderson and Bower draw on psycholinguistic concepts as the basis for an array of labeled associations.

To illustrate the way in which memory for an event is represented in Anderson and Bower's model let us assume that a subject in an experiment has observed the display of two single letters in succession on a closed-circuit TV screen. Anderson and Bower maintain that the subject draws upon his familiarity with the language to construct a proposition describing the events he has observed and then stores this proposition in long-term memory.

The form of the associative structure suggested by the presentation in Anderson and Bower's volume is illustrated in the upper panel of Figure 3.2. The nodes in the associative network, labeled by small letters, are abstract entities which correspond to concepts and exemplars of concepts. Those in the bottom row (d–h) correspond to instances of the concepts of past, screen, and so on in the subject's long-term memory system. The topmost node, a, corresponds to the individual's idea of the whole proposition. The arrow labeled C, extending from a to d, represents an associative connection signifying that the context in which the episode occurred existed at some time in the past. The arrow labeled F signifies a factual relation between some event and the given context. The arrows labeled S and P, leading downward from node b, signify that something is predicated (P) of a subject (S), which in this instance is the display screen. From the predicate node, *c*, there extend in turn a labeled association *V*, signifying that the verb is an instance of the subject's concept of display, and the arrows labeled *O*, which signify that the object corresponds to instances of the subject's concept of letter. This description may seem somewhat involved, but the concepts are easy to grasp. The rules assumed by Anderson and Bower for the process whereby an individual generates the associative structure are straightforward enough to be incorporated in a computer program that can simulate the behavior of an individual who is exposed to various kinds of events and then queried as to his memory for them.

The significance of the network structure is that it serves as the basis for either recognition or recall. Suppose, for example, that after the hypothetical individual had observed the letter displays in the above example and stored

1. Psycholinguistic Association Model

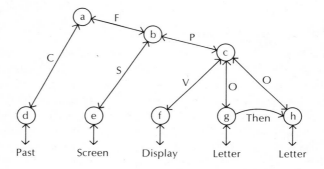

2. Associative Coding Model

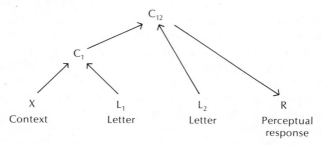

Figure 3.2

Comparison of the mnemonic representations of a hypothetical episode (observation of the successive display of two letters on a TV screen) in the models of (1) Anderson and Bower, 1973; and (2) Estes, 1972.

the episode in his memory, he was asked whether he had seen the given letters appear on the screen. He would construct a representation of the test sentence in memory and then compare the representation of the test sentence with the various networks already existing in his memory system; if he found a match, as would be the case in this example, he would answer yes, signifying that the test question described an episode he had actually experienced. Empirical testing of the model has proceeded largely by the generation and testing of various predictions concerning the relative reaction times that should be observed when, following a given experience, a subject's memory is probed by various test sentences that bear varying degrees of correspondence to the proposition he has presumably incorporated into his memory system.

Using this system, Anderson and Bower have been able to make impressively rapid progress in analyzing the way in which people retrieve from memory information concerning relatively complex verbal material. But rapid progress always involves a price, and in this instance the price has been the necessity of postulating *de novo* many elaborate properties of the memory system, for example, the various types of labelled associations. Further, these properties have been suggested primarily by psycholinguistic rather than psychological theory. Consequently, there is a gap between the research and theory formulated within the framework of the psycholinguistic association model and the well-established bodies of research and theory concerning perception and short- and long-term memory in simpler contexts. To fill this gap is a basic objective of the second approach to the revision of association theory, to which we now turn.

The Associative Coding Model

Basic Units and Relations

In developing the model with which I shall be largely concerned in the remainder of this chapter, the strategy has been to retain simple associative relations while modifying the assumptions about storage processes so that the associated units carry more information than in the classical models. This approach has been influenced primarily by conceptions of coding in memory (see, for example, Melton and Martin, 1972; Johnson, 1970). A basic assumption of the associative coding model is that when a behavioral event (stimulus or response) occurs in a background context, a *trace* of this experience is laid down in the nervous system. The trace may be reactivated later by similar stimulus inputs to generate a full or partial reinstatement of the original experience from the standpoint of the individual. This conception of a trace corresponds quite closely to that of the *image* of a stimulus or response in the EPAM model of Feigenbaum (1963).

The significance of the trace in the functioning of the memory system is that it acts as a *control element* (Estes, 1972) or *interactive filter* (Anderson, 1973), with the primary function of serving as a gate in a network of associations. It is assumed that the neural message arising from any stimulus input takes the form of a multidimensional vector, as does the memory trace left by any previous input. When a new message arrives at a control element in the associative network, the input and trace vectors are compared; if a match occurs, the message is transmitted intact, whereas if there is a mismatch, transmission is blocked; and for intermediate degrees of correspondence between input and trace vectors, the message is transmitted with some degradation. Thus the trace vector provides a logical *AND* function.

An immediate consequence of introducing the *AND* function is that we have a basis for recognition. Suppose that an individual has experienced an event, which we denote by E, in a background context, which we denote by X. The memory trace can be represented by a vector (T_{XE}). If, now, the same event recurs in the same context, the new stimulus input vector matches the trace vector, thus reactivating the latter and generating an output which we interpret as a recognition response. But if the test input comprises the same event E in a new context X' or a new event E' in the old context X, then there is a mismatch between input and memory vectors, and the control element is not activated to the point of yielding a recognition response.

Once an organism has had a number of experiences, a number of these trace vectors will have been laid down in the memory system. The result is that as new situations are encountered, the stimulus input from each in turn is directed to the system of trace elements and only if a match of the new input to one of the trace elements occurs is the input transmitted on through the system and allowed to activate associative connections of the matching control element with other elements in the memory system or the response system.

A second important property of the associative coding model is that of *recursiveness*. By this term I refer to the assumption that the output of a memory control element constitutes an event which may enter into the memory trace laid down upon the occurrence of a subsequent event. This property can be conveniently illustrated in terms of the same example used to illustrate the psycholinguistic model. If an individual observes the display of a letter on a TV screen, we can denote the letter by L_1, the context in which the letter appears (including the screen) by X, and the representation in memory by the trace vector (T_{XL_1}). If immediately following the display of the first letter, the individual sees a second letter, L_2, on the same screen, the context for the second letter presentation includes the trace of the first; the memory trace for the second presentation can be denoted $T_{[XL_1]L_2}$. If, now, the first letter is presented again, the input will match the trace T_{XL_1} and thus tend to reinstate the original response (perhaps naming the letter). However, since T_{XL_1} is a constituent of the trace $T_{[XL_1]L_2}$, the latter would also be partially activated, thus leading to some probability of reinstating the original response to the second event (that is, the individual would be likely to recall the second letter upon again seeing the first).

One consequence of these assumptions is that the associative structure generated by an experience can be represented by a hierarchical tree structure, as illustrated in the lower panel of Figure 3.2 for the example of the two-letter display. In this structure, the control element C_1, which is activated by the occurrence of the letter L_1 in the context X, corresponds to the memory trace T_{XL_1} and the control element $C_{1,2}$ corresponds to the memory trace $T_{[XL_1]L_2}$. Reactivation of the control element $C_{1,2}$ leads to reinstatement of the response R which occurred on the occasion of the original letter display.

A particularly important property of the AND function is that it leads immediately to the generation of higher-order units. If an organism encounters a situation that simultaneously activates two trace elements whose outputs occur concurrently in the memory system, a new trace element is established which henceforth will be activated only if the two, associated, lower-order elements receive inputs simultaneously. Thus we have a basis for organized systems of memory traces.

An intensively studied example of an organized trace structure is the memory system involved in the identification of letters and higher-order perceptual units in reading (see, e.g., Estes, 1975a, 1975b; LaBerge and Samuels, 1974). This system is illustrated in Figure 3.3. The elements at the successively higher levels in the figure denote memory trace elements corresponding to the critical features of letters (the Fs with subscripts), the letters themselves (the Ls), and letter groups (G). We assume that each F_i represents a trace element established by the stimulus input associated with a particular critical feature of a printed character. Each letter is associated with a specific combination of critical features, and hence the memory trace element corresponding to the abstract representation of a letter is activated only when inputs are received from the trace elements corresponding to the appropriate combination of features.

Thus in the situation illustrated in Figure 3.3, if a stimulus event occurs that involves the display of a printed letter A, this input activates feature elements F_1 and F_3 which in turn activate letter element L_A. If the display also includes a printed letter B, feature elements F_3 and F_4 are activated and their output activates L_B. If and only if the display includes both of the letters A and B will the system activate the trace element G, which corresponds to a representation of a letter group.

Interpretation of Free Recall

It will perhaps be evident, at least at an informal level, that the combinatorial and recursive properties posited for the memory-trace mechanism can readily account for the apparently hierarchical organization of memory that is mani-

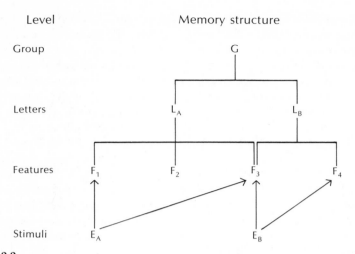

Level	Memory structure

Figure 3.3
Schematic account of the generation of progressively higher-order associative units. The bottom row represents letters presented in a stimulus display; these activate combinations of critical features, which in turn activate control elements in memory for letters, and finally, at the highest level, familiar letter groups.

fest in free-recall experiments. Let us sketch the way in which the system would operate if an individual in list context X were presented with a sequence of words $(W_1, W_2, \ldots, W_N)$ in which words W_1 and W_2 belong to a familiar category a, words W_3 and W_4 to category b, and so on, as in the case illustrated in Figure 3.1. In terms of the example, W_1 and W_2 are the words *hat* and *glove*, a is the category clothing, and so on. Although in many experiments the lists of words to be recalled are selected from familiar semantic categories, it should be noted that even when a list is uncategorized from the standpoint of the investigator, clusters of list words may nonetheless fall into categories from the standpoint of the subject, owing to his idiosyncratic previous experience and his rehearsal activities during list input.

In either case, we assume that recall is mediated by the several types of memory trace vectors listed in Table 3.1. In the case of a categorized list, the individual would already have stored memory trace vectors of the type T_{W_1a}, T_{W_2a}, which represent occurrences of the category label a in conjunction with the words W_1 and W_2. Now, as the list is presented, new trace vectors of several types would be established. Firstly, perception of the stimulus words in the given context during input of the list would give rise to traces $T_{xW_1}, T_{xW_2}, \ldots$. But also, the perception of W_1 and W_2 would in each case tend to reactivate the preexisting traces T_{W_1a}, T_{W_2a}. As a result, the individual would recall category a thus establishing a trace T_{xa}. Further, rehearsal of the related list words in conjunction with this recall would generate additional trace vectors $T_{[xa]W_1}$ and $T_{[xa]W_2}$.

Upon reinstatement of the list context during a later test for recall, there would be two associative routes for recall of the list words. Firstly, the recurrence of the original context would tend to reactivate the elements T_{xW_i}, but only weakly, since input from x alone would not yield a close match to any of the trace vectors. However, the context would also tend to reactivate trace T_{xa}, which corresponds to recall that the category label a has previously occurred in list context x; this in turn would tend to reactivate $T_{[xa]W_1}$ and $T_{[xa]W_2}$.

These multiple sources of reactivation of control elements for the list words would increase the probability of recall in comparison with the case of an uncategorized list and would result in clustering, that is, in a tendency for words associated with a common category to occur together during recall. Further, as observed in the study of Mathews and Tulving (1973), if list words are presented in conjunction with category labels, the probability of recall of a category should depend only on the frequency with which that category name has been activated in the list context (and not on communalities or differences in the particular exemplars of the category that were involved on different occasions). Thus, free-recall data from an individual whose memory system operates in accord with the assumptions of the associative coding model would accord with the conception of a hierarchical organization of items in long-term memory.

In order to demonstrate just how the associative-coding system would operate in various situations, we will of course have to go beyond informal remarks and formalize the assumptions in either a mathematical or a computer-simulation model, a task much beyond the scope of this article. For

Table 3.1 Characterization of Memory Trace Vectors Established during Various Phases of Acquisition of a Free-Recall List

Phase of Experiment	Units Associated	Trace	Effect on Recall
Prior to list presentation	List words (W_i) with category names (C)	T_{W_iC}	Word stimuli evoke recall of category names
During list presentation	List words with list context (x)	T_{xW_i}	List context (weakly) evokes recall of list words
During rehearsal	List words with traces of category names in list context	$T_{[xC]W_i}$	List context plus recall of category names evokes recall of list words

present purposes I shall conclude this brief sketch of the coding model by indicating how the model can deal with the critical question of why, during free-recall tests, response output generally ceases before all of the list words have been produced.

According to the model, upon partial reinstatement of the list context at the time of a recall test, the input vector from the context partially matches the trace vectors T_{xW_i} of list words. The consequent weak activation of these traces yields outputs sufficiently stronger than those of the inactive traces of nonlist words to provide a basis for recognition, and words thus recognized as members of the input list enter the response output. But then a complication arises. As a consequence of prior experiences, recall of some of the list words, in some instances, activates memory traces of category names that have not previously entered into the organization of the input list (a version of *encoding variability*), and these traces cause recall of nonlist words.

The activation of memory traces of nonlist words affects output in two ways. Firstly, it reduces the similarity between the list context present during recall and that present during list input, thus reducing the probability of activation of additional traces T_{xW_i} of list words. At the same time, the indirect recall of nonlist words raises an additional problem for the subject who must attempt to discriminate nonlist from list words on the basis of differences in level of trace activation. Similarly, if subjects are presented with nonlist, "distractor" words at the time of a free-recall test, as in the experiments of Tulving and Thomson (1971), detrimental effects on recall are expected on the basis of essentially the same processes.

Interpretation of Paired-Associate Learning

Other standard experimental paradigms that are readily susceptible to interpretation in terms of the associative coding model include ordered recall of digit or letter strings and paired-associate learning. I have discussed the former elsewhere, especially with reference to the phenomena of grouping and *chunking* (Estes, 1972, 1974). It will be instructive to consider briefly here the acquisition of paired associates in order to point up the contrasts between the present approach and the S-R association model that seemed reasonable at one time (Estes, 1959; Spence, 1956).

In the earlier model, which was based on an analogy to classical conditioning, it was assumed that upon presentation of the two stimuli, S_1 and S_2, of a paired-associate item, the response, R_2 originally evoked by S_2 became associated with, or conditioned to, S_1. The course of acquisition could be accounted for well enough, but there was no direct way of handling backward association or of interpreting the distinction between recall and recognition.

In the associative coding model, it is assumed that the consequence of an effective study trial is the establishment of a memory trace $T_{xS_1S_2}$ (conveniently abbreviated $T_{x_{12}}$) representing the joint occurrence of stimuli S_1 and S_2

in a list context, x. This trace vector provides the basis for recognition if either S_1 or S_2 or both are later presented again in the same context. Further, the evocation or rehearsal of R_2 while the trace $T_{x_{12}}$ is active results in the establishment of a trace $T_{[x_{12}]R_2}$, the basis for later recall of R_2 upon presentation of S_1 in the list context. Similarly, rehearsal of R_1, the response originally evoked by S_1, effects the establishment of an independent trace $T_{[x_{12}]R_1}$, which then mediates recall of R_1 upon presentation of S_2 in the list context. Such phenomena as "forward" and "backward" recall can be interpreted in a manner generally compatible with that of Wolford's *directional-association* model (Wolford, 1971). Wolford assumes that distinct associations form between S_1 and R_2 and between S_2 and R_1 during study of an item, and that these associations form the basis for forward and backward recall, respectively, and for various types of recognition performance. In the associative coding model, it is assumed that a single trace $T_{x_{12}}$ may be reactivated by the recurrence of either S_1 or S_2 in the list context, but that the output of this trace enters as a constituent into those involving R_1 and R_2 which may be formed during rehearsal. Predictions of the kind considered by Wolford (e.g., predictions of old and new recognition from forward- and backward-recall scores after one list presentation) appear to be indistinguishable for the two models, but differentiation might be possible when data from repeated acquisition trials are considered.

The associative-coding approach to paired-associate learning is similar in a number of essentials to that of Humphreys and Greeno (1970). Analyzing acquisition data within the framework of a discrete-state, Markov model, Humphreys and Greeno obtained evidence supportive of a two-stage conception in which the first stage is the establishment of a representation of the S_1–S_2 presentation in memory and the second stage is the discovery of a retrieval strategy that enables a subject to recover response R_2 once the representation is reactivated. The only material differences between my interpretation and theirs seem to be that the trace vector $T_{xS_1S_2}$ in the associative coding model takes explicit account of context and that the recursive property of the coding model, leading to the establishment of the second-order trace $T_{[x_{12}]R_2}$ during rehearsal, does away with the need for a qualitative distinction between encoding and retrieval strategies. Furthermore, the latter mechanism represents a formalization of the concept of a *retrieval cue*, which has been fruitfully applied to numerous phenomena of verbal memory by Tulving and his associates (e.g., Tulving and Thomson, 1971; Watkins and Tulving, 1975).

On the Structure of Memory Theory

The foregoing, summary examples of my own efforts to delve into structural aspects of memory, together with the many interesting examples brought forward by other contributors to this volume, lead me to think that the enormous range of problems confronting investigators of human cognitive activity requires a commensurate range of types and levels of theories. No one of the current approaches—information processing, psycholinguistic theory, associative coding theory—can be sufficient by itself. One reason is that the structural and organizational properties of memory are manifest in quite different ways at different levels of analysis. Owing to our inability to comprehend all aspects in a single manageable formalism, we find ourselves working with a number of different bodies of theory, and a particular investigator's choice of plots in this array depends on both his theoretical predilections and the empirical problems he happens to be addressing.

Looking over the assemblage of models that receive attention in this book, we can discern a semblance of order. As illustrated in Table 3.2, we can arrange a number of the models in order of increasing abstraction of theoretical elements or units and increasing complexity of subject matter. We start at what seems to be for our purposes the ground floor of this structure with Anderson's interactive-filter model for memory, in which the elements are traces left in the nervous system by patterns of sensory input and the principal theoretical relation or function is computation of correlations between new input patterns and traces of old inputs. To date the model has been applied in detail only to a limited class of experiments on recognition memory (Anderson, 1973).

At the next level we have the associative coding model, which I have discussed in the present paper. The basic structural units in this model are representations of events and contexts in memory. However these units need not be taken as primitive assumptions; rather they appear to be derivable from the elements of Anderson's model by a simple logical operation. The same logical operation applied to the elements of the coding model generates higher-order units that correspond to such psychological notions as words, categories, and concepts. The associative coding model is most directly

Table 3.2 Levels of Memory Theory

Model	Elements	Relations	Special Area of Competence
Computational Linguistics	Abstract concepts	Syntactic and semantic	Comprehension of language
Psycholinguistic association	Concepts and instances	Labeled associations	Semantic memory
Associative coding	Representations of events in context	Associations	Role of frequency, recency, grouping
Interactive filters	Traces of neural input patterns	Correlations	Recognition

applicable to phenomena having to do with the frequency, recency, and grouping of relatively simple events in memory.

But theories that build directly on concepts of sensory inputs and memory traces, even though considerably enriched conceptually as compared with traditional association theories, have theoretical resources that are too limited to keep up with the cognitive psychologist's voracious appetite for ever more complex and naturalistic phenomena. In order to investigate the comprehension of language, or memory for information conveyed by linguistic expressions at the level of sentences or even paragraphs, a number of current researchers have turned to a new level of theory that employs some of the relational structure of association theory but takes concepts as its basic units and distinguishes classes of concepts and classes of associative relationships among them according to semantic and syntactic properties. This type of theory, here termed psycholinguistic association theory, is represented in the recent work of Anderson and Bower (1973), Kintsch (1974), Rumelhart, Lindsay and Norman (1972). It is able to deal with questions like "Will it take longer to comprehend Sentence A than Sentence B?" or "Can a subject recall Sentence A if element p is presented as a cue?" Finally, at the top level of our structure we find a group of theoretical approaches deriving from computational linguistics, represented for example in the work of Schank (1972) and Winograd (1972); in these top-level theories, the elements are abstract concepts and the theoretical relations are derived entirely from linguistic rather than psychological theory.

Working in terms of these higher-level theories and relying increasingly on computer simulation rather than on experimentation, current investigators have obtained interesting results with reference to aspects of linguistic performance that would have been far out of the reach of research based on traditional association theory. These efforts will doubtless continue to flourish, for it is often an excellent idea to tackle complex problems with new techniques, unfettered by the constraints of older theoretical frameworks. However, if we seek not only to simulate successfully various types of data but also to understand the cognitive functioning of the living human being, we need to devote some attention to the problems of developing links between the various levels of theory. We must not only fill in the gaps between older and newer theoretical approaches, but also devote some of our efforts to deepening our understanding of simpler empirical problems that have been bypassed rather than solved in some of the newer and higher flights of cognitive psychology.

REFERENCES

Anderson, J. A. A theory for the recognition of items from short memorized lists. *Psychological Review*, 1973, *80*, 417–438.

Anderson, J. R., and Bower, G. H. *Human associative memory*. Washington, D.C.: Winston, 1973.

Atkinson, R. C., and Shiffrin, R. M. Human memory: A proposed system and its control processes. In K. W. Spence and J. T. Spence (Eds.), *The psychology of learning and motivation* (Vol. 2). New York: Academic Press, 1968.

Attneave, F. Some informational aspects of visual perception. *Psychological Review*, 1954, *61*, 183–193.

Bower, G. H., and Theios, J. A learning model for discrete performance levels. In R. C. Atkinson (Ed.), *Studies in mathematical psychology*. Stanford, Calif.: Stanford University Press, 1964.

Bower, G. H., and Winzenz, D. Group structure, coding, and memory for digit series. *Journal of Experimental Psychology Monograph*, 1969, *80* (2, Pt. 2), 1–17.

Collins, A. M., and Quillian, M. R. Retrieval time from semantic memory. *Journal of Verbal Learning and Verbal Behavior*, 1969, 8, 240–247.

Craik, F. I. M., and Lockhart, R. S. Levels of processing: A framework for memory research. *Journal of Verbal Learning and Verbal Behavior*, 1972, *11*, 671–684.

Ebbinghaus, H. [*Memory*] (H. A. Ruger and C. E. Bussenius, trans.). New York: Teachers College, 1913. Reprint. New York: Dover, 1964. (Originally published in 1885.)

Estes, W. K. Toward a statistical theory of learning. *Psychological Review*, 1950, *43*, 94–107.

Estes, W. K. The statistical approach to learning theory. In S. Koch (Ed.), *Psychology: A study of a science* (Vol. 2). New York: McGraw-Hill, 1959.

Estes, W. K. An associative basis for coding and organization in memory. In A. W. Melton and E. Martin (Eds.), *Coding processes in human memory*. New York: Winston, 1972.

Estes, W. K. Memory and conditioning. In F. J. McGuigan and D. B. Lumsden (Eds.), *Contemporary approaches to conditioning and learning*. Washington, D.C.: Winston, 1973.

Estes, W. K. Learning theory and intelligence. *American Psychologist*, 1974, 29, 740–749.

Estes, W. K. The locus of inferential and perceptual processes in letter identification. *Journal of Experimental Psychology: General*, 1975, *104*, 122–145. (a)

Estes, W. K. Memory, perception, and decision in letter identification. In R. L. Solso (Ed.), *Information processing and cognition: The Loyola symposium*. Hillsdale, N.J.: Erlbaum, 1975 (b).

Feigenbaum, E. A. Simulation of verbal learning behavior. In E. A. Feigenbaum and J. Feldman (Eds.), *Computers and thought*. New York: McGraw-Hill, 1963.

Greeno, J. G. Representation of learning as discrete transition in a finite state space. In D. H. Krantz, R. D. Luce, R. C. Atkinson, and P. Suppes (Eds.), *Contemporary developments in mathematical psychology* (Vol. 1). San Francisco: W. H. Freeman and Company, 1974.

Guthrie, E. R. *The psychology of learning*. New York: Harper & Row, 1935.

Hartley, D. *Observations on man. His frame, his duty, and his expectations*. London: Leake and Frederick, 1749.

Hovland, C. I. A "communication analysis" of concept learning. *Psychological Review*, 1952, 59, 461–472.

Hull, C. L. *Principles of behavior*. New York: Appleton-Century-Crofts, 1943.

Humphreys, M., and Greeno, J. G. Interpretation of the two-stage analysis of paired-associate memorizing. *Journal of Mathematical Psychology*, 1970, 7, 275–292.

Johnson, N. F. The role of chunking and organization in the process of recall. In G. H. Bower (Ed.), *The psychology of learning and motivation* (Vol. 4). New York: Academic Press, 1970.

Kintsch, W. *The representation of meaning in memory.* New York: Wiley, 1974.

LaBerge, D., and Samuels, S. J. Toward a theory of automatic information processing in reading. *Cognitive Psychology,* 1974, *6,* 293–323.

Lillie, R. S. Factors affecting transmission and recovery in the passive iron wire model. *Journal of General Physiology,* 1925, *7,* 473–507.

Mandler, G. Association and organization: Facts, fancies, and theories. In T. R. Dixon and D. L. Horton (Eds.), *Verbal behavior and general behavior theory.* Englewood Cliffs, N.J.: Prentice-Hall, 1968.

Mathews, R. C. and Tulving, E. Effects of three types of repetition on cued and noncued recall of words. *Journal of Verbal Learning and Verbal Behavior,* 1973, *12,* 707–721.

Melton, A. W., and Martin, E. *Coding processes in human memory.* New York: Winston, 1972.

Mill, J. *Analysis of the phenomena of the human mind.* London: Baldwin and Cradock, 1829.

Miller, G. A. What is information measurement? *American Psychologist,* 1953, *8,* 3–11.

Miller, G. A., Galanter, E., and Pribram, K. H. *Plans and the structure of behavior.* New York: Holt, Rinehart, and Winston, 1960.

Murdock, B. B., Jr. *Human memory: Theory and data.* New York: Wiley, 1974.

Pavlov, I. P. *Conditioned reflexes* (G. V. Anrep, trans. and ed.). Oxford: Oxford University Press, 1927.

Reitman, W. R. *Cognition and thought: An information processing approach.* New York: Wiley, 1965.

Rumelhart, D. E., Lindsay, P. H., and Norman, D. A. A process model for long term memory. In E. Tulving and W. Donaldson (Eds.), *Organization of memory.* New York: Academic Press, 1972.

Schank, R. C. Conceptual dependency: A theory of natural language understanding. *Cognitive Psychology,* 1972, *3,* 552–631.

Skinner, B. F. *Behavior of organisms.* New York: Appleton, 1938.

Spence, K. W. *Behavior theory and conditioning.* New Haven, Conn.: Yale University Press, 1956.

Thorndike, E. L. *Human learning.* New York: Century, 1931.

Tulving, E. Theoretical issues in free recall. In T. R. Dixon and D. L. Horton (Eds.), *Verbal behavior and general behavior theory.* Englewood Cliffs, N.J.: Prentice-Hall, 1968.

Tulving, E., and Donaldson, W. *Organization of memory.* New York: Academic Press, 1972.

Tulving, E., and Thomson, D. M. Retrieval processes in recognition memory: Effects of associative context. *Journal of Experimental Psychology,* 1971, *87,* 116–124.

Watkins, M. J., and Tulving, E. Episodic memory: When recognition fails. *Journal of Experimental Psychology: General,* 1975, *104,* 5–29.

Winograd, T. *Understanding natural language.* New York: Academic Press, 1972.

Wolford, G. Function of distinct associations for paired-associate performance. *Psychological Review,* 1971, *78,* 303–313.

4

Meaning, Memory Structure, and Mental Processes

David E. Meyer and Roger W. Schvaneveldt

1. Introduction: Recent Developments in Memory Research

Experimental psychologists have collected a large body of data on human learning and memory. Much of their research has dealt with how people acquire and retain new information. In contrast, there has been less work on how people recall familiar facts after using them continuously for many years. But the focus of research on learning and memory is shifting. Recently psychologists have begun to study long-term memory more carefully. They are seeking especially to discover how the human brain organizes and retrieves stored semantic information. Using this discovery as a basis for new research, they hope to achieve further insights into various mental processes involving words and concepts.

Part of the impetus for recent developments in memory research comes from a major change in experimental procedure. Current researchers are measuring the speed with which a person's brain can use various kinds of knowledge. Although this *reaction-time method* dates back many years (Cattell,

We thank A. S. Coriell, K. D. Gutschera, J. C. Johnston, R. L. Knoll, T. K. Landauer, S. Monsell, E. Z. Rothkopf, and S. Sternberg for their helpful comments.

1887; Donders, 1868/1969), the method was largely ignored until modern investigators introduced a number of refinements (for a review, see Smith, 1968; Sternberg, 1969a, 1969b, 1975). Instead, starting with Ebbinghaus (1885), most previous memory experiments involved measuring the errors that people make while trying to remember freshly learned material. The *error method* has been quite useful for examining the retention of new information (Cofer, 1971); however it is not a suitable method for studying how people recall very familiar facts, because memory failure seldom occurs as part of this long-term-memory process. By comparison, the reaction-time method provides a powerful tool for exploring the nature of long-term memory in which errors are a relatively rare phenomenon (Sternberg, 1975).

One reason for the current interest in the nature of long-term memory is that development of a logical, workable memory model offers a fascinating theoretical challenge. For example, a person normally has thousands of familiar words in his vocabulary; yet without being aware of any special mental process, he can usually recognize a word and retrieve its meaning within a split second. Moreover, it does not take him much longer to comprehend the words of a whole sentence. The high speed of the process combined with the exceptionally large capacity of long-term memory makes the underlying mechanism seem rather amazing (Norman, 1969).

Until recently, psychologists lacked a good foundation for thinking about this problem. But stimulating new ideas of linguists, artificial-intelligence experts, and researchers in other disciplines related to information-processing have helped to lay the necessary groundwork. Today psychologists are rapidly modifying and extending concepts from related disciplines to characterize the nature of human memory (e.g., Anderson and Bower, 1973). Although this work has just begun, it already promises to enhance our understanding of other intellectual abilities as well.

The purpose of the present paper is to illustrate some of the recent developments in memory research with examples from our own experimental studies. In collaboration with a number of colleagues, we have performed a series of psychological experiments on word recognition and sentence comprehension (Becker, Schvaneveldt, and Gomez, 1973; Gossman and Meyer, 1975; Landauer and Meyer, 1972; Meyer, 1970, 1973a, 1973b, 1975, in press; Meyer and Ellis, 1970; Meyer and Ruddy, 1973, 1974; Meyer and Schvaneveldt, 1971; Meyer, Schvaneveldt, and Ruddy, 1972, 1974, 1975; Ruddy, Meyer, and Schvaneveldt, 1973; Schvaneveldt and Meyer, 1973; Schvaneveldt, Meyer, and Becker, 1974, in press; Tweedy and Schvaneveldt, 1974). By informally surveying a few significant results of these experiments, we will try to show how the reaction-time method can be used to test ideas drawn from information-processing theories about human memory. Our discussion is directed to interested laymen and scientists from other areas, as well as to members of our own discipline.

The topic that concerns us especially is the role of meaning in the structure of memory. Several current theories suggest that people organize their long-term verbal memory somewhat like a thesaurus, wherein words with related meanings are filed in closer proximity than words with unrelated meanings (e.g., Quillian, 1969; Rumelhart, Lindsay, and Norman, 1972).[1] Such theories imply that the speed of mental processes involving written and spoken words depends on how closely related the meanings of the words are, the reason being that the proximity of related words in the memory structure affects how quickly words can be retrieved, much as the proximity of related words in a thesaurus affects how quickly a person finds them there. Our research was designed to test these implications experimentally. As will be seen later, the outcome of our experiments supports the notion that long-term verbal memory is organized according to meaning; further, the results of our experiments provide evidence about which mental processes may depend on this semantic organization.

2. Comprehension of Existential-Affirmative Sentences

We will start by considering one of our original experiments on sentence comprehension (Meyer, 1970). The experiment was designed to explore how people recall semantic information concerning common categories of objects such as furniture, vehicles, and animals. We began by selecting several dozen categories from several sources (e.g., Cohen, Bousfield, and Whitmarsh, 1957; Riegel, 1965; *Roget's International Thesaurus*, 1946; *Webster's New Collegiate Dictionary*, 1961), controlling the familiarity and length of the category names (Kůcera and Francis, 1967; Thorndike and Lorge, 1944). We then used the category names to form special sentences that we asked people to classify as true or false. The sentences were constructed such that semantic information from long-term memory would be required to classify them correctly. Our initial goal was to discover whether the speed of the retrieval process depends on relations among word meanings.

2.1 Method

Table 4.1 shows some examples of the sentences employed in our experiment. The experiment involved statements such as "Some pines are trees," which is a type of sentence called an *existential affirmative*.[2] Each sentence like this expresses a relation between two familiar categories of objects. To decide

---

[1]The brain could represent the proximity of semantically related words in various ways. For example, the groups of neural cells that store information about related words might be spatially nearer to each other, or the connections between them might be greater in number.

[2]Sometimes such sentences are also referred to as *particular affirmatives* (Copi, 1967; Meyer, 1970, 1973b, 1975, in press).

Table 4.1   Construction of Existential-Affirmative Sentences

Set Relations	Examples	Truth Values
Subset	Some pines are trees.	True
Superset	Some stones are rubies.	True
Overlap	Some writers are mothers.	True
Disjoint	Some clouds are wrists.	False

whether the sentence is true or false, a person must recall whether any members of the first category in the sentence are also members of the second category.

Within our special sentences, we varied the *set relation* between the first and second categories. The set relation depended on the relative number of members the two categories had in common. Sometimes the members of the first category formed a *subset* of (i.e., were all contained in) the second category, as in the statement "Some pines are trees." Alternatively, the first category was a *superset* of (i.e., contained all of) the second category, as in the statement "Some stones are rubies." On still other occasions, the two categories had just a *partial overlap,* as in the statement "Some writers are mothers." Finally, the two categories were sometimes *disjoint,* as in the statement "Some clouds are wrists."

As part of this variation in the set relation, we also changed the extent to which the meanings of the categories corresponded (cf. Rips, 1975; Smith, Shoben, and Rips, 1974). For example, if the first category was a subset of the second category, the two categories had closely related meanings. But if the two categories were disjoint, they had unrelated meanings.

We determined whether a sentence was true by following the formal rules of logic as shown in the right-hand column of Table 4.1 (Copi, 1967). A sentence was true whenever the two categories in it contained at least one common member, as in the subset, superset, and partial overlap relations. A sentence was false only when the categories had a disjoint relation.[3]

---

[3]This scheme may appear to violate the ordinary usage of existential affirmatives, in which such sentences sometimes mean "some but not all." If we adhered strictly to ordinary usage, both disjoint and subset relations would produce false sentences. However, Rips (1975) has shown that people actually experience more difficulty interpreting existential-affirmative sentences according to their "normal" meaning than according to their "formal" meaning. His results suggest that the normal meaning may not be so common after all. This observation is consistent with some of our own findings. For example, experimental volunteers comprehend the truth of existential affirmatives at least as fast when the first category of a sentence is a subset of the second category as when there is a superset or overlap relation instead (Meyer, 1970, 1973b). If the formal meaning of an existential affirmative were very unusual, it is unlikely that there would be such rapid acceptance of a sentence like "Some pines are trees."

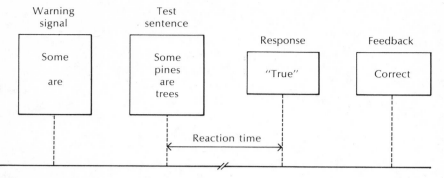

Figure 4.1
Procedure on a typical test trial of the sentence-comprehension experiment using existential affirmatives.

After constructing about 200 different examples of various existential-affirmative sentences, we selected a group of 32 college students who had to judge which sentences were true and which were false. Each person participated in a series of test trials during the experiment, which was conducted under the control of a digital computer. The procedure on a typical trial is shown in Figure 4.1. At the start of the trial, a warning signal appeared for 1 second on a display screen that showed a printed sentence arrayed vertically with two spaces in it (e.g., "Some _____ are _____.") Next the blanks of the sentence were filled with the names of two categories, forming a statement like "Some pines are trees." The person read the sentence and decided whether it was true or false. If he thought it was true, he pressed a key with one finger; if he thought it was false, he pressed a different key with another finger. In Figure 4.1, for example, the correct response is "true." Each person was instructed to respond quickly and accurately. We measured the reaction time from the moment the complete sentence appeared on the screen to the moment the response occurred. At the end of each trial, we gave feedback about whether the response had been correct. Then we went on to the next trial, using another sentence.

We followed the same procedure for each sentence, regardless of whether it was true or false.[4] Because the words were very familiar, the participants made mistakes on just a small fraction (4%) of the trials. By measuring the reaction times of the correct responses, we were able to make inferences

---

[4]Half of the sentences involved a disjoint set relation. Thus the relative frequencies of true and false sentences were the same, so that people could not anticipate the correct response. Among the true sentences, the subset, superset, and partial overlap relations occurred equally often.

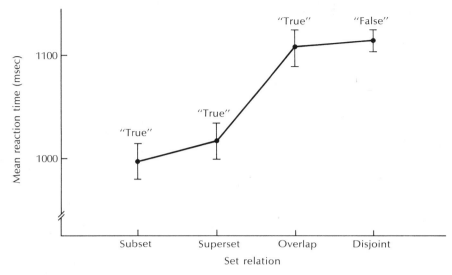

Figure 4.2
The correlation between mean reaction times and set relations between categories
in the comprehension of existential-affirmative sentences.

about the speed of the underlying retrieval process and its dependence on the
meanings of the words.

2.2 Results

Some results from the experiment are summarized in Figure 4.2, where reaction times (in milliseconds) of the correct responses have been averaged over
the individual people and sentences. The data are shown separately for each
set relation between the categories. It usually took little more than a second
to accept or reject a sentence, but the set relation had a significant effect on
reaction time. The effect cannot be attributed merely to a difference between
"true" and "false" sentences. For example, reaction times of "true" responses
were 110 ± 22 msec faster on the average when the first category had a subset relation with the second category than when there was just a partial overlap between the two categories. This result occurred reliably for both the
whole set of test sentences and the range of individuals who participated in
the experiment [$min\ F(1,121) = 24.8;\ p < .01$].[5] We may interpret the out-

_____

[5]Here and elsewhere we report the mean difference between the reaction times plus or minus
one standard error. We have based our computations on the *quasi-F statistic* recommended by
Clark (1973) and Winer (1971), which allows us to generalize our results simultaneously over the
sampled populations of sentences and people.

Table 4.2 Some Effects of Category Size on Reaction Time (RT) for Responses to Existential-Affirmative Sentences

Set Relation	Size of Second Category	Examples	Mean RT (msec)	Mean Change in RT due to Increase in Category Size (msec)
Subset	Small	Some pines are trees.	887	198 ± 30
	Large	Some pines are plants.	1085	
Superset	Small	Some stones are rubies.	1098	-164 ± 30
	Large	Some stones are gems.	934	

come in terms of meaning: when the meanings of the categories were closely related to each other, the reaction times tended to be shorter.[6]

There were also important results that depended on the sizes of the categories, which we varied using a technique introduced by Landauer and Freedman (1968). Some of the categories were small and contained relatively few members, while others were large and contained many members. Table 4.2 shows a few of these variations in category size and their effects on reaction times. In the top two rows of the table, the statements "Some pines are trees" and "Some pines are plants" illustrate cases where the first category is a subset of the second category, and the size of the second category varies from small to large, while the size of the first category remains constant. In the bottom two rows of the table, the statements "Some stones are rubies" and "Some stones are gems" illustrate cases where the first category is a superset of the second category, and the size of the second category again varies from small to large, while the size of the first category remains constant.[7] We found that increasing the size of the second category produced significantly slower responses if there was a subset relation [mean difference $= 198 \pm 30$ msec.; $min\ F(1,24) = 44.0, p < .01$]. In contrast, increasing the size of the second category produced significantly faster responses if there was a superset rela-

---

[6]Although closeness-of-meaning covaried with the set relation between the categories in our experiment, it is possible to separate the effects of these two factors. Closeness of meaning may be measured by asking people to rate the semantic similarity between connotations of different categories, instead of asking them to assess the actual amounts of overlap in their memberships (Smith, Shoben, and Rips, 1974). Results of further experiments indicate that the subjective closeness of meaning perhaps has a larger effect on reaction time than does the objective set relation.

[7]Although not shown in Table 4.2, we also varied the size of the first category while keeping the size of the second category constant. This type of manipulation produced sentences like "Some thrones are furniture" and "Some chairs are furniture." We did not restrict our manipulation of category size to sentences in which the first category was a subset or superset of the second category; we also varied the sizes of categories in sentences where there was a partial overlap or disjoint relation.

tion [mean difference $= 164 \pm 30$ msec.; $min\ F(1,21) = 30.8, p < .01$]. The pattern of effects suggests that reaction time is directly related to the difference between the sizes of the first and second categories, rather than to the size of the second category *per se:* the greater the difference between the sizes of the categories, the longer the reaction time.[8]

2.3 *Discussion*

The results of our research on the comprehension of existential-affirmative sentences have allowed us to test several basic ideas about the way in which human memory functions (Meyer, 1970). The comprehension of a sentence is accomplished very rapidly. It is not an instantaneous process, however. In particular, our findings reveal that people cannot immediately recall whether words have the appropriate meanings to make a sentence true. Instead, we have evidence that they must use a process of retrieval and inference to sift long-term memory for the desired information about the words. The speed of the process varies with the similarity and specificity of the meanings involved.

We believe it is useful to conceptualize our findings further in terms of the flow chart outlined in Figure 4.3, which illustrates how the comprehension process could handle sentences like the ones in our experiment. According to this view, comprehension starts with an encoding operation (Stage 1) that converts the names of the categories in a sentence to an internal representation of some kind. For example, a person might create visual (orthographic) images of the words and then transform them to an aural (phonemic) medium (Meyer and Ruddy, 1973; Meyer et al., 1974, 1975; Rubenstein, Lewis, and Rubenstein, 1971). Next the locations of the categories with these names are found in the structure of long-term memory (Stage 2), perhaps as the entries for words are found in a dictionary or thesaurus. Then stored information about each category is checked (Stage 3) to determine what set relation exists between the categories. Such an operation could rely on some type of cross referencing in the memory structure. Finally, depending on the outcome of the first three stages, the process leads to the execution of a response (Stage 4) indicating whether the sentence is true or false.

Within this general framework, the present data support the idea that stored information about familiar categories of objects is organized by mean-

---

[8]In addition to the data reported in Table 4.2, we observed other effects of category size on reaction time. If the two categories were disjoint, for example, increasing the size of the second category resulted in slower responses [$min\ F(1,53) = 3.7, p < .07$]. It took 37 ± 19 msec longer on the average to comprehend a sentence like "Some clouds are joints" than to comprehend a sentence like "Some clouds are wrists." Similar observations have been made by several investigators (e.g., Collins and Quillian, 1969, 1970b; Landauer and Freedman, 1968; Landauer and Meyer, 1972; Meyer and Ellis, 1970; Rips, 1975; Wilkins, 1971); however, the interpretation of these effects remains controversial.

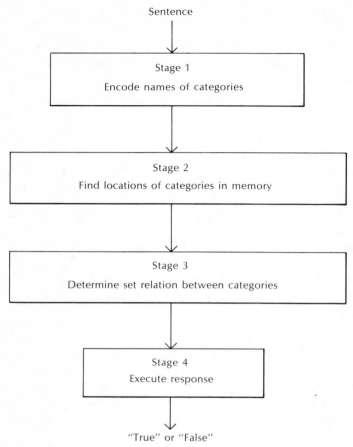

Sentence

Stage 1

Encode names of categories

Stage 2

Find locations of categories in memory

Stage 3

Determine set relation between categories

Stage 4

Execute response

"True" or "False"

Figure 4.3
Some operations completed during sentence comprehension.

ing, and that the semantic structure of memory influences how long some of the component operations take during comprehension. Indeed there are various detailed models along these lines that could explain our results more fully (e.g., Meyer, 1970; Smith et al., 1974). But for now we will focus mainly on one proposed by Quillian (1969) and his colleagues (Collins and Quillian, 1969, 1970a, 1970b, 1972). Our choice is motivated by both expository and historical considerations. Following other pioneers in the area of artificial intelligence, Quillian has tried to program computers so that they can understand sentences as people do. He has developed a formal system to store information about word meanings. The system has attracted the attention of many psychologists, because it also provides a possible model for representing the structure of human long-term verbal memory (Anderson and McGaw, 1973; Collins and Quillian, 1969, 1972; Conrad, 1972; Freedman and Loftus, 1971; Juola and Atkinson, 1971; Landauer and Meyer, 1972; Loftus, 1973; Rips, Shoben, and Smith, 1973).

Quillian's model represents familiar categories of objects like table, chair, and furniture, or robin, canary, and bird at distinct locations (nodes) of a network as illustrated in Figure 4.4 (Collins and Quillian, 1969). Links between these locations interconnect the various categories. The links are marked to specify how the categories are related to each other. For simplicity, only two different types of link have been included in the small section of memory outlined here. The solid links connect pairs of categories, such as canary and bird, in which one category is a superset of the other. The dashed links connect each category to different attributes that help to define it further, such as a canary "is yellow" and "can sing." In Figure 4.4, the arrowhead on each link designates the direction of the connection, pointing from a category to either one of its supersets or one of its attributes. Although attribute links may serve a critical function as discussed later, we will initially stress the role of the superset links.

There are two relevant properties of this memory structure. First, the categories with related meanings (e.g., canary and bird) have more direct connections than the categories with unrelated meanings (e.g., canary and furniture). Second, the categories are separated according to size. Varying the set relations and sizes of the categories involves changing the "distance" between their memory locations. As a result, one plausible interpretation of our reaction-time data is that the speed of sentence comprehension depends on how far apart the categories are stored in the memory structure.[9]

To be specific, Collins and Quillian (1972) have suggested that the distance separating category locations in the memory structure influences a mechanism like the one outlined in Figure 4.5, which is designed for Stage 3 of comprehension (Figure 4.4) to determine whether the categories from an existential-affirmative sentence have any members in common. The mechanism supposedly waits until encoding is done and each category of the sentence has been located in the memory structure during prior Stages 1 and 2. Then the mechanism searches a series of "paths" through the network (Stage 3a), starting from the locations of the original categories and moving to the locations of other categories that have various relations with the original categories. The

---

[9]At the same time, we must stress that Quillian (1969) did not think of the memory structure as being a strict hierarchy (Collins and Loftus, 1975). In his model he allowed for the possibility of direct links between two categories such that one is not an "immediate" superset of the other (e.g., horse and animal, even though mammal is technically an intermediate category that separates them). He also suggested that numerical values may be used to specify the "strength" of the direct links between categories (Collins and Quillian, 1972).

64

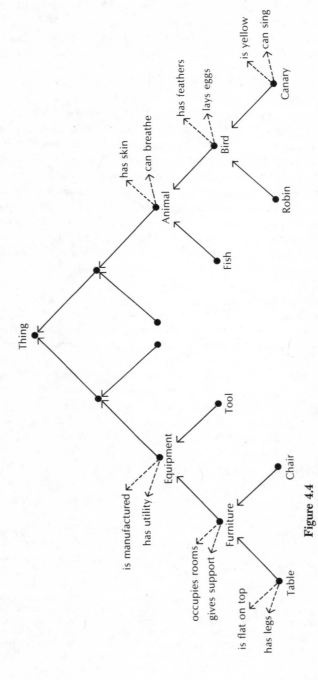

Figure 4.4

A schematization of Quillian's network model for storing information about word meanings. (Adapted with permission from A. M. Collins and M. R. Quillian. Retrieval time from semantic memory, in *Journal of Verbal Learning and Verbal Behavior*, 1969, 8, p. 241, published by Academic Press, New York.)

search proceeds by following the links that connect the different categories.[10] Along the way, checks are made to see if any of the paths extending from the first category intersect the paths extending from the second category. The duration of the search increases with the distance traversed through the network. If no intersections are found within a reasonable time, the search terminates and a decision is made that the categories have a disjoint relation. But if an intersection between the paths is found, then the composite links forming the paths are evaluated more carefully (Stage 3b).[11] The evaluation is done by analyzing which kinds of links form the paths connecting the categories. Again, the time required for the evaluation increases as the distance separating the categories in the memory structure increases. If the links satisfy certain restrictions, the third stage produces an affirmative outcome, yielding a decision that the categories of the sentence have either a subset, superset, or partial overlap relation with each other.[12] Subsequently a person would respond that the sentence is true. Otherwise, if the outcome of the third stage is negative for one reason or another, he would respond that the sentence is false, because the categories are disjoint. In fact, such a memory search and evaluation is similar to the one Quillian (1969) used in designing his sentence-comprehension program for computers.[13]

The proposed mechanism for Stage three of comprehending existential-affirmative sentences would explain why category size affected reaction times in our first experiment (Table 4.2). For example, let us consider a collection of "nested" categories such as python, snake, reptile, animal, and organism. Quillian's model has each of these categories linked to the immediately suc-

---

[10]As proposed by Quillian (1969), many different paths would be checked at the same time, so that the search is a "parallel" one. However, this is not an essential feature of the model. The different paths could be checked one at a time, so that the search would be "serial" instead of parallel (Anderson and Bower, 1973). The only necessary requirement is that a tag be left at the location of each intervening category encountered during the search along a path, thereby allowing the process to realize when two paths have intersected each other.

[11]Stage 3b is necessary because an intersection could be found between the locations of two disjoint categories like canary and robin, by virtue of their mutual proximity to bird in the memory structure.

[12]The evaluation process may apply several criteria to reach a positive outcome in Stage 3b. For example, suppose that the locations of two categories C_1 and C_2 are connected by a series of superset links through the memory structure. If each arrow along the way points from C_1 to C_2, then C_1 must be a subset of C_2. Conversely, if each arrow points from C_2 to C_1, then C_1 must be a superset of C_2. At least a partial-overlap relation would be indicated if a third intermediate category C_3 exists such that the path from C_1 to C_2 goes through the location of C_3, but the arrows all point from C_3 to C_1 and C_2, implying that C_3 is a mutual subset of C_1 and C_2. In contrast, if the arrows all point from C_1 and C_2 to C_3, then C_3 would be a mutual superset of C_1 and C_2, which could happen even if these first two categories are disjoint.

[13]The mechanism outlined in Figure 4.5 also resembles a two-stage model for sentence-comprehension that we have outlined elsewhere (Meyer, 1970). In the terminology of that earlier paper, the present Stage 3a represents a modification of our previous first stage, while Stage 3b represents a modification of our previous second stage. For further details about how these operations might work, see Meyer (1970) and Quillian (1969).

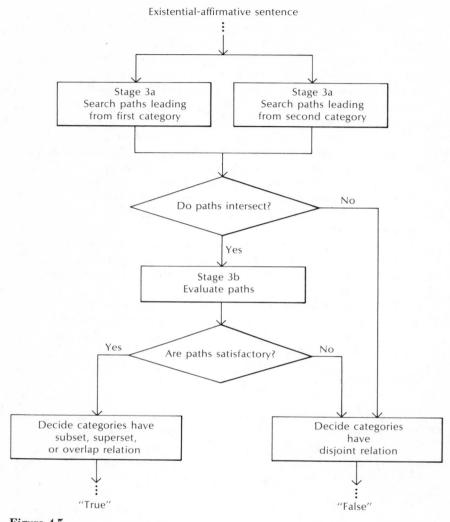

Figure 4.5

A mechanism using Quillian's memory network to determine the set relations among stored categories.

ceeding category, since they form a series of subsets and supersets whose sizes range from very small to very large. When a person must decide whether it is true that "Some pythons are reptiles," the model implies that paths leading from the locations of python and reptile are searched in the memory structure. Because these categories are stored relatively close together, an intersection should be found quickly at the location for snake, and an evaluation of the paths leading to the intersection would reveal that the sentence is true. But just as we observed, the decision should take much longer for a sentence like "Some pythons are organisms," which deals with two categories whose sizes differ much more than the sizes of the categories in the preceding example. It would take longer to find the intersection and evaluate the paths connecting python and organism because these two categories are stored farther apart in the memory structure.

Likewise it is possible to explain the observed effects of set relation in terms of path searching and evaluation. In Quillian's model, categories that have a disjoint relation or just overlap partially would usually be located farther from each other than subsets and supersets.[14] As a result, the third stage of comprehension should take longer for the overlap and disjoint relations than for the subset and superset relations, just as our reaction times indicate.[15]

Furthermore, Quillian's model has a certain logical appeal. It seems reasonable that people would store rather precise information about the nature of familiar categories of objects and that the semantic structure of memory could influence relatively "high-level" operations, such as those determining the set relation between two categories (Stage 3, Figure 4.3). In contrast, there is less reason to expect that the memory structure influences earlier stages of the comprehension process during which a visual or aural code for the words of a sentence is formed and used to locate designated categories (Stages 1 and 2, Figure 4.3).

3. Visual Recognition of Semantically Related and Unrelated Words

Nontheless we have reasons to doubt that the preceding account is entirely adequate. Our experiments on word recognition have shown that the semantic structure of memory may actually influence operations that occur before the later stages of sentence comprehension. It even appears that a person's ability to see printed words is in some sense affected by the memory structure, contrary to previous expectations.

3.1 Method

During one of our word-recognition experiments, for example, each of 16 people participated in more than 200 test trials. The procedure followed on a

[14]Two partially overlapping categories (e.g., mother and writer) in the memory structure should ordinarily have at least one other category (e.g., poetess) intervening between them. Thus a combination of two or more links would be required to connect them. But this would not be required for two categories (e.g., pine and tree) where one is an immediate superset of the other.

[15]For alternative explanations of the category-size and set-relation effects, see Landauer (1975), Landauer and Meyer (1972), Meyer (1970), Rips, Shoben, and Smith (1973), Schaeffer and Wallace (1969, 1970), and Smith, Shoben, and Rips (1974).

typical trial is shown in Figure 4.6 (Meyer et al., 1975). Each trial began with the presentation of two fixation points on a display screen. Then a row of letters appeared and the person participating in the experiment had to decide whether or not it was an English word (cf. Rubenstein, Garfield, and Millikan, 1970). He pressed a key with one finger to indicate an affirmative decision; he pressed a different key with another finger to indicate a negative decision. If the first row of letters was one like *wine*, then the correct response was "yes," because *wine* is an English word. Immediately after the response, the first row of letters disappeared, and a second row of letters was displayed below the spot where the first row had appeared. Again the person had to decide whether or not the row of letters was a word, and he indicated the decision by pressing the appropriate key. If the second row of letters was one like *plame*, the correct response was "no," because *plame* is not an English word.

We encouraged the participants in the experiment to respond quickly and accurately. After each trial, they received feedback about whether their responses to both rows of letters were correct. We measured the reaction time for each response from the moment a row of letters appeared on the screen to the moment a key was pressed. No row of letters was presented more than once to a particular individual.

Table 4.3 illustrates other rows of letters we presented as stimuli. We grouped the rows of letters into pairs, and used one pair for each trial of the experiment. Some of the pairs contained a mixture of words and nonwords such as *wine* and *plame* or *veath* and *hair*. Other pairs included two nonwords such as *nart* and *trief*. We constructed the nonwords so that they looked and sounded similar to English words but were not members of the English language (i.e., did not appear in *Webster's New Collegiate Dictionary*, 1961).

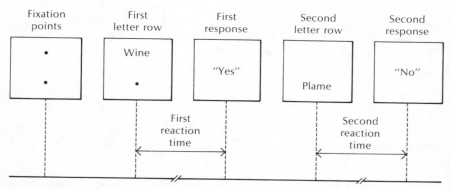

Figure 4.6
Procedure followed during a typical trial of the word-recognition experiment. (Adapted with permission from D. E. Meyer, R. W. Schvaneveldt, and M. G. Ruddy. Loci of contextual effects on visual word recognition. In P. M. A. Rabbitt and S. Dornic [Eds.], *Attention and performance* V. London: Academic Press, 1975.)

Table 4.3 Pairs of Letter Rows from the Recognition Experiment Using Normal Words, Visually Degraded Words, Nonwords, and Visually Degraded Nonwords

Type of pair	Examples	Correct responses
Word-nonword	*wine-plame* *glove-soam*	Yes-no
Nonword-word	*veath-hair* *jace-candy*	No-yes
Nonword-nonword	*nart-trief* *pable-reab*	No-no
Related words	*bread-butter* *nurse-doctor*	Yes-yes
Unrelated words	*nurse-butter* *bread-doctor*	Yes-yes

Still other pairs contained only words. One type of all-word pair contained words whose meanings were related to each other in the sense that they referred to similar categories of objects, such as *bread* and *butter*, which are both foods, or *nurse* and *doctor*, which are both medical professionals. We selected these pairs from standard word-association norms (e.g., Bousfield, Cohen, Whitmarsh, and Kincaid, 1961; Palermo and Jenkins, 1964).[16] Another type of all-word pair contained words with relatively unrelated meanings, such as *nurse* and *butter*, or *bread* and *doctor*; we constructed these pairs by randomly interchanging the words of the related pairs.[17]

We also varied the legibility of the rows of letters. On some trials, the words appeared in "normal" uppercase letters, as shown in Figure 4.7a. On other trials, we displayed the words with a pattern of dots over them as shown in Figure 4.7b. This pattern was chosen because it degrades the letters without obscuring the words so much that they are impossible to see. We degraded the nonwords on some trials as well. Regardless of legibility, however, a person merely decided which rows of letters were words and which were nonwords.

Our experiment on word-recognition therefore required fewer mental processes than our experiment on sentence comprehension (Section 2). Unlike

---

[16]We also included other pairs whose second words denoted synonyms (e.g., *pain-hurt*), antonyms (e.g., *hate-love*), supersets (e.g., *apple-fruit*), subsets (e.g., *flower-rose*), attributes of objects (e.g., *lemon-sour*), and parts of objects (e.g., *wagon-wheel*).

[17]Exactly the same words were used in both the related and unrelated pairs. This means that our results revealing differences in performance with such pairs cannot be attributed to idiosyncrasies of the individual words themselves.

Figure 4.7a
Example of a word displayed with "normal" legibility. (Reproduced with permission from D. E. Meyer, R. W. Schvaneveldt, and M. G. Ruddy. Loci of contextual effects on visual word recognition. In P. M. A. Rabbitt and S. Dornic [Eds.], *Attention and performance* V. London: Academic Press, 1975.)

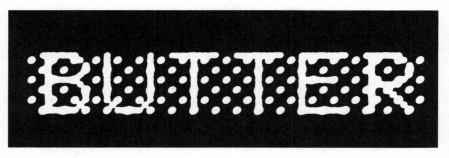

Figure 4.7b
Example of a word whose legibility was "degraded." (Reproduced with permission from D. E. Meyer, R. W. Schvaneveldt, and M. G. Ruddy. Loci of contextual effects on visual word recognition. In P. M. A. Rabbitt and S. Dornic [Eds.], *Attention and performance* V. London: Academic Press, 1975.)

the comprehension experiment, the recognition experiment did not call for people to determine whether the categories designated by the words had any members in common. Instead, before responding they only had to encode each row of letters individually and then try to find the location of the designated category in memory. If the duration of Stage 3 but not of Stage 1 or 2 (Figure 4.3) depended on the memory structure, as suggested previously, then relations among the meanings of the words should not have affected reaction times in the recognition experiment.

3.2   Results

Still we found that the meanings mattered considerably, as shown in Figure 4.8 where we have plotted the mean reaction times for affirmative responses to the second rows of letters from both related and unrelated pairs of words.

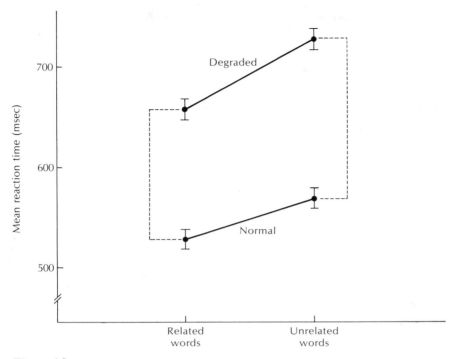

Figure 4.8
Mean reaction times to recognize the second words of related and unrelated pairs with normal and degraded letters.

Responses in the recognition experiment were significantly faster when the words had related meanings than when they had unrelated meanings [mean difference $= 55 \pm 7$ msec; $F(1,4) = 27.1, p < .01$]. For example, people were faster at recognizing that *butter* was a word when it followed the word *bread* than when it followed the word *nurse*. Furthermore, we found that degrading the words increased reaction times significantly [mean difference $= 146 \pm 12$ msec; $F(1,4) = 98.9, p < .01$]. Responses were much slower if the words had a pattern of dots over them than if they were displayed normally. But as the dashed brackets indicate, the harmful effect of degradation was not as great for words that had related meanings as for words that had unrelated meanings [mean difference $= 33 \pm 8$ msec; $F(1,14) = 5.2; p < .05$].[18]

[18]Like the participants in our sentence-comprehension experiment (Section 2), people seldom made errors during the word-recognition experiment. Incorrect responses to the words occurred on less than 4% of the trials, although there was a positive correlation between the mean reaction times and the error rates. Correct responses to the nonwords took about 200 msec longer than for the words, and the effect of degrading the letters was larger for the nonwords (cf. Stanners, Jastrzembski, and Westbrook, 1975). For further information about responses to nonwords, there are several other sources (e.g., Meyer and Schvaneveldt, 1971; Rubenstein, Lewis, and Rubenstein, 1971).

Paralleling these results, we have also found that a person takes less time to pronounce a printed word if its meaning is related to that of an immediately preceding word (Meyer et al., 1975). The decrease in the time required for pronunciation approximately equals the decrease that a close semantic relation produces in deciding that a row of letters is a word. Likewise the harmful effects of degradation on pronouncing words are reduced by close relations among their meanings. Although the facilitation tends to disappear when there is a delay between the occurrence of one related word and another, it is not eliminated by presenting an unrelated word during the interval (Meyer et al., 1972).

3.3 Discussion

Contrary to previous points of view (e.g., Collins and Quillian, 1969; Conrad, 1972; Glass and Holyoak, 1974; Loftus, 1973; Meyer, 1970; Quillian, 1969; Rips, 1975; Schaeffer and Wallace, 1970; Smith et al., 1974), our new findings indicate that the memory structure does more than just influence the stage of processing that determines the set relations among categories during sentence comprehension. The semantic structure of memory seems to facilitate the initial encoding of words and the accessing of their meanings. Close relations between the meanings of words may actually enable people to see the words more easily.

To explain these observations more fully, we have considered a variety of alternative models (Becker et al., 1973; Meyer and Schvaneveldt, 1971; Meyer et al., 1972, 1975; Schvaneveldt and Meyer, 1973). It is possible that people depend on the context established by prior words to form expectations about what words will occur subsequently (Bruner, 1957; Neisser, 1967). A complementary idea is that the recognition process relies on a set of word detectors to combine sensory and semantic information concerning rows of letters (Corcoran, 1971; Keele, 1973; Morton, 1969).

For example, Figure 4.9 illustrates one intriguing mechanism whereby word recognition is perhaps achieved. The system resembles other models proposed recently by several investigators (e.g., Collins and Loftus, 1975; Loftus and Cole, 1974; Morton, 1969, 1970; Norman and Rumelhart, 1970). It contains three parts, including a visual-feature analyzer, a set of word detectors, and a collateral network of memory locations linked according to relations among categories of objects as discussed earlier (Section 2.3). There are parallel connections between the feature analyzer and the word detectors. The word detectors have been arranged spatially to coincide with the locations in the memory structure of the underlying categories. The detectors of words with related meanings (such as *bread, butter,* and *food,* or *nurse, doctor,* and *person*) are closely interconnected through the memory structure, while the detectors of words with very different meanings (like *nurse* and *butter*) have only remote connections.

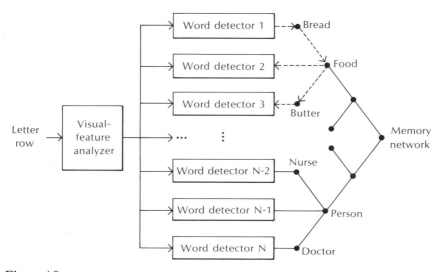

Figure 4.9

A hypothetical mechanism for combining sensory and semantic information during word recognition.

According to this model, the recognition process begins when a row of letters enters the feature analyzer, which produces a code representing the shapes of the letters, including their lines, curves, and angles, as well as the spatial relations among them. The output of the feature analyzer goes to the various word detectors, where counts are made of how many visual features the row of letters has in common with particular words.[19] The count by the detector of a word like *bread* presumably increases when appropriately oriented curves appear in the first, second, or fifth position of the letter row. Associated with each detector, there is a specified value that acts as a "threshold." When the count by a detector exceeds its threshold, an affirmative signal is produced to indicate that the corresponding word has just occurred. But it takes time to accumulate the necessary information, and its sensitivity may fluctuate. If none of the counts by the detectors exceeds a threshold within an established time period, the detector system produces a negative signal that the row of letters is not a word. In terms of the previous depiction of sentence comprehension (Figure 4.3), the analysis of visual features would form part of the encoding operation (Stage 1), while the signaling by the word

[19]Although we have omitted intermediate transformations between the visual-feature analyzer and word detectors, this is not a necessary restriction of the model. It may be expanded to incorporate additional components that convert collections of visual features to orthographic and/or phonemic representations before input to the word detectors, which would then operate on features of these higher-level codes. Indeed some data suggest that people rely extensively on such components under certain conditions (e.g., Meyer, Schvaneveldt, and Ruddy, 1974; Rubenstein, Lewis, and Rubenstein, 1971).

detectors could serve to locate the underlying categories in the memory structure (Stage 2).

Now let us suppose that the appearance of a word like *bread* has just caused its detector to exceed threshold. Our idea is that this event sends residual impulses through the memory structure to "excite" other nearby detectors, as illustrated by the dashed lines in Figures 4.9 (cf. Collins and Loftus, 1975; Morton, 1970). The excitation of these detectors facilitates the subsequent processing of words, such as *butter* and *food*, that have meanings related to *bread*. For example, after a word detector has been excited, it could accumulate sensory information more rapidly from the feature analyzer, or the minimum number of relevant features that the detector requires to produce an affirmative signal could be lowered. These changes would explain why people take less time to recognize words with related meanings than to recognize words with unrelated meanings. Assuming that the visual-feature analyzer does not completely remove distortions from a row of letters, the model would also account for why close relations of meaning help to overcome the harmful effects produced by visual degradation of the words.[20] The excitation probably dissipates after a while, since related words facilitate responses less as the time interval increases between them.

This view of the word-recognition process has some important implications. One is that after a person recognizes a word, subsequent operations occur even though the situation does not require them. Because an individual word can be identified out of context, we believe the operation that subsequently excites other detectors by sending residual impulses through the memory structure is not necessary for recognition. Instead the excitation seems more akin to the previously proposed operation in which paths are searched to determine the set relation between two categories (Stage 3a, Figure 4.5). However, we must still distinguish between the influence that the memory structure has on the processing of visual features and the influence it has on the search itself. As our recent experiments demonstrate, the proximity of stored categories may allow people to process the visual features of related words more quickly in addition to speeding the later discovery of what their relations are.

A second implication is that certain operations on printed words are not sufficient by themselves to facilitate subsequent recognition of other related words. For example, let us suppose that the initial processing of a word stops immediately after its visual features are analyzed. Then, according to the model in Figure 4.9, the appearance of this word will not facilitate the recog-

---

[20]One possibility is that degradation may eliminate some proportion of relevant visual features from a row of letters. If a word detector checks the remaining features more rapidly or requires fewer features to recognize the related word, it can reach its threshold without taking as much extra time as the degradation would otherwise cause it to consume.

nition of other words, because facilitation depends on eventually arriving at a specific stored meaning for the first word.

4. Recognition of Words with Ambiguous Meanings

Indeed the role that meaning plays during word recognition is revealed even more by the results from one of our further experiments (Schvaneveldt et al., 1974, in press). In this next experiment, we added a new type of stimulus known as a *homograph*, an ambiguous word that has the same spelling as another word but a different meaning; for example, *bank* can refer to either a financial institution or the ground beside a body of water. The presentation of homographic stimuli allowed us to determine precisely how the recognition of a word is influenced by the processing of the visual and semantic features of previously presented words.

4.1 Method

On every trial of the experiment, three rows of letters (instead of just two) were displayed successively, as illustrated in Figure 4.10. We asked the people participating in the experiment to decide which rows were words and which were nonwords. Both affirmative and negative responses typically occurred during a trial. Following our earlier procedure, we measured reaction times separately for each response.

4.2 Results

The most interesting results come from those trials on which all three rows of letters were actually words. Table 4.4 lists the mean reaction times for

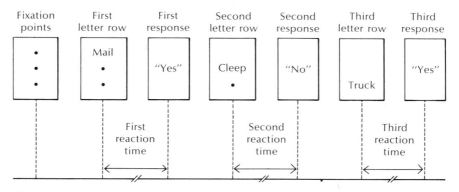

Figure 4.10
Procedure followed on a typical trial of the word-recognition experiment involving ambiguous words and nonwords.

Table 4.4 Mean Reaction Times (RT) to Recognize the Third
Row of Letters from Various Word Sequences

Type of sequence	Examples	Mean RT (msec)
Concordant related words	*save-bank-money* *day-date-time*	505 ± 7
Discordant related words	*river-bank-money* *fig-date-time*	558 ± 8
Initial related words	*river-bank-time* *fig-date-money*	551 ± 8

affirmative responses to the third rows of letters from some of the word sequences. In each of these sequences, the second word was spelled the same,
but it had at least two possible meanings and was therefore ambiguous. The
first word was chosen to bias the interpretation of the second word. We
measured how much this bias affected the later recognition of the third word,
whose meaning was either related or unrelated to the second word.

Now let us consider what happened for the sequences of *concordant related
words* like *save, bank,* and *money* in the upper row of Table 4.4. In this
case, the meaning of the third word was related to one possible meaning
of the ambiguous second word, and the first word biased the interpretation
of the second word toward the same meaning; that is *save* and *money* both
referred to the financial meaning of *bank* rather than to its geographical
meaning. We found that the reaction times to recognize the third word in
sequences of concordant related words were relatively short.[21]

On the other hand, significantly slower responses occurred for sequences of
discordant related words like *river, bank,* and *money*. In this case, the meaning
of the third word was again related to one possible meaning of the ambiguous
second word. But the first word biased the interpretation of the second word
toward a different meaning; that is, *river* referred to the geographical meaning of *bank*, while *money* referred to its financial meaning. We found that
the reaction times to recognize the third word in sequences of discordant
related words were 53 ± 10 msec longer than for the concordant related
words [$F(1,11) = 28.7, p < .01$].

---

[21]The fast responses for the concordant related words cannot be attributed solely to the
relation that was present between the meanings of the first and third members of these
sequences. To eliminate this possibility, we included a control involving sequences of "separated
related words" like *save, date,* and *money,* where the first and third words had related (e.g.,
financial) meanings, but the ambiguous second word had two unrelated meanings (e.g., temporal
and edible). Reaction times to recognize the third words in the sequences of separated related
words revealed less facilitation than occurred for the sequences of concordant related words.

In fact, the reaction times for the discordant related words were about the same as the reaction times for sequences of *initial related words* like *river*, *bank*, and *time*, where only the first and second words were related to each other [mean difference = -7 ± 11 msec; $F(1,11) < 1.0$]. This result occurred even though the meaning of the third word (e.g., *time*) in sequences of initial related words was different from both meanings of the ambiguous second word.

4.3   Discussion

The experiment using homographs suggests that merely processing the visual features of the second word in a three-word sequence does not influence the recognition of the third word, even when there is a potential semantic relation between the words. Instead it appears that the speed of recognizing a subsequent word depends primarily on how the meaning of a prior word has been specifically interpreted. This finding supports the view of the recognition process outlined in Figure 4.9.

The data are consistent with the idea that an ambiguous word like *bank* has separate detectors corresponding to each distinct meaning of the word (Morton, 1969; Rubenstein et al., 1970). The excitation induced by prior semantic context could control which detector signals the occurrence of an ambiguous word. Such a mechanism would explain why a relation with one meaning of the ambiguous word precludes facilitation in recognizing a subsequent word with a different relation.[22] It also helps to explain why people usually notice only one of several potential meanings that a sentence may have (Lackner and Garrett, 1972; MacKay, 1973).

5. Comprehension of Universal-Affirmative Sentences

Still there are some basic questions to be answered. So far we have discussed three mental processes that the semantic structure of memory might influence: detecting the visual features of printed words (Figure 4.9), finding paths that

---

[22]For example, consider a sequence of concordant related words like *save*, *bank*, and *money*. Recognizing the word *save* presumably excites the detector corresponding to the financial meaning of *bank*, rather than the detector corresponding to its geographical meaning. Hence a person is primed to recognize the word *bank* as having a financial meaning, since the detector corresponding to that meaning should produce an affirmative signal rather quickly. In turn, accessing the financial meaning of *bank* would excite the detectors of other related financial words like *money*. But the first two members of a sequence of discordant related words like *river*, *bank*, and *money* could prime a person to recognize subsequent words with geographical rather than financial meanings, thereby preventing the prior excitation of the detector for *money* (Schvaneveldt, Meyer, and Becker, in press).

connect stored categories in the memory structure (Figure 4.5, Stage 3a), and evaluating any paths discovered (Figure 4.5, Stage 3b). It is possible that only the feature-detecting and path-finding operations actually depend on the proximity of the categories, because this proximity alone could have produced the facilitation of responses in both our sentence-comprehension (Section 2) and word-recognition (Sections 3 and 4) experiments. We are unable to tell for certain yet whether the path-evaluation operation also depends on the categories' proximity. Furthermore it is not certain whether the proximity of categories always facilitates the use of information from the memory structure. To determine the effects of proximity more fully, we must consider another experiment on sentence comprehension (Meyer, 1970) that was done in conjunction with the previously discussed experiments.

5.1   Method

In the final experiment that we will discuss here, our method was similar to the one described previously for studying sentence comprehension (Section 2.1). We again measured how long it took to decide whether various statements about familiar categories of objects were true or false. But rather than asking people to respond to existential-affirmative sentences such as the statement that "Some pines are trees" (Table 4.1), we asked them to respond to universal-affirmative sentences such as the statement that "All pines are trees" (Table 4.5).

As before, we varied the set relations and the sizes of the categories from one sentence to another. Unlike the existential affirmatives, however, the universal affirmatives were true only if the first category had a subset relation with the second category; the universal affirmatives were false whenever the two categories had a superset, overlap, or disjoint relation. For example, it was true that "All pines are trees," but false that "All stones are rubies."[23]

Because of this property, the universal affirmatives required a more careful determination of the set relations between the categories than did the existential affirmatives (Section 2.2). To decide whether a universal affirmative (e.g., "All pines are trees") was true or false, a person needed to check his long-term memory for information about whether the first category had a subset relation with the second category. With existential affirmatives, (e.g., "Some pines are trees"), he needed only to check whether the two categories shared any of the same members (Section 2). The added requirement for universal affirmatives allowed us to learn more concerning the influence of the memory structure on later stages of sentence comprehension, and our findings about the compre-

---

[23]Half of the sentences in the experiment with universal affirmatives actually involved a subset relation, so that the relative frequencies of true and false sentences were equated as in our other comprehension experiment (Section 2). Among the false universal affirmatives, the superset, partial overlap, and disjoint relations occurred equally often.

Table 4.5 Construction of Universal-Affirmative
Sentences

Set relations	Examples	Truth values
Subset	All pines are trees.	True
Superset	All stones are rubies.	False
Overlap	All writers are mothers.	False
Disjoint	All clouds are wrists.	False

hension of universal-affirmative sentences differed somewhat from our findings about the comprehension of existential-affirmative sentences.

5.2 Results

In Figure 4.11 we have plotted the mean reaction times of correct responses to the universal affirmatives as a function of the set relations between the categories. For purposes of comparison, the reaction times from our first experiment with the existential affirmatives are also shown (cf. Figure 4.2).[24]

The effects of the set relation on the reaction times differed greatly for the two types of sentences. Whereas responses to the existential affirmatives were slowest when the categories of a sentence had a disjoint relation, the slowest responses to universal affirmatives occurred when there was a superset relation. For example, people took about 185 ± 27 msec longer to respond that a sentence like "All stones are gems" is false than to respond that a sentence like "All clouds are wrists" is false $[min\ F(1,85) = 47.6, p < .01]$. Unlike our earlier observations (Section 2.2), these data indicate that close relations of meaning can increase the reaction times for responses to universal affirmative sentences. Similar results have been reported recently by other investigators (e.g., Collins and Quillian, 1969; Rips et al., 1973; Schaeffer and Wallace, 1970).[25]

----

[24]The confidence intervals in Figure 4.11 (mean reaction-times plus or minus one standard error) allow us to assess the effects of set relation while holding the type of sentence constant. They show, for example, that responses to the universal affirmatives were significantly slower when the categories had a superset rather than a disjoint relation. But we need to compute another set of confidence intervals (not shown in Figure 4.11) to assess the differences between the mean reaction times for the two types of sentences while holding the set relation constant. This is because the experiment with the universal-affirmative sentences involved a different group of people than the experiment with existential affirmatives (Meyer, 1970).

[25]One important aspect of our procedure should be emphasized. We asked participants to respond to the universal-affirmative sentences during groups of trials separate from the ones on which we asked for responses to existential-affirmative sentences. Some investigators have found that differences in reaction times for the two types of sentence are not as great when mixed presentations of both universal- and existential-affirmatives occur during the same block of trials (Glass and Holyoak, 1974; Rips, 1975). A possible reason is that mixing the sentence types may force a person to use exactly the same operations for comprehending each type.

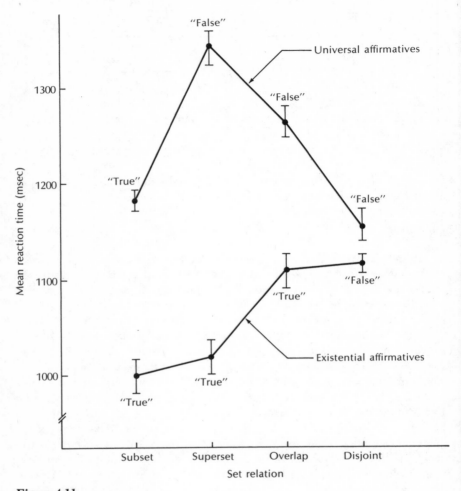

Figure 4.11
Mean reaction times as a function of set relations for the universal-affirmative sentences compared to the existential-affirmative sentences (cf. Figure 2).

Further differences between universal and existential affirmatives appear when we compare Tables 4.6 and 4.2, which summarize some of the effects that variations in category size had on reaction times for the two types of sentences. If the first category of a sentence was a subset of the second category, increasing the size of the second category slowed responses to the universal affirmatives [$min\ F(1,38) = 4.5, p < .05$]. People took about 54 ± 26 msec longer with a sentence like "All pines are plants" than with a sentence like "All pines are trees." But this effect of category size on reaction time was not as great for responses to universal affirmatives as it was for the correspond-

Table 4.6 Some Effects of Category Size on Reaction Times (RT) for Responses to Universal-Affirmative Sentences

Set Relation	Size of Second Category	Examples	Mean RT (msec)	Mean Change in RT due to Increase in Category Size (msec)
Subset	Small	All pines are trees.	1142	54 ± 26
	Large	All pines are plants.	1196	
Superset	Small	All stones are rubies.	1351	146 ± 52
	Large	All stones are gems.	1497	

ing responses to existential affirmatives. (Table 4.2 shows an increase in reaction time of about 200 msec.) In fact, the category-size effects for the two types of sentences differed by about 144 ± 44 msec when the first category had a subset relation with the second category [$min\ F(1,51) = 10.8, p < .01$].

Likewise we found that the category-size effects for the universal and existential affirmatives differed greatly when the first category was a superset of the second category. In this case, increasing the size of the second category increased reaction times for the universal affirmatives (Table 4.6), whereas increasing the size of the second category decreased reaction times for the existential affirmatives (Table 4.2). People took about 146 ± 52 msec longer with a sentence like "All stones are gems" than with a sentence like "All stones are rubies" [$min\ F(1,13) = 7.8, p < .05$].[26]

5.3 Discussion

We can interpret our findings by referring again to Quillian's (1969) network model of long-term verbal memory (Figure 4.4). The variation of set relations and category sizes during the experiment with universal-affirmative sentences presumably involved changing the distance between the locations of stored categories, just as it did in the experiment with existential-affirmative sentences (Section 2). The fact that the results of the two experiments differ suggests that the proximity of categories in the memory structure inhibits comprehension under some conditions, even though proximity facilitates comprehension under other conditions.

It seems unlikely that any inhibition occurs before a person finishes analyzing the visual features and detecting the words of a sentence (Figure 4.9).

---

[26] As in our first experiment with existential-affirmative sentences (Section 2), there were other reliable effects of category size on reaction times that we will not discuss here. For example, when the first and second categories of the universal affirmatives were disjoint, increasing the size of the second category increased reaction time [$min\ F(1,11) = 5.3, p < .05$]. People took about 58 ± 25 msec longer to respond to a sentence like "All clouds are joints" than to respond to a sentence like "All clouds are wrists."

All the results from our word recognition experiments imply that people initially process words with related meanings faster than words with unrelated meanings (Sections 3 and 4). Instead the inhibition probably occurs during subsequent attempts to determine the set relation between two categories by searching and evaluating paths through the network of memory links (cf. Figure 4.5). As Quillian (1969) originally proposed, the discovery of such paths may be faster if the categories are stored close together.[27] However, the path evaluation may involve a mechanism whose operation is slowed by the proximity of stored categories.

In particular, we suspect that the mechanism outlined in Figure 4.12 plays a role in the path-evaluation process for universal-affirmative sentences like "All pines are trees." The purpose of the mechanism is to check whether the first category of a sentence has a subset relation with the second category. Rather than directly evaluating the composite links of any paths discovered earlier between the two categories, the mechanism relies on a different kind of information. It assumes that in addition to the set relations represented by marked links in the memory network, each category is also connected separately to a collection of defining attributes (including size, shape, color, etc.) that together specify the nature of the category members (cf. Figure 4.4; Kintsch, 1972; Meyer, 1970; Rosch, 1973; Schaeffer and Wallace, 1970; Smith et al., 1974). When the attribute mechanism operates, the defining attributes of the second category (e.g., trees) in a sentence are retrieved from memory and compared with the defining attributes of the first category (e.g., pines). If each attribute (e.g., greenness) of the second category is found to match some attribute of the first category, then a decision is made that the first category has a subset relation with the second category, and the sentence is classified as true. In contrast, the attribute mechanism would determine that a sentence like "All stones are rubies" is false. In evaluating such a sentence, the mechanism would find some defining attribute (e.g., preciousness) of the second category (e.g., rubies) that has no counterpart among the defining attributes of the first category (e.g., stones); it would then make a decision that the first category does not have a subset relation with the second category. The mechanism produces correct evaluations because all the defining attributes of the second category would also characterize the first category if the first category forms a subset of the second.[28]

---

[27]There is additional evidence to support this proposal. Facilitation for stimuli involving close relations of meaning was considerably greater in some of our sentence-comprehension experiments (e.g., Section 2) than in any of our word-recognition experiments. Such a result suggests that the proximity of stored categories in memory has beneficial effects beyond those that occur during the earliest stages of visual-feature analysis and word detection.

[28]Of course, special provisions must be made for certain idiosyncratic subsets that lack a defining attribute of their supersets, such as some Japanese maple trees have red rather than green leaves. Smith, Shoben, and Rips (1974) have discussed how the attribute mechanism could be extended to handle these unusual cases.

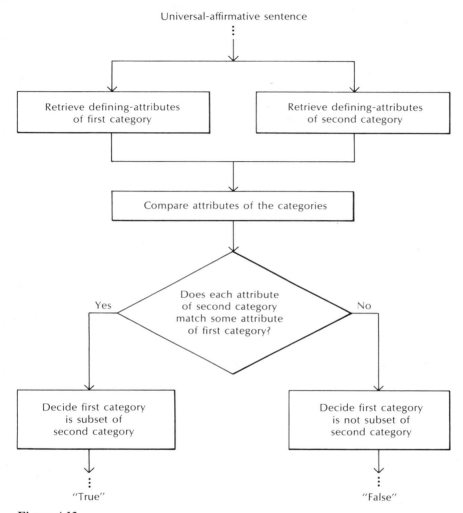

Figure 4.12
An attribute mechanism for evaluating whether the first category of a universal-affirmative sentence is a subset of the second category.

The attribute mechanism would increase reaction times for false universal-affirmative sentences in which the categories have closely related meanings. For example, let us again consider a sentence like "All stones are rubies," in which the first category is a superset of the second category. Even though stones in general do not have certain characteristics (i.e., preciousness) that are defining attributes of rubies, it would be relatively difficult to determine that stones are not a subset of rubies. This is because the two categories still have many other attributes in common (i.e., hardness, inanimateness, etc.), and a considerable amount of checking would be required to find some defining attribute of rubies that is not shared by stones. On the other hand, consider a sentence like "All clouds are wrists," in which the categories are disjoint. If a person relies on the attribute mechanism, it would be relatively easy to determine that clouds are not a subset of wrists. This is because the two categories have few if any attributes in common so that just a little checking would uncover some defining attribute (e.g., solidity) that wrists do not share with clouds.

Hence, with the attribute mechanism we can explain why it took longer for subjects to respond to false universal-affirmative sentences when their categories had a superset relation than when they had a disjoint relation (Figure 4.11). Depending on various parameters of the mechanism, close relations of meaning would extend the retrieval and comparison of attributes sufficiently to obscure any prior facilitation. Moreover the attribute mechanism would account for some of the observed category-size effects (Table 4.6), because changing category size also changes the number of shared attributes (Meyer, 1970).

However, the success of this explanation raises other questions. Since close relations of meaning did not have an inhibitory effect in our earlier experiment using existential affirmatives (Section 2), we must ask whether the attribute mechanism played any role at all in the comprehension of existential-affirmative sentences like "Some stones are rubies." A likely answer is no. Contrary to our original application of Quillian's model (Figure 4.5), it is possible that the participants in our first experiment did not have to evaluate carefully any of the paths between the categories in the existential affirmatives. These sentences were true when the categories had either a subset, superset, or overlap relation with each other. The discovery of a relatively short series of memory links between the categories may have been sufficient to produce a correct response without subsequent operation of an attribute mechanism or some other device (cf. Meyer, 1970). In analyzing existential-affirmative sentences, people may therefore have bypassed the operations included in Stage 3b of Figure 4.5 (which are not facilitated by the proximity of stored categories) and only carried out the prior operations contained in Stage 3a of the diagram (which are facilitated by the proximity of stored categories). This explanation

---

[29]We can even deal with exceptional cases in which the reaction times for the two types of sentences did not differ significantly. When the first and second categories had a disjoint relation, "false" responses to the universal affirmatives were nearly as fast as "false" responses to the existential affirmatives. People took about the same amount of time for sentences like "All clouds are wrists" and "Some clouds are wrists" [*min F* < 1.0]. This result, combined with our other findings, implies that the comprehension of universal affirmatives did not always require a path-evaluation process. Only unsuccessful attempts to find a path linking the stored categories (Stage 3a, Figure 4.5) may have occurred for the existential affirmatives and the universal affirmatives with a disjoint relation (cf. Meyer, 1970).

would also account for the observation that responses to the existential-affirmative sentences were usually much faster than responses to the universal-affirmative sentences (Figure 4.11).[29]

We must also ask why people ever bother to rely on the proposed attribute mechanism. If the memory links between locations of stored categories are marked to designate their set relations, as Quillian (1969) proposed, then it would seem more efficient to examine the marks immediately to determine how the categories are related. The use of a more primitive attribute mechanism instead suggests that the links may not be marked precisely. It therefore appears that, in some form, a person can know that two categories are related without having stored the exact nature of their relation. Consequently, details about the relation may have to be computed from other information that is available.

6. Conclusion

In conclusion, we have found that the speed of various mental processes depends on relations among the meanings of familiar words. Our findings involve a pattern of reaction times obtained from word-recognition and sentence-comprehension experiments. Although the process of retrieving verbal information from long-term memory is usually rapid and accurate, it still remains sensitive to semantic factors. Available data support the view that long-term verbal memory is organized by meaning, but not all information is stored directly. The proximity of underlying categories in the memory structure facilitates the initial encoding of printed words and the accessing of their meanings, while sometimes inhibiting the subsequent determination of set relations between the designated categories.

We believe that our research is also relevant to the development of computer programs that can simulate certain mental processes. Some artificial-intelligence experts realize that meanings are not just the end product of sentence comprehension. Semantic relationships may play a critical role during the comprehension process itself. Several programs have used stored semantic information to guide the grammatical parsing of sentences and to formulate inferences about their specific meanings (Schank, 1972; Winograd, 1972). However, such programs typically assume that the letters and words of a sentence arrive in a form that is already suitable for the computer to begin higher-level analyses. Thus the creators of these programs have separated the process of comprehension from the process of pattern recognition, whereas these processes are not necessarily separate in the human brain. Our findings suggest that for computers as well as people, relations among the meanings of words could help to guide the recognition process as well as the comprehension process.

REFERENCES

Anderson, J. R., and Bower, G. H. *Human associative memory.* Washington, D.C.: Winston, 1973.

Anderson, R. C., and McGaw, B. On the representation of meanings of general terms. *Journal of Experimental Psychology,* 1973, *101,* 301–306.

Becker, C. A., Schvaneveldt, R. W., and Gomez, L. M. Semantic, graphemic, and phonetic factors in word recognition. Paper presented at the meeting of the Psychonomic Society, St. Louis, November 1973.

Bousfield, W. A., Cohen, B. H., Whitmarsh, G. A., and Kincaid, W. D. *The Connecticut free associational norms.* Tech. Rep. No. 35. Storrs: Department of Psychology, University of Connecticut, 1961.

Bruner, J. S. On perceptual readiness. *Psychological Review,* 1957, *64,* 123–152.

Cattell, J. McK. Experiments on the association of ideas. *Mind,* 1887, *12,* 68–74.

Clark, H. H. The language-as-fixed-effect fallacy: A critique of language statistics in psychological research. *Journal of Verbal Learning and Verbal Behavior,* 1973, *12,* 335–359.

Cofer, C. N. Properties of verbal materials and verbal learning. In J. W. Kling and L. A. Riggs (Eds.), *Woodworth and Schlosberg's experimental psychology.* New York: Holt, Rinehart, and Winston, 1971.

Cohen, B. H., Bousfield, W. A., and Whitmarsh, G. A. Cultural norms for verbal items in 43 categories. Tech. Rep. No. 22. Storrs: Department of Psychology, University of Connecticut, 1957.

Collins, A. M., and Loftus, E. F. A spreading-activation theory of semantic memory. *Psychological Review,* 1975, *82,* 407–428.

Collins, A. M., and Quillian, M. R. Retrieval time from semantic memory. *Journal of Verbal Learning and Verbal Behavior,* 1969, *8,* 240–247.

Collins, A. M., and Quillian, M. R. Facilitating retrieval from semantic memory: The effect of repeating part of an inference. In A. F. Sanders (Ed.), *Attention and performance III.* Amsterdam: North-Holland, 1970. (a)

Collins, A. M., and Quillian, M. R. Does category size affect categorization time? *Journal of Verbal Learning and Verbal Behavior,* 1970, *9,* 432–438. (b)

Collins, A. M., and Quillian, M. R. How to make a language user. In E. Tulving and W. Donaldson (Eds.), *Organization of memory.* New York: Academic Press, 1972.

Conrad, C. Cognitive economy in semantic memory. *Journal of Experimental Psychology,* 1972, *92,* 149–154.

Copi, I. M. *Symbolic logic.* New York: MacMillan, 1967.

Corcoran, D. W. J. *Pattern recognition.* Baltimore: Penguin, 1971.

Donders, F. C. [On the speed of mental processes.] In W. G. Koster (Ed. and trans.), *Attention and performance II.* Amsterdam: North Holland, 1969. (Reprinted from *Acta Psychologica,* 1969, *30;* originally published in 1868.)

Ebbinghaus, H. [Memory] (H. A. Ruger and C. E. Bussenius, trans.). New York: Teachers College, 1913. Reprint. New York: Dover, 1964. (Originally published in 1885.)

Freedman, J. L., and Loftus, E. F. Retrieval of words from long-term memory. *Journal of Verbal Learning and Verbal Behavior,* 1971, *10,* 107–115.

Glass, A. L., and Holyoak, K. J. The effect of *some* and *all* on reaction time for semantic decisions. *Memory and Cognition,* 1974, *2,* 436–440.

Gossman, J. R., and Meyer, D. E. Coordination of search processes in short-term and long-term memory. Paper presented at the meeting of the Midwestern Psychological Association, Chicago, May 1975.

Juola, J. F., and Atkinson, R. C. Memory scanning for words versus categories. *Journal of Verbal Learning and Verbal Behavior,* 1971, *10,* 522–527.

Keele, S. *Attention and human performance.* Pacific Palisades, Calif.: Goodyear, 1973.

Kintsch, W. Notes on the semantic structure of memory. In E. Tulving and W. Donaldson (Eds.), *Organization of memory.* New York: Academic Press, 1972.

Kucera, H., and Francis, W. N. *Computational analysis of present-day American English.* Providence, R. I.: Brown University Press, 1967.

Lackner, J. R., and Garret, M. F. Resolving ambiguity: Effects of biasing context in the unattended ear. *Cognition,* 1972, *1,* 350–372.

Landauer, T. K. Memory without organization: Explorations of a model with random storage and undirected retrieval. *Cognitive Psychology,* 1975, *7,* 495–531.

Landauer, T. K., and Freedman, J. L. Information retrieval from long-term memory: Category size and recognition time. *Journal of Verbal Learning and Verbal Behavior,* 1968, *7,* 291–295.

Landauer, T. K., and Meyer, D. E. Category size and semantic-memory retrieval. *Journal of Verbal Learning and Verbal Behavior,* 1972, *11,* 539–549.

Loftus, E. F. Category dominance, instance dominance, and categorization time. *Journal of Experimental Psychology,* 1973, *97,* 70–74.

Loftus, E. F., and Cole, W. Retrieving attribute and name information from semantic memory. *Journal of Experimental Psychology,* 1974, *102,* 1116–1122.

MacKay, D. G. Aspects of a theory of comprehension and attention. *Quarterly Journal of Experimental Psychology,* 1973, *25,* 22–40.

Meyer, D. E. On the representation and retrieval of stored semantic information. *Cognitive Psychology,* 1970, *1,* 242–299.

Meyer, D. E. Correlated operations in searching stored semantic categories. *Journal of Experimental Psychology,* 1973, *99,* 124–133. (a)

Meyer, D. E. Verifying affirmative and negative propositions: Effects of negation on memory retrieval. In S. Kornblum (Ed.), *Attention and performance IV.* New York: Academic Press, 1973. (b)

Meyer, D. E. Long-term memory retrieval during the comprehension of affirmative and negative sentences. In R. A. Kennedy and A. L. Wilkes (Eds.), *Studies in long-term memory.* London: Wiley, 1975.

Meyer, D. E. Semantic memory, sentence comprehension, and reaction time. *Bulletin de Psychologie,* in press.

Meyer, D. E., and Ellis, G. B. Parallel processes in word recognition. Paper presented at the meeting of the Psychonomic Society, San Antonio, Texas, November 1970.

Meyer, D. E., and Ruddy, M. G. Lexical-memory retrieval based on graphemic and phonemic representations of printed words. Paper presented at the meeting of the Psychonomic Society, St. Louis, November 1973.

Meyer, D. E., and Ruddy, M. G. Bilingual word-recognition: Organization and retrieval of alternative lexical codes. Paper presented at the meeting of the Eastern Psychological Association, Philadelphia, April 1974.

Meyer, D. E., and Schvaneveldt, R. W. Facilitation in recognizing pairs of words: Evidence of a dependence between retrieval operations. *Journal of Experimental Psychology*, 1971, *90*, 227–234.

Meyer, D. E., Schvaneveldt, R. W., and Ruddy, M. G. Activation of lexical memory. Paper presented at the meeting of the Psychonomic Society, St. Louis, November 1972.

Meyer, D. E., Schvaneveldt, R. W., and Ruddy, M. G. Functions of graphemic and phonemic codes in visual word-recognition. *Memory and Cognition*, 1974, *2*, 309–321.

Meyer, D. E., Schvaneveldt, R. W., and Ruddy, M. G. Loci of contextual effects on visual word recognition. In P. M. A. Rabbitt and S. Dornic (Eds.), *Attention and performance V*. London: Academic Press, 1975.

Morton, J. Interaction of information in word recognition. *Psychological Review*, 1969, *76*, 165–178.

Morton, J. A functional model of memory. In D. A. Norman (Ed.), *Models of human memory*. New York: Academic Press, 1970.

Neisser, U. *Cognitive psychology*. New York: Appleton-Century-Crofts, 1967.

Norman, D. A. *Memory and attention*. New York: Wiley, 1969.

Norman, D. A., and Rumelhart, D. E. A system for perception and memory. In D. A. Norman (Ed.), *Models of human memory*. New York: Academic Press, 1970.

Palermo, D. S., and Jenkins, J. J. *Word association norms: Grade school through college*. Minneapolis: University of Minnesota Press, 1964.

Quillian, M. R. The teachable language comprehender: A simulation program and a theory of language. *Communications of the Association of Computing Machinery*, 1969, *12*, 459–476.

Riegel, K. F. The Michigan restricted association norms. Report No. 3. Ann Arbor: Department of Psychology, University of Michigan, 1965.

Rips, L. J. Quantification and semantic memory. *Cognitive Psychology*, 1975, *7*, 307–340.

Rips, L. J., Shoben, E. J., and Smith, E. E. Semantic distance and the verification of semantic relations. *Journal of Verbal Learning and Verbal Behavior*, 1973, *12*, 1–20.

Roget's International Thesaurus. New York: Crowell, 1946.

Rosch, E. On the internal structure of perceptual and semantic categories. In T. E. Moore (Ed.), *Cognitive development and acquisition of language*. New York: Academic Press, 1973.

Rubenstein, H., Garfield, L., and Millikan, J. A. Homographic entries in the internal lexicon. *Journal of Verbal Learning and Verbal Behavior*, 1970, *9*, 487–494.

Rubenstein, H., Lewis, S. S., and Rubenstein, M. A. Evidence for phonemic recoding in visual word recognition. *Journal of Verbal Learning and Verbal Behavior*, 1971, *10*, 645–657.

Ruddy, M. G., Meyer, D. E., and Schvaneveldt, R. W. Context effects on phonemic encoding in visual word-recognition. Paper presented at the meeting of the Midwestern Psychological Association, Chicago, May 1973.

Rumelhart, D. E., Lindsay, P. H., and Norman, D. A. A process model for long-term memory. In E. Tulving and W. Donaldson (Eds.), *Organization and memory.* New York: Academic Press, 1972.

Schaeffer, B., and Wallace, R. J. Semantic similarity and the comparison of word meanings. *Journal of Experimental Psychology,* 1969, *82,* 343–346.

Schaeffer, B., and Wallace, R. J. The comparison of word meanings. *Journal of Experimental Psychology,* 1970, *86,* 144–152.

Schank, R. C. Conceptual dependency: A theory of natural language understanding. *Cognitive Psychology,* 1972, *3,* 552–631.

Schvaneveldt, R. W., and Meyer, D. E. Retrieval and comparison processes in semantic memory. In S. Kornblum (Ed.), *Attention and performance IV.* New York: Academic Press, 1973.

Schvaneveldt, R. W., Meyer, D. E., and Becker, C. A. Contextual constraints on ambiguous word recognition. Paper presented at the meeting of the Psychonomic Society, Boston, November 1974.

Schvaneveldt, R. W., Meyer, D. E., and Becker, C. A. Lexical ambiguity, semantic context, and visual word recognition. *Journal of Experimental Psychology: Perception and Performance,* in press.

Smith, E. E. Choice reaction time: An evaluation of the major theoretical positions. *Psychological Bulletin,* 1968, *69,* 77–110.

Smith, E. E., Shoben, E. J., and Rips, L. J. Structure and process in semantic memory: A feature model for semantic decisions. *Psychological Review,* 1974, *81,* 214–241.

Stanners, R. F., Jastrzembski, J. E., and Westbrook, A. Frequency and visual quality in a word-nonword classification task. *Journal of Verbal Learning and Verbal Behavior,* 1975, *14,* 259–264.

Sternberg, S. Memory scanning: Mental processes revealed by reaction time experiments. *American Scientist,* 1969, *57,* 421–457. (a)

Sternberg, S. The discovery of processing stages: Extensions of Donders' method. In W. G. Koster (Ed.), *Attention and performance II.* Amsterdam: North-Holland, 1969. (b)

Sternberg, S. Memory scanning: New findings and current controversies. *Quarterly Journal of Experimental Psychology,* 1975, *27,* 1–32.

Thorndike, E. L., and Lorge, I. *The teacher's wordbook of 30,000 words.* New York: Columbia University Press, 1944.

Tweedy, J. R., and Schvaneveldt, R. W. Context validity and the effects of context on word recognition. Paper presented at the Mathematical Psychology Meeting, Ann Arbor, Michigan, August 1974.

Webster's New Collegiate Dictionary. Springfield, Mass.: Merriam, 1961.

Wilkins, A. T. Conjoint frequency, category size, and categorization time. *Journal of Verbal Learning and Verbal Behavior,* 1971, *10,* 382–385.

Winer, B. J. *Statistical principles in experimental design.* New York: McGraw-Hill, 1971.

Winograd, T. Understanding natural language. *Cognitive Psychology,* 1972, *3,* 1–191.

5

Memory for Prose

Walter Kintsch

Studies of memory for prose require some means of dealing with the meaning of texts, apart from the actual words and sentences used to express this meaning. The psychologist must be able to score recall in terms of meaning, and he needs a description of the stimulus events—the texts to be remembered—in terms of their most relevant aspect: their semantic content.

The ability to represent the meaning of texts (recall protocols being one kind of text) is therefore a prerequisite for experimental work on prose memory. Usefulness in psychological research should be the criterion for any model formulated to represent meaning. Such a model need not be an original contribution to linguistics or logic, but it must be sufficiently sophisticated to deal explicitly with the traditional problems of semantic analysis such as quantification, modality, time, tense, and the inference rules involved in semantic memory.

Researchers have recently suggested several such representations of meaning, but I shall concentrate here only upon the one I have been working on (Kintsch, 1974). I shall outline very briefly the chief features of this proposed

The research reported here was supported by Grant No. 15872 from the National Institute of Mental Health.

representation of meaning, without trying to either justify or explain it. Instead, I would like to show how this representation has been used in our laboratory as a tool for the investigation of prose memory.

The model under discussion represents the meaning of a *text* by *text bases* consisting of lists of *propositions*. Propositions are *n*-tuples of *word concepts*, formed according to a set of rules which are part of a person's *semantic memory*. In this context, semantic memory is synonymous with a person's "knowledge of the world." Let me explicate by means of the example presented in Table 5.1, which shows a brief text of 22 words and the eight-proposition text base from which this text is derived. The actual rules of derivation of texts from text bases do not concern us here and can be left to computational linguists. It is sufficient for us to agree that the text shown is, indeed, one way of expressing the corresponding text base (in general, there may be several paraphrases that express the same meaning equally well). For present purposes the main interest lies in analyzing the characteristics of text bases so that they can be used as independent variables in experiments on prose memory. Returning therefore to the eight propositions of Table 5.1, note first the proposition (FORM, TURBULENCE), which is a very simple verb frame consisting of the predicator *form* (usually expressed in English by means of the verb *form*) followed by one argument, the word concept *turbulence*. Like all word concepts, *turbulence* is defined in a person's lexicon, both by stating its relationships with other word concepts and by means of appropriate sensory imagery and motor programs. It is not known precisely how *turbulence* is defined, and surely this definition differs slightly from person to person, but the general principles are nevertheless clear: people define word concepts implicitly by the propositional contexts in which they appear.

The second proposition in Table 5.1 (the numbers are merely for convenience of reference) has the predicator *location:at* and two arguments: one

Table 5.1   Sample Text Base and Text

Propositions	Connections and Levels
1 (FORM,TURBULENCE)	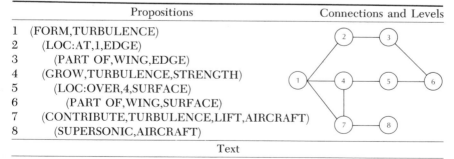
2 (LOC:AT,1,EDGE)	
3 (PART OF,WING,EDGE)	
4 (GROW,TURBULENCE,STRENGTH)	
5 (LOC:OVER,4,SURFACE)	
6 (PART OF,WING,SURFACE)	
7 (CONTRIBUTE,TURBULENCE,LIFT,AIRCRAFT)	
8 (SUPERSONIC,AIRCRAFT)	

Text

Turbulence forms at the edge of a wing and grows in strength over its surface, contributing to the lift of a supersonic aircraft.

is simply a word concept, *edge*, the other is itself a proposition, namely Proposition 1. Instead of writing out this embedded proposition as (LOC:AT, (FORM,TURBULENCE),EDGE)—a very clumsy procedure for longer expressions, each proposition is written on a separate line and propositions are referred to by their corresponding line number. The third proposition relates the word concepts *edge* and *wing* by means of the predicator *part of*. In order to understand Proposition 4, consider the proposition frame of *grow* from the lexicon: *grow* is a frame with two slots, one to be filled by whatever is growing, the other to be filled by the dimension of growth; in the present case, *turbulence grows in strength*. Propositions 5 and 6 are a locative and a "part-of" proposition, respectively. The next proposition introduces a more complex frame, *contribute*, which has a slot for an animate or inanimate agent (here filled by *turbulence*), an object slot (*lift*), and a goal slot (*aircraft*), in addition to an instrument slot (left empty in Proposition 7). The final example of a proposition introduces an instance where the predicator is expressed as an adjective, *supersonic*.

The eight propositions in Table 5.1 form a connected list. They are connected by the repetition rule, which states that repeated arguments are identical. Thus, the *turbulence* that *grows* in Proposition 4 is the same *turbulence* as in Proposition 1. In longer texts, when identity of reference is not intended, this difference must be specially marked. A text base, then, by definition, consists of a list of connected propositions, with argument overlap providing the connections.

The repetition rule not only connects the propositions of a text base, it also serves to order them. This ordering is a partial one that permits us to define the *level* of a proposition in the text base. Given a set of propositions (such as the eight in Table 5.1) and the designation of one (or more) of that set as superordinate (Table 5.1 is about the *formation of turbulence*, hence Proposition 1 is the superordinate proposition), the repetition rule objectively orders all propositions of a set according to levels as shown in Table 5.1: Proposition 1, the designated superordinate, is connected to Propositions 4 and 7 via the repetition of the argument *turbulence*, and to Proposition 2, because the first proposition itself is repeated as an argument of the second proposition. Hence these three propositions form Level 2 of the text base. Three other propositions (3, 5, and 8) are connected to these level-2 propositions and therefore form the third level of propositions. Finally, Proposition 6 is a level-4 proposition, because its only connections are to level-3 propositions. We can thus distinguish four levels of propositions in the short text base of Table 5.1.

When someone writes a text he intends to communicate a message. We assume this message can be represented by a text base. Writing consists in expressing this text base in natural language. The reader uses this natural-language text as a set of cues for the construction of a new text base, which represents the information that he has obtained from the text. If the text is well written, and the reader is careful, the original text base in the writer's mind and the derived one in the reader's mind will correspond. But frequently there are discrepancies: the reader does not process all of the cues that are available to him and fails to construct some propositions, or he misconstructs others. He also may go beyond the text and use his inference capabilities to elaborate the text base. In fact, one of the most interesting and important unsolved problems in the study of text comprehension is how far this elaboration actually proceeds during comprehension. To remain with the example presented in Table 5.1, consider again the proposition (CONTRIBUTE, TURBULENCE,LIFT,AIRCRAFT). It is based upon the frame for the predicator *contribute*, which takes as argument an agent or event that contributes, something that is being contributed, someone or something to whom that is being contributed, and finally some action of the contributor that serves as the immediate cause in the process of contributing. In our example this latter instrument slot is vacant. It appears quite likely that some reader may fill it in by the following inference process: what is missing is some action of the contributor (*turbulence*, in our case); immediately preceding the "contribute" proposition some such actions are mentioned (*turbulence forms* and *grows*); under these circumstances it is reasonable to infer (and it happens to be correct, too) that the formation of turbulence causes the contribution. Formally, this may be represented either by a separate proposition (CAUSE, 1,7), or by just filling in the instrument slot in Proposition 7: (CONTRIBUTE, TURBULENCE,LIFT,AIRCRAFT,1). Note that the writer easily could have provided an explicit cue for this proposition, for example, by a *thereby* after the comma in the sample sentence presented in Table 5.1.

Clearly, it is impossible to present the proposed theory for the representation of meaning in detail here. I have merely tried to introduce its main concepts and to give the reader enough of an idea about the proposal to enable him to understand the experimental work based upon that theory, which will be discussed below. But before turning to that work, I must point out explicitly one rather important feature of the theory. I do not propose to decompose lexically complex word concepts into their semantic elements. I hypothesize, and have tried to substantiate this hypothesis experimentally, that lexically complex word concepts are treated as unitary chunks in cognitive operations, except when a task specifically demands that they be decomposed. This hypothesis has important consequences for the way in which one conceives of propositions: what the model under discussion treats as a single proposition may, in other systems, be decomposed into several propositional elements. Consider, for one last time, the example (CONTRIBUTE, TURBULENCE,LIFT,AIRCRAFT). I treat this quadruple as a propositional unit, unlike, for instance, Anderson and Bower (1973) who require all propositions to be binary, or Schank (1972) who would decompose a complex predicate like *contribute* into a set of semantic primitives in which *contribute* is described as "a TRANS act where actor and originator are identical, performed jointly with other actors." I need to point this out specifically, because what one treats as a unit makes a great difference when it comes to counting propositions, as we shall do below.

1. Reproductive Memory as a Function of Text-Base Characteristics

In several studies conducted in our laboratory, we have investigated people's ability to comprehend a text and to recall it as a function of the properties of the underlying text base (Kintsch, 1974; Kintsch, Kozminsky, Streby, McKoon, and Keenan, 1975). The experimental procedure followed in these studies was quite simple: a subject read a text at his own rate and then attempted to recall it in writing, not necessarily verbatim. We obtained two dependent measures during the experiments: we recorded how long it took a subject to read a text, which indicated how easy or hard the text was for that subject, and we counted the number of text-base propositions the subject was able to reproduce in his recall protocol, which told us which portions of the text the subject had actually processed. There were of course other aspects of the subject's recall protocol, such as inferences, intrusions, and distortions, but we chose to neglect these for the moment in order to concentrate upon the subject's ability to reproduce the meaning of different types of texts.

The first text variable that we investigated is the most obvious one, namely, the number of propositions in the base structure of texts. In normal texts, the number of propositions in the base structure is, of course, correlated with the number of words in the text; however, it is possible to construct texts that contain an equal number of words but differ in the number of propositions forming the underlying base. One such set of sentences that Janice M. Keenan and I used consisted of 14–16-word sentences with 4 to 9 propositions in the sentence bases. The interesting result that we obtained with these sentences was that reading times increased regularly with an increase in the number of propositions in the sentence base, although the sentences did not differ in the number of words to be read. Thus, readers appear to be sensitive to the amount of information they have to process in a sentence, as measured by the propositional model.

We have since replicated this original result a number of times. The basic finding is illustrated in Figure 5.1 where we have plotted average reading times as a function of the number of propositions recalled. The subjects participating in the proposition-recall experiment read 70-word paragraphs, each based upon 25 propositions. The paragraphs were taken from articles in *Scientific American,* and they were much like the short paragraph on turbulence that I used as an example earlier. Figure 5.1 shows that the number of propositions a subject recalled right after reading a paragraph depended upon how long he had studied the text: for each additional proposition recalled an extra 1.26 seconds of reading time was required on the average. There is, of course, a great deal of variability around the regression line in Figure 5.1, but that merely demonstrates something that should be obvious anyway: even though the number of propositions in a text base partially determines the difficulty of the text (and hence reading times), it is surely not the only variable capable of producing such an effect. In fact, we have estimated that the number of propositions in the base accounts for about 25% of the variance of the reading times if the number of words in the text is controlled.

What are some of the other factors that affect the difficulty of a text? Dorothy Monk and I, as well as others (King and Greeno, 1974), have shown that even if the propositional base of a text remains the same, variations in the way the base is expressed syntactically can have strong effects upon reading times: a writer can say the same thing in either a straightforward or a very complicated manner. In both cases the meaning that is communicated to the

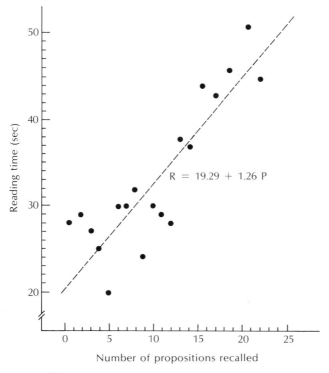

Figure 5.1
Reading time as a function of the number of propositions recalled.

reader is the same, that is, requires the reader to construct the same text base, but the reader will take longer to decode the complex message than the easy one.

Another factor that influences the difficulty of a passage is the mere length of the text. If one plots functions (like the one illustrated in Figure 5.1) for texts of different lengths, the slope of these functions varies from less than 1 second for short sentences to over 4 seconds for very tough 60-word paragraphs (containing definitions of psychological terms). We have tried to find out why readers need only 1.26 seconds per proposition to recall *Scientific American* paragraphs, but more than three times that long to recall psychological definitions approximately equal in length to the magazine texts. In addition to the mere number of propositions in the base, we have been able to identify experimentally a property of text that is clearly related to text difficulty, namely, the number of different arguments that are employed in the text base. If we take another look at Table 5.1, we note that the eight text-base propositions employ seven different word concepts as their arguments: *turbulence,edge,strength,surface,wing,lift,* and *aircraft.* For comparison consider the following text: *Although it had been expected that Mercury would not show a magnetic field, satellites detected such a field around it.* It is about the same length as the text analyzed in Table 5.1 and its text base also contains eight propositions; but it employs only three different arguments: *mercury, field,* and *satellite.* We (Kintsch et al., 1975) compared texts like these, including longer ones, in our experiments and found that the number of different arguments in a text base affects processing difficulty quite strongly. Readers require considerably more time (around 12% in our studies) to read texts with many different arguments than texts with few different arguments, even if the texts are as comparable in all other respects as we can make them. However, people recall about the same amount of information from both kinds of text. If reading times are fixed, on the other hand, a difference in the amount of material recalled appears. Given a fixed time, readers can process more propositions from the few-different argument paragraphs than from the many-different argument paragraphs.

There are many other problems that can be studied with the tools we have developed. For instance, we can ask, given a particular text, what determines which propositions from that text will be recalled and which will be missed? A partial answer to that important question is that the level of a proposition in the text base significantly affects the probability that it will be processed and recalled. The concept of level was introduced above; it is objectively defined by the repetition rule, given a set of propositions and a superordinate, topical proposition to start with. Figure 5.2 shows some representative data from our experiments investigating the effect of level on recall. We again used the 70-word *Scientific American* paragraphs as texts. Our findings indicate that people recall superordinate, level-1 propositions 80% of the time after one reading, but the more subordinate the position of a proposition in the text hierarchy, the less likely it is to be recalled; the likelihood of recall decreases to about 30% for propositions on the most subordinate levels in these texts. Comparably large effects have been observed in all the studies we have conducted so far. The levels variable is of course correlated with a number of other possible confounding variables, but as far as we have been able to determine, it appears to be the basic determinant of recall.

What might the processing strategy of the reader be like to produce the strong levels effect shown in Figure 5.2? Remember how the repetition rule permits us to define levels: the repetition of arguments connects level-2 propositions to the topical, level-1 propositions; the third level of propositions in a text base consists of propositions connected via argument repetition to the level-2 propositions, and so on. Suppose that when a reader constructs a text base, he too is guided by argument repetitions. Assume that he first processes the most important superordinate propositions and then preferentially processes other propositions that are connected to the ones he has already processed. Figure 5.3 shows that this is indeed the case. The figure is based upon data (unpublished, collected by Gail McKoon at the University of

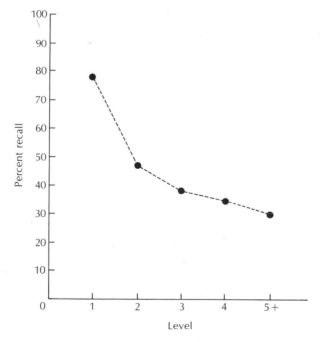

Figure 5.2
Recall probability of propositions as a function of their level in the text base hierarchy.

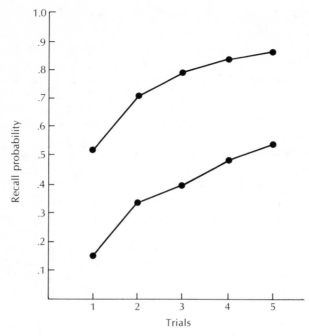

Figure 5.3
Recall probability of propositions as a function of their level in the text base: upper curve indicates recall probability for texts in which the superordinate proposition connected to the proposition in question has been recalled; lower curve indicates recall probability for texts in which the superordinate proposition has not been recalled.

Colorado Laboratory) from an experiment in which each of 30 subjects read four paragraphs (from the set already discussed) during each of five study/recall trials. For each trial we computed the probability that a proposition would be recalled (A) if its immediately superordinate proposition (to which it is connected via argument repetition) had been recalled or (B) if its immediately superordinate proposition had not been recalled. Clearly, readers are much more likely to process propositions they can connect to other propositions that have already been processed than to start with propositions they cannot yet connect to the growing network. The fact that the lower curve in Figure 5.3 increases over trials may mean either that readers do not always follow this strategy or that although they use this strategy in general, the propositional network they construct from the text differs somewhat from the theoretical one we used to score the data.

2. Memory for Inferences During Reading

Psychologists have been aware of the reconstructive nature of recall at least since 1932 when Bartlett published his studies of the phenomenon. Frequently, what people recall from reading a story is not really part of the story at all, but rather something added to it at the time of recall. The most dramatic instances of such reconstructions that we have observed in our work occurred when we gave subjects texts to read about topics with which they were quite familiar (e.g., the biblical story of Joseph and his brothers). If the recall test was delayed until 24 hours after a subject had read a text, an almost complete lack of differentiation occurred between the contents of the paragraph read a day ago and the subjects' general knowledge of the story. Many subjects simply wrote down everything they knew about Joseph and his brothers, whether it had been mentioned in the experimental paragraph or not. Interestingly, this confusion between the specific contents of a text and a person's general knowledge did not occur at all if recall immediately followed reading. Immediate recall produced very little reconstruction for the materials we used, and with few exceptions, the only errors subjects made were errors of omission. Only when recall was delayed did our subjects begin to fill out their meagre memories with reconstructions.

People may add to a text not only at the time of recall but also while they are reading. Readers often infer propositions that are not directly expressed in the text. In a sense, of course, propositions are always inferred from a text, but there is a difference between those propositions that are cued specifically by a text and those that must be inferred entirely on the basis of other propositions, without the benefit of a textual cue. We shall call these latter propositions *implicit propositions,* to distinguish them from propositions explicitly represented in the text.

To study memory for implicit propositions, we must be able to determine for a given text which propositions, if any, readers would reliably infer during the process of comprehension. Even though we cannot give a general answer to this question, it is possible to set up specific situations for which we can predict that certain implicit propositions must be inferred during reading. One such situation occurs when a text violates the connectedness property. The only way a reader can construct a text base from such a text is if he makes an inference that connects the separate parts of the text. This prediction follows from the requirement of the theory that text bases be connected lists of propositions. As I have mentioned, the theory defines connection in terms of argument repetition between propositions. Given a set of propositions that is not connected by this criterion, we assume that the reader infers a proposition that provides the missing link between the unconnected proposition sets and thus turns them into an orderly, structured text base.

Table 5.2 Inferences during test comprehension

Read	Delay	True-false Test
Explicit: A carelessly discarded burning cigarette started a fire. The fire destroyed many acres of virgin forest. or **Implicit:** A burning cigarette was carelessly discarded. The fire destroyed many acres of virgin forest.	$\longleftarrow \left\{ \begin{array}{c} \phi \\ 15\text{ min} \end{array} \right\} \longrightarrow$	A discarded cigarette started a fire.

Consider the two versions of text shown in Table 5.2. A reader can derive a text base from the explicit version of the text in which all propositions are connected by argument repetition, as required. This is not the case for the implicit version of the text, where there is no connection between the *discarded cigarette* and the *fire*. Nevertheless, readers have no trouble understanding texts of that nature (and in fact read texts like that all the time in their newspapers). According to the theory, the only way to comprehend such a text is to infer a proposition, for example, (CAUSE,CIGARETTE,FIRE), that links the disconnected parts of the text.

In a series of experiments, Janice M. Keenan, Gail McKoon, and I obtained evidence that people do indeed make this kind of inference during reading, and we explored the rather interesting memory properties of such inferred propositions (Kintsch, 1974, pp. 153–176). The design of the experiment is shown in Table 5.2: subjects read either the explicit or the implicit version of a paragraph, and then either immediately thereafter or following a 15-minute delay, they read a test statement corresponding to the critical proposition that was explicit in one version of the text but implicit in the other. We asked subjects to indicate whether the test statement was true or false, depending upon whether they thought it was an acceptable part of the story they had just read or not. The reaction times of these true-false judgments are shown on Figure 5.4. Subjects almost always called the test statements true, whether they had actually read them or not (for this analysis, we can disregard the false sentences that were presented). However, on tests administered immediately after subjects had read a paragraph, there was a significant difference in reaction time between responses based on the explicit version of the text and those based on the implicit version. Subjects verified explicit statements half a second faster than implicit statements, implying they had to infer a proposition when the implicit statement was presented, while they could respond directly from memory to the explicit statement. This interpretation, however, becomes untenable when we consider what happened when the test was administered after a 15-minute delay: reaction times were equally fast for responses based on both the explicit and the implicit statements, and they were approximately equal to the reaction times for responses given immediately after readings of the implicit version of the text. Hence it cannot be the case that subjects infer the implicit statements at the time of test. Since in the delayed tests response times were the same for explicit and implicit statements, we can assume that both types of response were based on the same type of memory trace for the proposition in question. What, then, could have caused the reaction-time difference on the immediate test?

We propose that this difference is evidence for the multilevel nature of memory for texts. There is, first of all, the propositional memory trace; responses based upon this propositional trace require, in our experimental situation, a little more than 4.5 seconds. When subjects infer an implicit

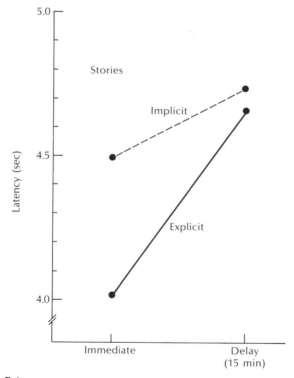

Figure 5.4
Reaction times to verify explicit and implicit presented test sentences.

Study sequence:

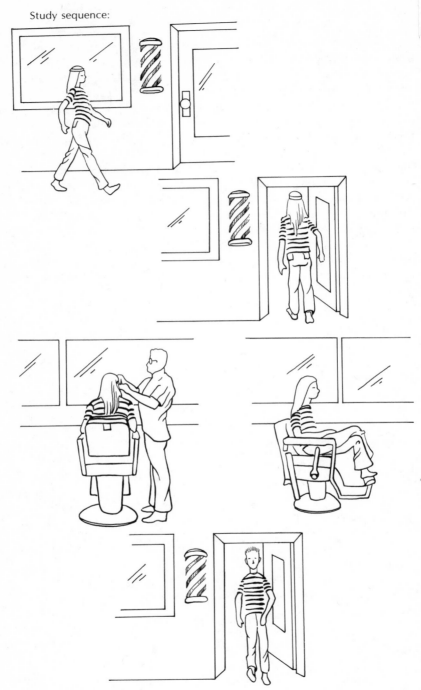

Figure 5.5A
Stimulus sequences in the picture-inference experiment.

proposition, this is the only trace they have available, and it is also the only memory trace left for explicit propositions after a 15-minute delay. However, on the immediate test, subjects who have read the explicit text have another memory trace upon which they can base their response, namely, the actual perceptual memory trace for the sentence they have just read. In this case, subjects remember not only the meaning of what they have read (i.e., the proposition) but also the actual words used or their visual appearance. This second memory trace gives them a reaction-time advantage. Memory for the surface form of a text is, however, more subject to interference than memory for meaning. Therefore, after a delay, the advantage gained by having this second memory representation is lost, and subjects must rely upon their memory for the meaning of the story—the same as subjects who have read the implicit text must do; for these latter subjects, there never was any other memory representation but the propositional one.

Recently, Patricia Baggett, also of the University of Colorado, has shown that these results are not peculiar to the linguistic medium; she obtained parallel results by telling subjects a story via cartoons (Baggett, in press). Figure 5.5 shows one of Baggett's picture stories; both the explicit and implicit versions present the same images. In the actual experiment, subjects saw the four pictures of the story sequentially and were then given a test slide, with instructions to indicate whether or not it was an acceptable, probably true part of the story they had just seen. (False text pictures were of course also used, just as false test statements were used in the verbal experiments). In the explicit condition the test slide was identical with one of the study slides— just as the test sentence in the former experiment was identical to one of the sentences of the story. In the implicit condition the test slide had never been seen before, but it depicted an action that subjects could infer by looking at

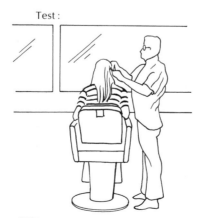

Figure 5.5B
Test item in the picture-inference experiment.

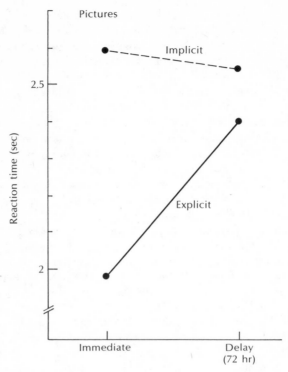

Figure 5.6
Reaction times to verify explicitly and implicitly presented test pictures.

the cartoon sequence. Figure 5.6 shows Baggett's results, which are strikingly similar to the story results just discussed. Again, almost all answers were correct, but when the test came right after the presentation of a sequence of pictures, subjects responded faster if they had actually seen the picture than if they had to infer the content of the picture. This indicates that people developed two memory traces that could provide a match to the explicit test slide: the surface-picture memory and the abstract, conceptual, presumably propositional memory for the meaning of the story. For all implicit test slides and for explicit slides presented after a 72-hour delay (note the much longer delay here than for the verbal tests—people's recognition of pictures is notoriously good!), all responses must be based on the memory trace for the meaning of the story, and the reaction time difference between responses to explicit and implicit test slides almost disappears.

The parallelism between the inferential processes used during reading and looking at pictures is worth noting. It illustrates the abstract, conceptual, nonlinguistic nature of meaning. Text bases are conceptual, not linguistic, structures. Meaning is not something restricted to the verbal domain; pictures, too, have meaning, and human actions in general are meaningful. Learning how to deal with the meaning of texts may prove helpful in eventually tackling the broader problems of the nature of meaning.

3. The Macrostructure of Texts: Summaries

Suppose someone reads a short story, or even a whole novel: What does he remember? It is obvious that he does not remember proposition lists such as those I have been talking about. At least, such proposition lists are not his only memory traces. The latter consist primarily of a summary of the story, supplemented at certain points by the more detailed type of propositional information that we have been concerned with up to now. When a reader recalls a story, this abstract provides him with a framework by means of which he can organize the bits and pieces of detailed information still available and from which he can reconstruct other parts of the story.

No representation of the meaning of texts can be satisfactory unless it provides an account of the overall structure of the text. Up to now, I have been dealing with the microstructure of texts: lists of propositions organized into a hierarchy of levels via the repetition rule. Now the concept of the macrostructure of a text must be introduced. Fortunately, this can be done without introducing much new theoretical apparatus.

There are many different types of texts, and hence many different types of macrostructures. Quite familiar to psychologists is the rigid structure of psychological research reports, which are divided into a certain number of sections and subsections, indicated by headings. Each section fulfills a very specialized function with respect to the whole report. The reader of such reports is aware of all these conventions, which greatly facilitates his task: in order to comprehend the report he must construct in his working memory a representation of its meaning, that is, a text base, but at least the general form of the macrostructure of that base is already available to him so that all he needs to do is to fill in the relevant details.

I have analyzed this example in some detail elsewhere (Kintsch, 1974, pp. 15–22), so let me discuss here a different, somewhat-less-rigid structure: the macrostructure of natural narratives. These structures are reasonably simple (unlike artificial, literary narratives), and although the various subsections of the macrostructure are not cued by headings in the text, they are quite stereotypic.

In our culture, a reader (or listener) has certain expectations about the structure of a natural narrative. He anticipates that the story will have a hero or main character (in long stories there may be more than one) and that it will recount some interesting event concerning this hero. The story will consist of various episodes, which, in the simplest type of narratives, are organized into higher-order units. These units differ in their functions. The first unit introduces the main character, places him in a setting, and outlines the background of events relevant to the story. The second unit consists of episodes that relate an unusual and remarkable complication involving the hero. Finally, the third unit tells how these complications are resolved. In longer narratives there may be several cycles of complications and resolutions. The reader of a natural narrative expects these episodes to be sequentially ordered in time and, indeed, to be causally connected. What happens in one episode must be relevant to the rest of the story; in other words, a causal chain must run through the story. I cannot discuss the theory of narration schemata in any detail here. Linguists (e.g., van Dijk, 1972) and students of literature have developed this concept as well as other useful descriptions of various literary forms. For the purposes of this discussion, all I want to do is to propose that a reader has available (as part of his knowledge) a set of expectations about natural narratives as described above. I will call these expectations a *narration schema*. Table 5.3 outlines the structure of such a schema. The reader expects

Table 5.3   The empty boxes are slots for the episode headings, as well as for higher-order labels. Each episode has slots for a proposition list.

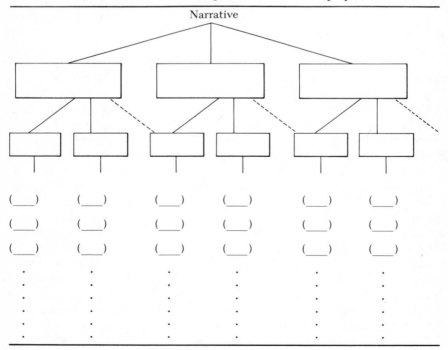

to encounter a hierarchically ordered sequence of episodes. Table 5.3 does not show the constraints placed on the function and interrelationship of these episodes (i.e., that the three units must function as introduction, complication and resolution, respectively; that the episodes must be related temporarily and causally; that something remarkable must happen in the story, etc.). A reasonable working hypothesis that I would like to explore is that comprehension of a story consists in filling in the slots of a schema such as the one shown in Table 5.3: the reader organizes the story into episodes by means of the schema, with each episode consisting of a label (the superordinate or thematic proposition of that episode) plus a proposition list that represents the content of this episode as it was presented in the story. The text base that is the end result of the comprehension process is therefore a filled-out version of Table 5.3, in which the reader has filled in the empty slots for the macrostructure labels as well as the microstructure propositions from the specific narrative being processed. When asked to recall the story, a reader uses the macrostructure as a retrieval cue to gain access to the proposition lists derived from the text and stored in his memory. When the reader is asked to summarize the content of the story, he bases his summary directly upon the various episode headings that he constructed during comprehension in order to organize the story.

The claim that a reader has available in his mind a schema like that shown in Table 5.3 does not imply that he is aware of this schema or that the comprehension processes in which this schema is used are transparent to introspection. The rules involved in comprehending language rarely are. All that is claimed is that the reader's schema is formally equivalent to the one shown.

The notion of a macrostructure is taken from literary analysis, where it has a long tradition, but it is not an unfamiliar one in psychology. The term "schema" has been used extensively by Selz (1922) and Bartlett (1932), and "frame" is a closely related concept (Minsky, 1975). The question that I want to discuss here is how readers go about extracting the macrostructure of a story from a given text. The microstructure propositions that are part of the text base developed by a reader during comprehension have explicit cues in the sentences of actual text, but the macrostructure organization of the story is not cued explicitly in the text at all.

Theoretically, there seem to be two types of processes that could produce macrostructures. One might assume that a reader constructs all the propositions that are directly cued in a text, or at any rate many of them. He would then have a list of propositions such as the one presented in Table 5.1, except very much longer. He could next use an algorithm that generates episode headings from this long list of propositions by deleting all but the most "important" propositions of the list. For instance, either the level of a proposition or the number of connections that a proposition possesses might be used as a criterion for this deletion process. I have three arguments against such a model. First, for the proposition lists that we used in our work, such schemes do not produce satisfactory summaries. (This does not mean that other systems for the representation of meaning, which are more structured than the present proposition lists, could not be more successful). Secondly, deletion schemes strike me as unreasonable. I find it hard to believe that readers first construct a mass of propositions and then work out its structure by deleting unimportant details from that mass. Thirdly, many abstracts produced by subjects are based upon propositions that are never represented explicitly in the text. Thus, they require inferences of some sort and cannot be obtained merely by deletion. The alternative to this procedure of deletion is a process wherein the building of a macrostructure goes hand in hand with the building of the microstructure.

I have chosen to work with this latter hypothesis and have collected pilot data on how readers summarize narratives. I selected several short stories from Boccaccio's *Decameron* as experimental material. These stories, which are about 1600 words long, are close to natural narratives and usually follow the schema outlined in Table 5.3. Boccaccio has provided summaries of them that stay close to the story line. Both the stories and the summaries are pleasantly devoid of the typical literary devices that make many other sources unsuitable for our purposes. The question is "How can a reader generate 60–80-word summaries for these stories?"

The basic assumption of the model we choose to follow is that the reader constructs a text base by filling in the empty slots in a schema (see Table 5.3). The lists of propositions that are subordinated under each episode heading are derived directly from the text. Our main problem is to understand how a reader divides the text into episodes and how he obtains the actual episode headings; the word abstract is derived directly from these episode headings.

Our model assumes that a reader chooses a central character or hero for each story. There are many possible bases for this choice: the reader may pick the first character in the story as his candidate for the hero and later modify this choice if some other character is mentioned more frequently, or there may be explicit hints ("This story is about the incredible misfortunes of a certain . . . ."). All episode headings refer to the state of this central character.

Our model further assumes that the reader divides a story into episodes, just as subjects who learn a long list of words divide the list into chunks. The cues in the text that signal the beginning of a new episode to the subject are not yet clear. If one tracks the number of connections among propositions throughout the text, episodes may begin at points where the connectivity is low. In addition, an obviously important factor is the way in which the text is printed: new episodes are often signalled by new paragraphs in the text. In the example discussed below I provisionally equate episodes with the paragraphs the author made in his text—which is a simplistic but objective procedure. Finally, our model assumes that throughout each episode, the reader monitors what happens to the hero. At the end of the episode, the content of the monitor becomes the heading for that episode. Episode headings (and hence abstracts) therefore consist of the outcomes of each episode with respect to the hero.

Clearly, such a strategy can be applied quite specifically to the Boccaccio stories we used in our experiments. But there are some obvious ways to generalize such a scheme. Table 5.4 gives an example of how the model works. It shows the second paragraph from one of Boccaccio's stories (Second Day, Fourth Story) together with its text base. The column labelled *Abstract Monitor* indicates the way in which a reader might track the central character's fate throughout the episode. When the reader turns to a new episode, he presumably stores the statement that is currently in the abstract monitor in the appropriate slot of the narrative schema he is working with, subordinating to it all the other propositions he has processed from that episode. Thus, in our example, (RUINED,LANDOLFO) becomes the episode heading, and subordinated under it are whichever of the 34 propositions the reader has actually processed while reading this episode. If we proceed similarly with all the other episodes that make up this story, we arrive at the macrostructure shown in Table 5.5. This table is simply a filled-in version of the schema shown in Table 5.3, written as a proposition list rather than presented graphically. Table 5.5 is, of course, not a complete text base, because the actual proposition lists for each episode are missing. To complete the text base in Table 5.5, we would need to expand the episode heading (RUINED,LANDOLFO) by adding propositions from the list shown in Table 5.4, and similarly for the other episodes.

I have mentioned earlier that in determining the level of a proposition in a text base (see Table 5.1 and Figure 5.2), it is necessary to select one or more of the propositions as the superordinate propositions in that text base on the basis of intuition; from then on, levels can be determined objectively by the repetition rule. What has been shown here is that in the context of a longer text, it is not necessary to intuitively determine superordination; the abstract monitor described above provides a more objective basis for determining superordination in that it subordinates the whole proposition list that constitutes an episode to the episode heading.

A natural language abstract derived from the propositional macrostructure of Table 5.5 is shown in Table 5.6. Note that the sentence connectives used, such as *and, then, finally,* need not be represented specifically in the macrostructure because the schema for narratives contains the temporal order implicitly, and one can use this general knowledge about narratives when producing an abstract. Clearly, the model abstract is a sensible one, but do readers actually produce similar abstracts, and by similar processes? Two nonrepresentative and non-randomly selected abstracts are shown in Table 5.6 for comparison. Boccaccio's own abstract (GB) adds two modifiers, about the woman who nurses the hero and about the jewels, omits two statements

Table 5.4 Episode from a short story with the corresponding text base and abstract monitor

Text	Text Base	Abstract Monitor
This Landolfo,° then, having made the sort of preliminary calculations merchants normally make, purchased a very large ship, loaded it with a mixed cargo of goods paid for out of his own pocket, and sailed with them to Cyprus.	1(PURCHASE,L,SHIP) 2(LARGE,SHIP) 3(VERY,2) 4(AFTER,1,5) 5(MAKE,L,CALCULATION) 6(PRELIMINARY,CALCULATION) 7(LIKE,5,8) 8(MAKE,MERCHANTS,CALCULATION) 9(NORMALLY,8) 10(LOAD,L,SHIP,CARGO) 11(MIXED,CARGO) 12(CONSIST OF,CARGO,GOODS) 13(PAY,L,GOODS,MONEY) 14(OWN,L,MONEY) 15(SAIL,L,GOODS,CYPRUS)	(PURCHASE,L,SHIP) (LOAD,L,SHIP) (PAY,L,GOODS) (SAIL,L,CYPRUS)
But on his arrival, he discovered that several other ships had docked there, carrying the same kind of goods as those he had brought over himself.	16(WHEN,17,18) 17(ARRIVE,L,CYPRUS) 18(DISCOVER,L,19) 19(OTHER,SHIP') 20(SEVERAL,SHIP) 21(DOCK,SHIP) 22(LOC:IN,21,CYPRUS) 23(CARRY,SHIP,GOODS') 24(SAME KIND,GOODS,GOODS') 25(BRING OVER,L,GOODS)	(ARRIVE,L,CYPRUS) (DISCOVER,L,SHIP')
And for this reason, not only did he have to sell his cargo at bargain prices, but he was forced to give away his goods, thus being brought to the verge of ruin.	26(THEREFORE,24,27) 27(FORCED,L,28) 28(SELL,L,CARGO,PRICE) 29(BARGAIN,PRICE) 30(NOT ONLY-BUT,28,31) 31(FORCED,L,32) 32(GIVE AWAY,L,GOODS) 33(RUIN,32,L) 34(ALMOST,33)	(SELL,L,CARGO) (GIVE AWAY,L,GOODS) (RUINED,L)

°Landolfo is abbreviated as L.

Table 5.5 Macrostructure of a short story from the *Decameron*.

	Episodes
1	(CONSIST OF,NARRATIVE,2,6,12)
2	(CONSIST OF,EXPOSITION,(AND,3,4,5))
3	(ISA,LANDOLFO,MERCHANT)
4	(RUINED,LANDOLFO)
5	(ISA,LANDOLFO,PIRATE)
6	(CONSIST OF,COMPLICATION,(AND,7,8,9,10,11))
7	(CAPTURE,GENOESE,LANDOLFO)
8	(SHIPWRECKED,LANDOLFO)
9	(SURVIVE,LANDOLFO)
10	(CLING,LANDOLFO,SPAR)
11	(CLING,LANDOLFO,CHEST)
12	(CONSIST OF,RESOLUTION,(AND,13,14,15,16,17))
13	(NOTICE,WOMAN,LANDOLFO)
14	(NURSE,WOMAN,LANDOLFO)
15	(FIND,LANDOLFO,JEWELS) and (LOCATION:IN,JEWELS,CHEST)
16	(RETURN,LANDOLFO,HOME)
17	(RICH,LANDOLFO)

of the model abstract that are intuitively redundant (presumably, a more sophisticated analysis of the story into episodes would not distinguish separate episodes at these points), and omits the setting. The second subject considerably elaborated both the setting of the story and its final outcome, added a few modifiers that are absent in the model abstract, and omitted reference to the same two redundant statements that GB omitted.

I have analyzed a number of stories in this way and found that the model abstracts are sensible in general and not too different from what pilot subjects have produced. With a few additional rules (like when to add modifiers to concepts used in the abstract—such as the woman or jewels in our example), a fairly good algorithm for generating abstracts of narratives might be obtained.

The main problem of the model is that the inference rules used to generate monitor statements from the actual text need to be worked out explicitly. In Table 5.4 the monitor propositions stay rather close to the text propositions. (Usually they are generalizations that omit an argument from a text proposition). But in general much more powerful inference rules will be required to produce the monitor propositions (see Rumelhart, 1975; and Kintsch and van Dijk, 1975).

An interesting empirical implication of the model proposed here is that it should be impossible, or at least very hard, to comprehend texts for which one does not possess the proper macrostructure schema. To read scientific research reports, one must be conversant with the conventions of science writing; in order to understand a narrative, one must be familiar with the proper narration

Table 5.6 Model abstract compared with the data from two subjects.

Model	GB		EK	
Landolfo was a merchant	φ		√	+ rich merchant,
who was ruined	√		√	who hoped to
and became a priate.	√		√	double his
He was captured by the Genoese	√		√	fortune
and shipwrecked,	√		√	
but he survived	√		√	+ barely
by clinging first to a spar	φ		φ	
and then to a chest.	√		√	
Finally, a woman saw him.	φ		φ	
She nursed him,	√	+ woman on Corfu	√	
and he found some jewels				
in the chest,	√	+ very precious	√	+ valuable
so that he could return home	√		√	
as a rich man.	√		√	+ twice as rich
				and lived in
				splendor for
				the rest of
				his life.

schema. A child, or a member of a culture using a different narration schema, should be unable to organize the details of a story into a whole. When a young child who is asked to retell a movie she has seen responds with a vivid description of some obscure detail, apparently missing the point of the story altogether, the lack of an appropriate schema to integrate the story, rather than some other intellectual deficit, could be responsible for the poor performance.

To conclude, I would like to discuss a few questions that have been present implicitly throughout this chapter: To what does meaning pertain? Does the meaning of a text exist independently of a person processing it? Are propositions and macrostructures memorial phenomena, or are they abstract properties of texts? The answers given here are purely psychological ones. The meaning of a message exists in the mind of the speaker. A particular formalism has been used here to represent this meaning—propositional text bases, complete with macrostructures. Text bases are conceptual, not linguistic, entities; it just so happens that people frequently express messages linguistically, though this is by no means always the case. Once a message is expressed, say verbally or pictorially, an independent, physical stimulus event—the text or picture—is obtained. The meaning is something in the speaker's (or artist's) mind at the moment he generates that text. For the comprehender, the text is a cue that allows him to regenerate more or less faithfully the meaning that someone wanted to communicate by this text. In so doing, the comprehender reconstructs, as well as he can or desires, the original text base, that is the meaning of the message. Texts have meaning in so far as they are derived from a meaningful message in one mind and produce a meaningful communication in another mind. The model proposed in the present chapter represents the content of that meaningful communication by means of propositional text bases and views the act of comprehension as the decoding of texts into text bases.

REFERENCES

Anderson, J. R., and Bower, G. H. *Human associative memory.* Washington, D.C.: Winston, 1973.

Baggett, P. Memory for explicit and implicit information in picture stories. *Journal of Verbal Learning and Verbal Behavior,* in press, *14.*

Bartlett, F. C. *Remembering.* Cambridge, England: Cambridge University Press, 1932.

van Dijk, T. A. *Some aspects of text grammars.* The Hague: Mouton, 1972.

King, D. R. W., and Greeno, J. G. Invariance of inference times when information was presented in different linguistic formats. *Memory and Cognition,* 1974, *2,* 233–235.

Kintsch, W: *The representation of meaning in memory.* Hillsdale, N.J.: Erlbaum, 1974.

Kintsch, W., and van Dijk, T. A. Comment on se rappelle et on résume des histoires. *Langages,* 1975, *9,* 110–128.

Kintsch, W., Kozminsky, E., Streby, W. J., McKoon, G., and Kennan, J. M. Comprehension and recall of text as a function of content variables. *Journal of Verbal Learning and Verbal Behavior,* 1975, *14,* 196–214.

Minsky, M. A framework for representing knowledge. In P. H. Winston (Ed.), *The psychology of computer vision.* New York: McGraw-Hill, 1975.

Rumelhart, D. E. Notes on a schema for stories. In D. G. Bobrow and A. Collins (Eds.), *Representation and understanding.* New York: Academic Press, 1975.

Schank, R. C. Conceptual dependency: A theory of natural language understanding. *Cognitive Psychology,* 1972, *3,* 552–631.

Selz, O. *Zur Psychologie des produktiven Denkens.* Bonn: Cohen, 1922.

6

On the Role of Active Memory Processes in Perception and Cognition

Donald A. Norman

and

Daniel G. Bobrow

Our goal is to understand human cognitive processes. The phenomena of attention, perception, memory, and cognition are interrelated—intertwined might be a better word—and the explanation for one set of phenomena helps to elucidate the others. Because of this interdependence, we believe it possible to uncover a single, unified story of processing structure for human cognitive processes.

Human processing capabilities are powerful yet limited in interesting ways. Consider a limitation: concentration on one task generally causes a deterioration in performance of other tasks. The results of numerous laboratory experiments on people's ability to perform several tasks simultaneously point to limitations in the amount of processing resources available at any given time. Now consider some positive aspects of human cognitive processes: Subjects can perceive a visual image more easily and with greater accuracy the more familiar it is or the more closely it matches their expectations of

Research support to D. A. Norman was provided by grant NS 07454 from the National Institutes of Health.

what was to be presented. Familiarity and expectations play a major role in human processing. A task that is practiced for a sufficiently long period appears to become "automated": it can be performed with little or no conscious attention. Novel tasks or unexpected aspects of familiar tasks demand conscious attention, and what ever demands are placed on conscious processing resources tend to cause severe interference with whatever other cognitive task is going on at the same time.

Information within human memory can be accessed quickly for some purposes but may be difficult to retrieve for other purposes—sometimes retrieval takes only tenths of a second; at other times it requires days, weeks, or months. Finally, people have a tendency to understand events in terms of their similarity to and difference from other events, which reveals an analogical or metaphorical use of memory structures. When we think of one event, we are sometimes "reminded" of others that have unexpected similarity to the one under consideration. This property is valuable because it allows us to discover previously unnoticed relations among concepts.

The traditional view of information processing considers the analysis of incoming information as a sequence of stages: first sensory analysis, then short-term memory, and finally long-term memory. This traditional view has difficulty accounting for any process that uses long-term memory information in the stage of sensory processing. In this chapter, we briefly sketch some possible organizational structures for memory that overcome this difficulty and permit the type of interactions with long-term memory we believe to be necessary at even the initial stages of perceptual processing. As a result, we propose a new method of viewing the human information-processing system.

Cognitive Processing

In the field of problem solving, it has long been known that considerable time may pass between the initial phases of active, conscious work on a problem and the arrival of a solution. The solution sometimes arrives long after the initial phase of work has been completed, and we often characterize a delayed solution by such statements as "it just popped into my head" or "I haven't thought about that problem for months." Psychologists call this time lapse the *period of incubation*. A person cannot use this autonomous problem-solving method as a way of being lazy. On the contrary, incubation periods seem only to be successful when preceded by a considerable amount of hard work on a topic.

An Anecdote

Let us relate a simple anecdote that illustrates the above process. Later in our discussion of cognitive processing we will introduce the notion of autonomous memory units that provide a structural framework to guide the analysis of data. While writing this chapter, we sought a name for these units. In an earlier work we had used the term *schema*, but we have never been satisfied with that term, both because of the confusion with Piaget's use of the same term and also because it is clumsy (the plural form is *schemata*). What other word could we use? In our search, we rejected the word *frames* because that too had been taken over by others and infused with a meaning different from the one we had in mind (Minsky, 1975). Then, one of us remembered that Lashley (1950) had used a specific word to designate memory units. In fact, Lashley had conducted an extensive investigation looking for the site of these units: he would teach an animal some skill and then excise various parts of its brain, hoping to find the area where that skill resided. He called this set of experiments "the search for the . . . ." What was the word?

The one of us who was trying to remember the term had taught classes about Lashley's work and had thus talked about it extensively, but this had occurred at least eight years prior to the writing of this chapter. So what was the word? No recollection came to mind. Realizing that this was a possible case study in the difficulties in recall, we decided to record the recall attempts which had started at 2:00 PM. There was no knowledge about the word—no knowledge about its size or sounds; it was *not* on the tip of the tongue. Our subject attempted to invent new terms, hoping they would either be useful or would lead to Lashley's term: *memorite, memite, cell, structure.* The other author tried to help by volunteering terms: *plex, plexis, plexiform.* A search of the Oxford English Dictionary brought forth *mem* and *mentum.* But our subject had no luck in recalling Lashley's word. So, after a few more furtive attempts at completing the sentence "Lashley searched for the . . . ummm (considerable mental effort) . . ." the conscious effort was ended. Back to writing the chapter. Then, while rewriting the section on stages of processing, the word *engram* came to mind. It was 3:39 PM: 1 hour and 39 minutes after the start of the recall attempt. The word came without hesitation. There was no doubt that it was correct. For the hour prior to the solution, there was no recollection of thought on the topic. When the solution arrived, the only other thoughts in mind at the time were unrelated to it.

What kind of mechanism supplied the answer? Evidently, something kept on processing the recall long after the conscious attempts had ceased. Our problem is to account for this phenomenon. The mechanism we propose must also be able to account for the phenomena described earlier as well as for other relevant data from the experimental literature; these data provide important constraints. We can base our considerations of possible processing mechanisms on previous work on memory processes. In his published work, Hebb (1949) discusses special kinds of active units, which he calls *cell assemblies,* that have some of the characteristics required by our model of cognitive processing. Reitman (1965) pushes this idea further and shows how active memory units can do a great deal of processing by themselves, without recourse to some central processor or controlling mechanism. In the recent computer-science literature there is talk of autonomous program units—actors or demons—that take programming resources and perform computations, passing useful results or unsolved problems to some higher controlling mechanisms (Hewitt, Bishop and Steiger, 1973). Minsky and Papert (Note 1; also, see Winston, 1975) contrast hierarchical and heterarchical processes. We are sympathetic with these approaches, and because we believe the organizational properties of memory to be critical, we base our approach on the properties of memory.

The Conventional Processing Structures

The common view of human cognitive processing is that it proceeds in a linear, sequential fashion through stages as shown in Figure 6.1. Transduction of the physical signals occurs at the sensory organs, and is followed by some processing and, perhaps, storage within a sensory memory. After pattern recognition, the signals enter short-term and long-term memory. Studies of attention show that there is a limit to how much a person can attend to at once. The natural question to ask, and the one that has occupied the efforts of psychologists who study attention, is: At what stage is the limit in processing capability imposed? Unfortunately, the form of processing summarized above restricts the possible classes of answers to the question.

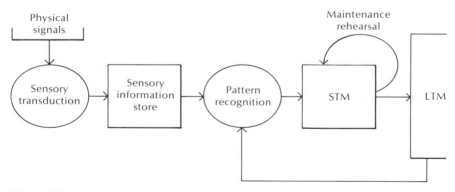

Figure 6.1
The traditional, linear stage theory of processing. Details of the system vary from author to author, but the intent is always the same. Processing is assumed to proceed from left to right, from sensory transduction to final storage in long-term memory. Information from long-term memory is used in pattern recognition, and rehearsal processes can recycle material in short-term memory.

The different theories of attention based on the linear model of processing do not agree as to which stages account for the bottlenecks in processing. Some propose that problems occur at early stages, others assume that they occur at later stages. Some indicate it is a problem in analysis, others that it is a problem in making responses. In spite of these differences, all seem to agree that difficulties are caused by the limited amount of processing effort that can be exerted. In addition, there is agreement that attention does not switch completely from one input task to another; rather, some mechanism (that differs depending upon the theory) enables every sensory input to receive some amount of processing. Finally, there is agreement that some amount of information flows back towards the initial stages of processing; to account for

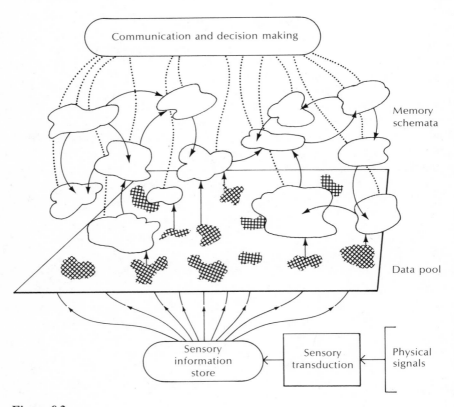

Figure 6.2
The memory schemata view of the human information-processing system. Incoming data and higher-order conceptual structures all operate together to activate memory schemata. Short-term memory consists of those schemata that are undergoing active processing. There is no set of sequential stages; the limits on processing capability are set by the total amount of processing resources available to the system.

the fact that context heavily affects pattern recognition, it must be possible for information gained at later stages of analysis to affect the earlier stages.

Our view is that this linear sequence of processing stages is not an appropriate description of what happens. Instead, we propose that there are large numbers of semi-independent procedures that analyze the data sent to them and return results to some common data pool, somewhat as shown in Figure 6.2. A variety of procedures continually examine the data pool and operate on whatever data fit their specifications. Some applicable procedure is automatically activated by the arrival of any new data.

Even before we describe how our proposed set of mechanisms operates, it should be clear that it provides a new view of the problem of attention. For example, the question of what limits a person's attentional processes receives a different kind of answer, one that is not stated as a particular stage of processing.

Active Memory Schemata

We believe that the aim of cognitive processes is to form a meaningful interpretation of the world. That is, the sensory information available to a person at any moment must be gathered together and interpreted in terms of a coherent framework. We assume that past experience has created a vast repertoire of structural frames or *schemata* that can be used to characterize the propositional knowledge of any experience. The problem of the perceptual processes is to determine the appropriate schema and to match the present occurrences with the frame provided for them. If there are too many discrepancies, either a new schema must be selected or the current one must be reorganized.[1]

We assume that when sensory information enters through the sensory system, the processes which operate upon it do so automatically, up through the extraction of features. Then, as a result of these processes, the sensory memory is active, with different regions representing the different feature sets. Imagine, if you will, a memory space in which regions of activity are flourishing here, fading away there. Each new sensory input initiates new activity, and the system must attempt to organize the structures that have been activated into

---

[1]The notion of structural frameworks or schemata is central to our ideas. These notions are not novel. The concepts play a fundamental role in the large literature on apperception written around the turn of the century. The concept of schemata plays an important role in Bartlett's (1932) work, and it is from him that we have borrowed the term. Piaget uses schemata as a major theoretical concept. Norman uses the terms *structural framework* and *knowledge frames* to help explain why subjects make conceptual distortions in drawing such things as the floor plan of the apartment in which they have lived for two years (Norman, 1973). Minsky (1975) uses *frames* to describe visual pattern recognition; see, also, Moore and Newell (1974) and the review by Cofer (1973).

some meaningful schema. This is a botton-up analysis: an analysis driven by the sensory input.

There are other ways to analyze information. Consider a schema that has been activated by suggestion from an input or a context. What else does this schema require? Use the requirements to guide a search of the feature space. Does the schema require a contour to the left? Ask if any procedure can provide data about one. Does the system postulate that it is perceiving a room? Then look for corners, walls, ceiling. Ask if the feature space is consistent with the interpretation. These are top-down analyses: analyses driven by the conceptual organization.

An Example from Visual Perception

An analysis of the interaction of information in the recognition of simple visual objects provides a good example of the activities of both the bottom-up and the top-down processes. (This analysis is inspired by the work of Palmer, 1975.) Consider, for example, the basic components shown in Figure 6.3: none of them are readily identifiable. Yet put them together, as shown in Figure 6.4, and a face emerges.

As Palmer points out, an appropriate configuration of elements can be recognized as a face despite the fact that none of the components of the face—eyes, ears, nose, mouth, head shape—can be recognized apart from the configuration. Clearly the relationships among the elements are important. The schema representing an object within the memory system must contain information about the relationships among the parts of the object, and whenever some corresponding relationships or identifiable subparts are observed in a perceptual input, that schema must be activated as a potential organization for the input. It is important to note that a schema can be excited either by the individual sensory elements or by perception of the appropriate relationships among sensory elements. Competing hypotheses (schemata) may

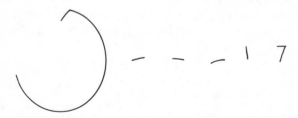

The component parts

Figure 6.3
The parts of a meaningful figure. None of these parts is recognizable in isolation, yet, when they are put together, a meaningful configuration emerges. For the result, see Figure 6.4.

The complete image

Figure 6.4
The complete image. The face emerges from the appropriate configuration of the component parts shown in Figure 6.3.

sometimes be activated. When this happens, each must evaluate how well it accounts for the entire input. If two schemata are equally appropriate, then the selection process may alternate between the two.

The image shown in Figure 6.4 might be analyzed as follows. The schema for a face contains the information about the relations among the parts: the triangular configuration of the eyes and nose, the relationship between the ears and the rest of the elements, the relationship of the mouth to the eyes and to the eye-nose triangle. When one or more of the relevant relationships are present, they activate the schema for a face.

The face schema interrelates the sensory evidence. Once the schema has been hypothesized, it then guides the processing. The face schema requires that there be evidence for the component parts of a face, so it examines the evidence, checking, for example, whether there is some feature on the left that could be identified as an eye. If so, can the schema verify the evidence for another eye on the right? Is there something located in the appropriate position relative to the eyes that could serve as a mouth? As a nose? In Figure 6.4, even though the shape of the head is incomplete there is no evidence for a second ear, nothing is present to contradict a complete head shape or another ear, and the positive evidence that is present is sufficient to cause the suggested hypothesis of a face to be accepted. The first few tentative indications of features drive the system to make conceptualizations about the input and to eventually discover sufficient confirming evidence to accept the hypothesis.

A simple illustration of this analysis is shown in Figure 6.5. Proceeding vertically from Level 1 to Level 6 of the figure, we have arranged the drawings in order of the increasing acceptability of the percept of a face. As more and more elements are added inside the enclosure, the quality of the face percept improves. Working down from the top, the naive observer will start to perceive a face someplace around Level 4 or 5. Once the percept is formed, the missing elements are suggested by conceptually generated processing. As a result, once a face is seen, the conceptualization will allow the percept to be accepted with less evidence than was needed to establish it in the first

Level

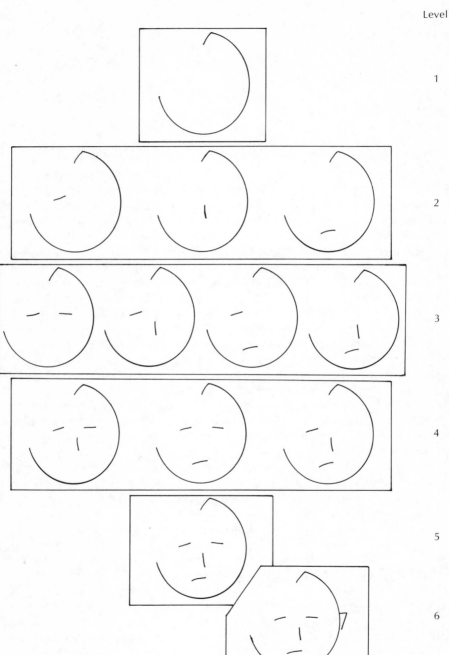

1

2

3

4

5

6

place. Hence, starting at Level 6 and working back up to Level 1, it is possible to maintain a satisfactory suggestion of a face perhaps up through Level 3 or 2.

The amount of perceptual evidence needed to perceive an object diminishes as the amount of conceptual evidence increases. Thus, conceptual processing interacts with sensory processing: an excess in one can compensate for a deficit in the other. As more and more contextual information is added to a scene, less and less specific sensory information is required. All that matters is that an appropriate conversion of bottom-up and top-down processing occurs to select a unique interpretation of the information. Thus, in Figure 6.6a the number of details allows the picture to be perceived easily as an eye, even with no context. As contextual information is added (Figures 6b and 6c), fewer details are required until only the barest hint of the eyes need be provided in the context of a face (Figure 6d).

The "fruit face" shown in Figure 6.7 (taken from Palmer, 1975) illustrates how powerful the relationships among elements can be in the selection of schemata. Even when individual components are recognizable objects, they can trigger the analysis of a figure that is unrelated to their identity. The drawings of the apples and the banana can be recognized as those fruits while simultaneously serving as the eyes and mouth in a face: the interrelationships of the fruits are sufficient cues to allow the face schema to operate. (Similar examples can be discovered in works of such artists as Magritte and Dali. Magritte's painting *The Rape*, 1936, illustrates just this point.)

Some Processing Principles

We propose that the cognitive processing system is based on the following properties:

- There is a single, limited pool of resources from which processes must draw.
- Memory is constructed of active units—schemata—that use the data available in a common pool, perform computations upon these data, and then both send new results back (into the common pool or to other schemata) and/or request specific information from other schemata. Schemata communicate with one another either directly or through the data pool.

Figure 6.5

Stages in recognizing a face. As more elements are added within the enclosure, the appropriateness of the face percept increases. This figure provides an approximate ordering of the acceptability of the percept. Starting from the top and working down, a reasonably complete image is required to accept the percept of a face. Once a face schema is accepted, however, conceptually driven processing suggests the missing components. Once the conceptualization process has been activated, it is possible to back up to lower-numbered levels of the drawing and still accept the image as a face.

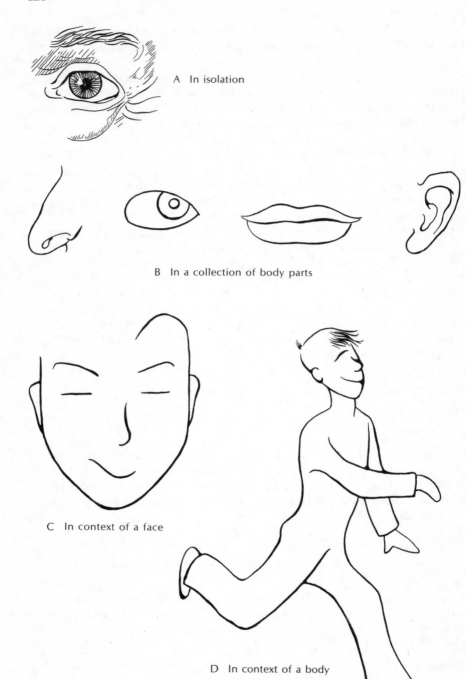

A In isolation

B In a collection of body parts

C In context of a face

D In context of a body

Figure 6.7   Palmer's fruit face

With sufficient information that the item being seen is a face, none of the component parts need be identified as legitimate parts of the face. Thus, in this figure, each of the components can be recognized as a fruit, yet the whole is perceived as a face. (From Palmer, 1975.)

- Schemata are required. A schema consists of a framework for tying together the information about any given concept or event, with specifications about the types of interrelations and restrictions upon the way things fit together. Schemata can activate procedures capable of operating upon local information and the common pool of data.
- Schemata can be invoked by the occurrence of data in the common data base relevant to their operations, or by requests from either other schemata or the central communication mechanism. A schema can request information of other schemata.
- There are no fixed memory locations in the head; therefore, memory structures must refer to one another by means of descriptions of the information that they seek. We call such references *context-dependent descriptions*.

Access to Schemata

We have discussed how multiple schemata might act simultaneously in the processing of information. A critical question now arises: How do schemata refer to one another?

Figure 6.6

Conceptual or contextual information can substitute for sensory information. In A, where there is no contextual information, the picture of an eye must be drawn in some detail in order to be recognized. In B, with some context, less detail is required. In C, a simple horizontal line will suffice for an eye, and in D, the two eyes need not even be distinguished from one another when, as in this case, there is sufficient contextual information.

The human memory system consists of neurological structures. The details of the physiological operations of the memory system are not known nor need they be known in order to establish the functional properties of the system. But some aspects of the structure do bear upon our discussion of the possible ways in which one memory unit might refer to another. In a digital computer, or in any large filing system for that matter, information is placed within some specific physical location, and that location constitutes the *address* of the information. Then, indices must be prepared to allow some knowledge of the information to be used as an indicator of the physical location. One item refers to another by cross-references (i.e., through lists of attributes known to be useful in the index scheme). Thus, for example, an article can refer to other articles by stating the names of the authors of those articles; we refer to other works on a subject by such phrases as "see the discussion on memory addressing in the article by Bobrow and Norman, 1975." To locate the cross-reference, a reader must first find the authors' names (along with a date which can serve as both a partial clue and as a means of disambiguating some references) in the reference section of this chapter. That reference section gives either a book title or a journal name, and that, in turn, can be used to process yet another set of indices. Eventually, the actual article being referred to can be found and the cross-referenced item can be read. The problem with this method is that it depends upon a rigid set of referencing procedures. It will fail whenever one wishes to find an article not referenced in this manner. Thus, as everyone who attempts to file papers discovers, organizing the file cabinets by the authors' names is useful, but it makes it very difficult to search for a paper by the topic or by the name of the second author. Organizing the files by topics has two disadvantages: first, it makes searching for a particular author difficult; second, it imposes a rigid structuring of topic labels that soon becomes outdated. It is possible to create cross-indices, of course, but soon the labor of keeping all the indexing schemes up-to-date defeats even the most industrious cataloger.

Similar problems must arise with respect to the location of information in human memory. Surely, indices of physical location cannot provide decent references to information. Reference to the content of the desired item would appear to be the sensible procedure, but careful examination of this referencing scheme reveals a series of problems. First, it is not clear which aspects of the contents ought to be referenced. Certainly, one cannot refer to an item by all of its contents, for then one wouldn't need to go to the item at all; furthermore, it is obvious that one couldn't contain all the relevant information for each item of memory. So, in describing the contents of a desired new item, choices are made as to what aspects to describe. Here the problem is that what appears to be an appropriate description today might not be at a later time.

We suggest that memory units refer to one another through the use of descriptions. A description has the positive property of providing a relative addressing mechanism that gives flexibility, reliability, and generality to the memory structure. There are different levels of descriptions possible. At one extreme, a description can be so complete that it unambiguously specifies a unique memory referent. At the other extreme, a description can be so vague that it fits almost every memory referent. We suggest that descriptions are normally formed to be unambiguous within the context in which they are first used. That is, a description defines a memory schema relative to a context. In novel contexts, a description yields novel results. We call such descriptions *context-dependent descriptions* (please do see Bobrow and Norman, 1975).

Context-dependent descriptions. A context-dependent description must be only precise enough to specify the desired referent with respect to the context in which it is used. Such a description contains the important properties of the information relative to the context. This reliance on the power of context is perhaps the most important aspect of retrieval through description. It means, in essence, that a retrieval mechanism uses two sources of information in determining the referent it seeks: the description and the context.

Properties of context-dependent descriptions. Use of partial description and context for reference provides a number of features that are important in a memory system. These are:

- *Efficiency* Because context is used as part of the address specification, the descriptions within a schema can be short and efficient, providing only enough information to distinguish the referent in context.
- *Generalizability* A description makes a schema a generalizable form. The same schema can be used in different contexts without changing the descriptions. In the new context, the descriptions contained within the schema will refer to memory structures that have the same relative properties with respect to the new context as the originally intended memory structures had to the original context. Thus, memory access by context-dependent description automatically makes a unique, particular schema into a generalized schema whenever the context is changed. Metaphorical and analogical uses of schemata result directly from the representational scheme without any special mechanism. (In fact, it requires special mechanisms to prevent analogical and metaphorical extension.)
- *Reliability* A context-dependent description allows for graceful degradation of function in case of error, either in processing structures or in memory structures. Because descriptions are relative and because the system is designed to cope with descriptions that yield only partial matches or ambiguous matches, any error that produces these results can be handled smoothly. An error in description or process is treated simply as a case of analogical or metaphorical match, and when a failure to match a description occurs, the system can still return with the best possible match (plus a statement of the mismatching aspects).
- *Partial knowledge* Even if the description and context are insufficient to specify the referent, some knowledge is still available. First, it is apparent in the schema

that there is a referent. Second, some aspects of the referent are known and can be used by the system. Finally, a memory procedure can be set in operation to monitor memory for the appropriate referent. As processing continues and the information relevant to the development of the contextual setting accumulates, previously uninterpretable referents may suddenly be found.

Depth of Processing

Much of the current literature on human memory examines the topic characterized by Craik and Lockhart (1972) as the relationship between *retrieval* from memory and the *depth* to which a particular item is processed when it is first received. Craik and Lockhart argue that the initial depth of processing is the major determinant of the probability that an item will later be retrievable, and that the more usual notions of the length of time an item has resided in short-term memory or the amount of rehearsal given to an item are not true determiners of later retrieval.

Consider an experiment in which people would be asked to make semantic judgments on a group of spoken, concrete nouns by saying whether each word represented an animate or inanimate object. Most of these words would be retrievable later, even if no conscious attempt had been made to learn them. The same words would be less retrievable in an experiment where the subjects were again given the same amount of time but asked to judge whether each word was singular or plural, or spoken by a male or a female. (It is interesting that people asked to remember only the words themselves often recall fewer items than people asked to make some semantic judgment about the words.) Obviously, in these experiments, all other factors—such as length of time each item is available for processing—would be held constant.

The results of experiments similar to this hypothetical example (as well as the interpretation placed upon them by Craik and Lockhart) seem to be quite compatible with the memory-access mechanism we have just discussed. Consider, again, the problems of gaining access to information within human memory. How does one specify which information one desires to retrieve? There must be some method of addressing the memory structure that yields results even some time after the original presentation. A description such as "the last item presented" suffices only as long as no other items are presented. A description based on the physical features of the item works only as long as those physical cues are relevant to the addressing structure of the memory. We would expect temporal and spatial descriptions to be effective just after the presentation of an item, but we would expect cues based on simple physical properties to become more and more ambiguous, and thus less and less useful, with the passage of time. Some description of the contents or meaning of the items appears to be necessary for future retrieval.

Our examination of the literature on depth of processing leads us to the view that memory units use different types of descriptions at different levels of processing. Shallow depth of processing often produces descriptions of the limited physical context in which the material to be retained was presented. Slightly deeper analysis yields descriptions based on the initial encoding of the information. Still deeper analyses yield descriptions based on the semantics of the items. Each "deeper" description disambiguates the item further from a wider range of possible retrieval contexts. This idea is worth pursuing in more detail in future research.[2]

Subconscious Problem Solving

Let us return briefly to the original anecdote with which we started the chapter: the account of searching for the word *engram*. It should be obvious how we propose to handle the issue of unconscious problem-solving behavior. Processing by memory schemata can take place autonomously, without conscious awareness. Thus, we believe that just as the lowest levels of sensory and perceptual processing operate subconsciously by autonomous schemata, so too do the higher-level schemata form and proceed without conscious direction. Note, however, that something must drive the system. In the case of perceptual processing, it is the arrival of sensory data that automatically invokes the relevant schemata. In the case of problem-solving activity, the data that drive the schemata must be provided internally. As we mentioned previously, a prolonged period of concentration on a problem is required before the higher-level autonomous processes can take over (see Woodworth and Schlosberg, 1954, pp. 838–841). We believe that the necessity of generating sufficient data to drive the memory schemata over the length of time required to reach a solution establishes this prerequisite. Once sufficient internal data are generated, the process becomes self-sustaining. Occasionally, resource conflicts or decision points are reached that require conscious intervention, but this too is consistent with the literature: problems do recur in consciousness at odd moments during the day's activities.

Although problem-solving activities can take place autonomously, with little or no conscious awareness or guidance, they do require processing resources from the system. Thus, low-level, "background" problem-solving activities slightly degrade the performance of other ongoing cognitive tasks. The following passage from Woodworth and Schlosberg's discussion of problem solving illustrates the point; they quote a chemist's recollection of his own problem-solving activities:

---

[2]Craik and Tulving (in press) have modified the depth-of-processing formulation to emphasize the active processing involved in learning and remembering, and the "degree of elaboration of the encoded trace" rather than "depth." We agree.

I remember one morning I took my bath, shaved, took another bath, and in reaching out for a dry towel suddenly became aware that this was my second bath and that my mind had been deeply concentrated on a problem for half-an-hour. (Platt and Baker, 1931, quoted in Woodworth and Schlosberg, 1954, p. 839.)

Concluding Remarks

We have proposed some principles of the organization and operation of the human memory system. Although we have used perceptual examples to illustrate the properties of the system, it should be clear that the basic principles apply to a wide variety of cognitive processes. We suggest that active memory units—schemata—work autonomously and simultaneously to both analyze incoming data and make suggestions to one another about possible interpretations. These memory schemata interact in one of two ways: they either communicate with each other indirectly by adding the results of their analyses to the common data pool, thereby making them available to other schemata; or they communicate directly by referring to each other through context-dependent descriptions.

The experimental literature on divided attention suggests that each person has a limited pool of processing resources. Whenever these resources are not adequate to meet the demands placed upon them by active schemata, some deterioration of performance must occur. It is possible to examine the nature of performance decrements with changes in resource allocation to particular processes. Such an analysis produces findings that seem to be quite compatible with the existing literature on the effects of divided attention, despite the fact that quite a different set of assumptions about the underlying processing mechanisms is used (see Norman and Bobrow, 1975).

The basic principle of human information processing is that the cognitive system attempts to create a cohesive structure of the data presented to it. It does this through the activation of schemata that guide the interpretation of data. Each memory schema contains a framework upon which to organize incoming information. We assume that each situation causes a new schema to be constructed: the cognitive system uses the first parts of the incoming information to select an appropriate, existing schema as a basis for interpreting the stimuli; as more and more information accumulates, either the new information is fit into an appropriate spot in the existing schema or the schema is modified. According to this view, the cognitive system interprets each new situation as being similar to some previously encountered situation, except for specifically noted differences (a related scheme has been proposed by Moore and Newell, 1974). The result, of course, can be that the processing mechanism generates a new schema that is quite unlike any other memory unit, including the schema selected as the original base upon which the new one was constructed. Schemata provide not only a framework for the interpretation of perceptual information but also information to guide one's expectations.

What drives the system? What determines which tasks get performed? We have proposed that humans respond to events in the environment and that their cognitive processes are driven by the set of stimuli arriving at the sense organs. But we have also proposed that human behavior is controlled by high-level principles. The sensory data help determine which schemata are selected to represent the scene; the selected schemata provide conceptual guidance in determining both where else to seek new data and how to interpret current data. Whenever new data enter the perceptual analysis, they automatically invoke the schemata for which they might be relevant. Simultaneously, the selected schemata attempt to fit these new data into the existing framework. The system is thus both data-driven and conceptually-driven.

REFERENCES

Bartlett, F. C. *Remembering*. Cambridge: Cambridge University Press, 1932.
Bobrow, D. G., and Norman, D. A. Some principles of memory schemata. In D. G. Bobrow and A. M. Collins (Eds.), *Representation and understanding: Studies in cognitive science*. New York: Academic Press, 1975.
Cofer, C. N. Constructive processes in memory. *American Scientist*, 1973, *61*, 537–543.
Craik, F. I. M., and Lockhart, R. S. Levels of processing: A framework for memory research. *Journal of Verbal Learning and Verbal Behavior*, 1972, *11*, 671–684.
Craik, F. I. M., and Tulving, E. Depth of processing and the retention of words in episodic memory. *Journal of Experimental Psychology: General*, in press.
Hebb, D. O. *The organization of behavior*. New York: Wiley, 1949.
Hewitt, C., Bishop, P., and Steiger, R. A universal modular ACTOR formalism for artificial intelligence. Stanford, California: Proceedings of the Third International Joint Conference on Artificial Intelligence, 1973.
Lashley, K. S. In search of the engram. *Symposium of the Society of Experimental Biology* (No. 4). New York: Cambridge University Press, 1950.
Minsky, M. A framework for the representation of knowledge. In P. H. Winston (Ed.), *The psychology of computer vision*. New York: McGraw-Hill, 1975.
Moore, J., and Newell, A. How can MERLIN understand? In L. W. Gregg (Ed.), *Knowledge and cognition*. Potomac, Maryland: Lawrence Erlbaum Associates, 1974.
Norman, D. A. Memory, knowledge, and the answering of questions. In R. Solso (Ed.), *The Loyola symposium on cognitive psychology*. Washington, D.C.: Winston, 1973.
Norman, D. A., and Bobrow, D. G. On data-limited and resource-limited processes. *Cognitive Psychology*, 1975, *7*, 44–64.
Palmer, S. E. Visual perception and world knowledge: Notes on a model of sensory-cognitive interaction. In D. A. Norman, D. E. Rumelhart, and the LNR Research Group, *Explorations in cognition*. San Francisco: W. H. Freeman and Company, 1975.

Platt, W., and Baker, B. A. The relation of the scientific "hunch" to research. *Journal of Chemical Education*, 1931, *8*, 1969–2002.

Reitman, W. R. *Cognition and thought.* New York: Wiley, 1965.

Winston, P. H. (Ed.) *The psychology of computer vision.* New York: McGraw-Hill, 1975.

Woodworth, R. S., and Schlosberg, H. *Experimental psychology.* New York: Holt, 1954.

NOTES

1. Minsky, M., and Papert, S. *Artificial Intelligence Progress Report* (Tech. Rep. 252). Cambridge, Mass.: Massachusetts Institute of Technology, Artificial Intelligence Laboratory, January 1972.

7

Computer Memories:
A Metaphor
for Memory Organization

Terry Winograd

The Computer as Metaphor

A casual reader who stumbles across a book on current ideas in psychology and one on the latest developments in computer science may find it hard to be sure at first glance just which is which. Both will contain chapters on information-processing and buffers, on coding and retrieval in memory stores, and on "intelligent" computations (with quotation marks around "intelligent" in both books).

Of course this is no accident. One of the most important changes in the study of psychology has been the appearance of a new metaphor—a new way of looking at phenomena of memory and reasoning. Just as the development of complex physical machines a few hundred years ago resulted in the elaboration of mechanistic models for every aspect of the human environment and of humankind itself, our newfound ability to devise information-processing machines has inspired novel ways of thinking about what goes on when a person thinks, says, or does something.

For computer scientists working in the new area of *artificial intelligence,* the computer metaphor is the most important aspect of our work. The building of devices useful to our everyday lives is a challenge, but it is not as exciting as the application of the computational paradigm to the study of the human mind. In building programs that do things that might be called "intelligent," we add a new dimension to the investigation of the principles of human intelligence. There is no guarantee that all aspects of the human mind are amenable to the computational metaphor. Philosophers have argued for thousands of years about whether we are nothing more than very complex machines. Just as the simple mechanical metaphor has failed to provide enough conceptual tools to talk sensibly about thinking, our current notions of computation may fall short as well. But there is ample reason to believe that there are many aspects of human cognition which can best be characterized by analogy to the artificial cognitive devices we are learning to build. One of the main lessons learned from programming is that very different programs can produce behavior that is uniform in many ways; we can imply from this observation that any complex behavior is probably the result of an interaction between many mechanisms, each with its own characteristics, operating in a complex environment with ever changing demands. No single notion of memory or computation will have the power to explain the diverse phenomena that psychologists have noted. Rather the usefulness of the computational metaphor is in providing a whole range of different possible mechanisms that enable us to examine how structures of information are related to the processes that use them.

What I hope to do in this chapter is to present some of the interesting notions that researchers working on the design and operation of computers and programs have developed, and to illustrate through these concepts the nature of the computer metaphor, that is, to give some idea of the kinds of computational processes that can be modelled and the kinds of complexity these processes would generate. Others in this book are far more qualified than I to relate these models to the vast literature detailing the response of human memory systems to varied tasks and conditions. I hope that for some readers, this chapter will stir new thoughts about the sorts of considerations involved in understanding the computational implications of any model. The sections below present several sets of ideas. Section 1 describes the basic notions of what comprises a unit of memory; it is written for people with no background in computer science. Section 2 explores different schemes through which memory elements can be integrated for use by a coherent process; it introduces ideas that are the topic of current research in organizing computer systems. Section 3 looks in detail at specific schemes for organizing recall and attempts to present some idea of the ways in which issues of timing and computational complexity arise. The algorithms it describes are very simple. The section is designed for people who want to get a basic idea of how we can analyze the implications of different retrieval algorithms for performance. Section 4 is an introduction to the fundamental notions and terminology developed for programming the multilayered memories used in digital computers.

1. The Elements of Memory

The most obvious difference between computer memories and human memories is that they are built out of different stuff. A brain is made up of neurons that have a complicated internal behavior, based on the flows and potentials of chemical ions, and a bewildering network of branchings and connections. The computer is built up of wires and transistors, magnetic doughnuts, and silicon chips. It might seem (and does to some people) that it is a hopeless quest to find a common ground between things that start with such a different base. But we can talk about memories on a more abstract level without regard to the details of how they are wired together.

Many descriptions of computers begin with a lengthy description of the binary number system and make a major point of the fact that all the information in a computer is represented with two signals—on–off, plus–minus, etc. In fact, this is true of most of the physical computers currently used, but it is not really the critical aspect of the capabilities of the computer memory. All that is important from a more theoretical viewpoint is that the memory is built up out of a set of elements, each of which is capable of existing in various recognizable *states*. These states can be any sort of physical phenomenon—a voltage, an amount of charge, a physical position, or even a chemical concentration. The only requirements are:

It must be possible to change each element from state to state
    at will.
An element must not change state spontaneously.
It must be possible to determine the state of an individual element.

Most current computers treat each element as if it has a finite number of distinct states. In fact, the physical memory elements do not have a finite number of actual states: any of a continuous range of states is interpreted as belonging to one state of a small set. A simple analog is the flag on an old-fashioned rural mailbox: there are an infinite number of different positions it could be in, but the mail carrier and householder have an understanding that it will be viewed as being in one of two recognizable states. The circuitry in a computer operates with a continuous range of voltages; the ends of that range are used to signal different states and the middle is considered an *error condition*.

Memory structure is a conceptualization imposed upon the physical states, not a simple reflection of the underlying device. Just as the same picture can be painted in oils or scratched into a metal plate, the same organization of memory can be implemented by magnetized ceramic elements, by bits of charge, by currents flowing in semiconductor circuits, and even by waves in a bath of mercury. The underlying unity comes from the fact that each device can be used in a uniform way to code the same set of entities at a higher level of abstraction.

Coding and Symbols

The cliche that the computer is "nothing but a giant adding machine" is misleading in many ways. The greatest inaccuracy is in not recognizing the importance of a stored program that enables the machine to compute the sequence of operations to be done, rather than just performing one operation at a time on human command. For our discussion of memory, the adding-machine image presents another problem in its emphasis on numbers. The computer is by nature a symbol-handling machine, not a specialized device for doing arithmetic. It is a general processor of anything that can be encoded into a finite alphabet of symbols, whether they be numbers, letters, or musical notes. As computers come into wider and wider use, their numerical functions will become less and less prominent compared with all the ways in which they can deal with other human symbols and languages.

The basic power of computers to remember symbols comes from the organization of memory elements into small groups and the interpretation of their combined states as representing a single symbol. There were many examples of this kind of coding in use long before computers. Letters of the alphabet could be represented in Morse code, for example, using sets of elements having only two states (dot and dash). There is a standard computer code (called *ASCII* for *American Standard Code for Information Interchange*) that is much like Morse code, except that it includes the other characters on the typewriter (such as the special keys like carriage return, tab, backspace, etc.) and is uniform in using exactly seven elements for each character. Each of these elements (called a *bit*) has two states, often represented by the numbers *0* and *1*. Of course there is nothing sacred about this particular code. It was designed to be convenient for the existing equipment, and many arbitrary choices were made as to which combinations would correspond to which symbols. What is important is that it provides a uniform way of encoding symbols chosen from a large set (128) into strings of elements whose states are chosen from a much smaller set (in this case only 2). This particular coding involves a fixed number of elements per symbol and is therefore limited to a fixed number of different symbols. There are other codes that have an extendable size and can be used to encode arbitrary numbers of symbols.[1]

---

[1]There is a whole field of coding theory which explores issues like error detection and correction in codes, the efficiency of various coding schemes, etc. Lin (1975) is a good introductory text to this field.

Hierarchies of Symbols

Human language is based on the ability to take strings of sounds (phonemes) or letters and interpret them as words, and on the capacity to combine these words into phrases and sentences. This sort of coding is an extension of the combination of elements described in the last section. It begins with the letters of the alphabet, which can be thought of as elements having 26 possible states. Small numbers of these are combined to provide many thousands of unique words. In computer systems, this ability to build up layers of encoding is the vital tool that allows arbitrarily complex entities to be encoded into memory.[2]

In many programming languages, there is a symbolic entity called an *atom*, which corresponds roughly to an English word. Information can be stored in the memory of systems using these languages through structures composed of lists of atoms. I will use examples from a particular system (Winograd, 1972) that was designed to carry out a dialog (in English sentences typed on a teletype) involving questions and commands in the simulated world of a robot manipulating toy blocks on a tabletop. Many other systems have been developed using similar principles to carry out a wide range of tasks that might be said to involve intelligence.

In the program under discussion, the memory included among other things a set of symbols corresponding to the set of objects on the table where the robot worked. These symbols had arbitrary forms (e.g., BLOCK17 and BLOCK24), and served as unique references to objects whose descriptions were much more complex, involving properties such as color, size, shape, and location. The programmed memory also contained symbols corresponding to general types of objects (e.g., BLOCK and TABLE), types of actions the robot could take (e.g., PICKUP and CLEAROFF), and properties that objects might have (e.g., COLOR and SIZE). To interpret a command like "Pick up the big red block," the system first built up a description of the object:

(X IS BLOCK)(COLOR X RED)(SIZE X BIG)

It then searched its memory to find the symbol for the object fitting this description (like BLOCK17). Finally, it coded the command into a specific form:

(GOAL (PICKUP BLOCK17))

In the process of carrying out the command, the system used a means-end planning strategy so that it could itself generate other goals:

(GOAL (CLEAROFF BLOCK17))
(GOAL (GRASP BLOCK17))
(GOAL (RAISEHAND))

---

[2]For details of how symbols are coded in different programming languages, see Sammet, 1960.

After carrying out the command, the system stored away a record of what had happened, including the time (another arbitrary symbol), and also generated a new symbol representing the whole event. If other events were involved in carrying out an action, each of them was given a unique name as well. A typical memory of an episode might look like:

EVENT25 (TYPE PICKUP)
      (OBJECT BLOCK17)
      (TIME 12:44:23)
      (HOW (EVENT22 EVENT23 EVENT24))
      (WHY COMMAND)

A

(:EVENT17

      (#GIVE :JOHN :DAVID :DIME :TIME17)
      TYPE #GIVE
      (:TIME17 START UNKNOWN END :NOW)
      HOW --
      WHY --)

B

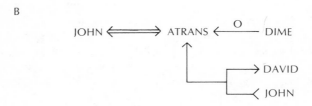

C

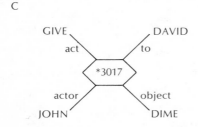

Figure 7.1
Memory representations for events: (A) SHRDLU (Winograd, 1972), (B) conceptual dependency (Schank, 1973), (C) active structural network (Norman and Rumelhart, 1975).

LEVEL	EXAMPLE
Physical states	Voltages in computer circuits
Bits	Interpretations of the voltages as 1 or 0
Symbols	A, B, . . . , 0, 1, 2, . . .
Words	BLOCK17 COLOR
Propositions	(COLOR BLOCK17 RED)
Schemata	EVENT25
	(TYPE PICKUP)
	(OBJECT BLOCK17)
	(TIME 12:44:23)
	(HOW (EVENT23 EVENT24))
	(WHY COMMAND)

Figure 7.2
Levels of coding.

Much of the work that goes into designing such a program involves specifying the details of exactly how the symbols are organized into larger structures. The specific forms are not important to the point here, and it is worth noting that there are many schemes for representing concepts containing objects and actions encoded as lists of symbols, each of which is associated in the memory with a set of properties. This type of model is obviously related in some ways to the notions of *chunking* that play such a large role in studies of human memory. Figure 7.1 shows several different schemes for representing a simple fact: "John gave David a dime." The figure gives a pictorial representation, which in turn is coded into simple strings of symbols.

If we build "hierarchies of symbols," we can introduce multiple levels of structure. To enable the robot program to remember facts about its world, we must resolve the issues of how to represent goals, how to connect that representation to the way in which the memory of events is stored, and so on. The answers to all these questions originate in decisions made at the level of how to organize the atomic symbols (representing individual objects and concepts) into structures. There is no need to be concerned with just how the machine works, or how it represents symbols, or even how it stores words, as long as we know that it has a consistent way of storing and retrieving the individual symbols on which we are building. Figure 7.2 summarizes the levels of coding involved in the robot program.

The "conceptual invisiblity" of lower levels of structure is one of the most important properties of computational systems. It means that the same program can be run on many different computers as long as each of them has its own way of structuring (at a lower level) those elements that are atomic concepts at the higher level on which the program is written. It means that one computer can simulate another by building up structures that correspond to the primitive ingredients of the simulated system. One of the most important fundamental concepts of computer theory is the fact that any machine with a certain very small minimum of capabilities can be programmed in such a way as to mimic the results of any digital computer that could possibly be built. This simulation does not include such factors as how long computations take or how much storage they require, but it guarantees the same eventual result.

2. Addressing and Recall

In Section 1, I discussed sequences of elements without describing how a processor accesses a sequence. Figure 7.3 illustrates this simplified view in which memory consists of a set of independent elements at appropriate levels of abstraction; the use of the elements is controlled by a central processor that carries out tasks involving input and output. When it needs to access some of the information stored in memory, the central processor probes the appropriate element, which in turn passes the information back to the central processor. In general, finding the desired information involves a mixture of *search* and *active message processing.* In search, the central processor can examine

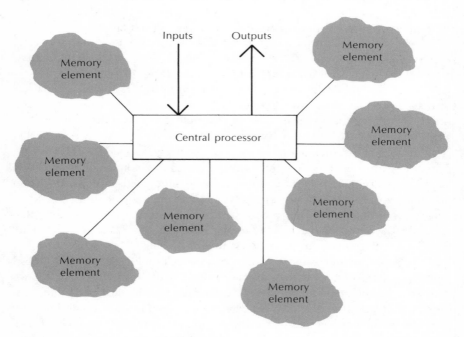

Figure 7.3
Processor organization.

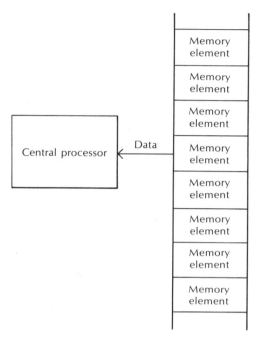

Figure 7.4
Sequential access.

the contents of an individual memory element; it examines all of the elements
in some systematic way to find the desired information. In active processing,
each element has the power to do its own computations on a message that is
sent to the memory elements, and each element can decide independently
what action it should take.

Computer designers have developed a number of different mechanisms by
which a central processor can communicate with a set of memory elements.
Figures 7.4 through 7.7 illustrate some of the basic techniques. The basic
issues the design must resolve are:

How much independent computation can each memory element
accomplish?

How does the central processor indicate what it wants from
memory?

How do the elements communicate their contents to the central
processor?

What sorts of communication can go on between the elements?

Memories with Passive Elements

The simplest sort of computer memory has individual elements that are nothing more than "mailboxes." They can store contents and dump their contents when probed. The central processor must decide which one to probe and then ask specifically for its contents. The two standard ways of organizing the set of memory elements are called *sequential access* and *random access*.

In sequential access (Figure 7.4), the memory elements are lined up in a built-in sequence. This is often a series of locations along a physical storage medium like a magnetic tape or disk, but it can also be, for example, a time sequence of signals flowing through a loop. The central processor has the ability to step along this sequence in either direction, and it can count the steps to decide where to stop and ask for the contents of a single element or to store something in that element. The amount of time it takes to find or store an item depends strongly on how far away that item is from the current position being read; retrieval time increases linearly with the amount of material stored.

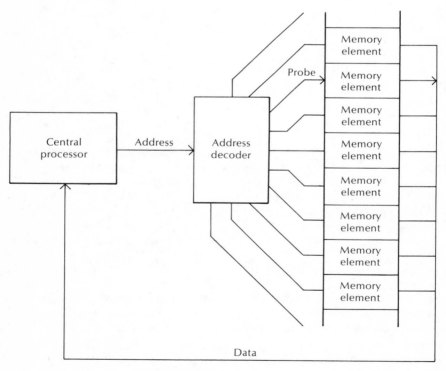

Figure 7.5
Random-access memory.

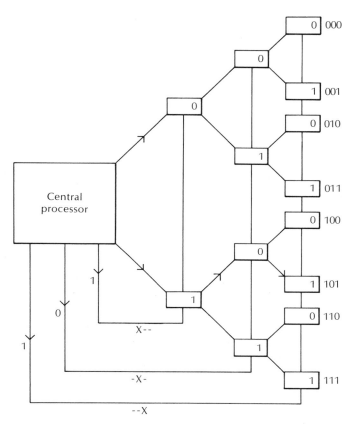

Figure 7.6
Addressing network.

In random access, there is a device that can decode a symbolic *address* to probe the appropriate element in memory. Figure 7.5 illustrates an organization in which the central processor sends a numerical address to the decoder, which in turn sends a probe signal to the single designated memory element. The element then dumps its contents into a communication path returning to the central processor. Of course, in this arrangement a good deal of complexity must be built into the decoding mechanism. Typically, it is restricted to taking simple numerical addresses that refer to a sequentially ordered set of memory elements. This can be done with a *decoding network* made up of simple logical elements. Each element (represented by a box in Figure 7.6) has two input lines and sends an output signal whenever it gets particular inputs along both connections. Figure 7.6 illustrates the decoding of the address *101*. Each decoding element is looking for a "start" signal coming from the element to its left, and for either a *1* or a *0* (as designated in the box) coming from the central processor. The central processor codes the desired address as a binary number and sends its digits along the three lines, while sending a "start" signal to the pair of elements to its right. One or the other of these will match the digit sent and send a "start" signal to the two elements on its right. One of these in turn will match, continuing the signals to the third layer, and one of these will probe one of the memory elements with a "start." The memory element will then dump its contents back along the communication path to the central processor.

What is important here is not the use of specific elements or of binary numbers, but the general notion of using simple logical elements in combination with the memory elements in order to make desired selections.

Active Memory Elements

The simplest way of thinking about associative memory is to imagine a collection of nodes (each representing a symbol or concept) physically linked together in a network. There is some analog of a wire connecting pairs of nodes, and processing can involve some sort of signals flowing along this wire. Each element is able to process in some way the signals it is receiving and to send out other signals.

Cueing

The simplest scheme for retrieval in a network of active elements is a *content-addressable* memory, in which there are active elements each communicating only with the central processor. When something is desired from memory (for example the information associated with a single word), the central processor sends out a message describing what is wanted (i.e., giving a cue). Each element processes the description and decides whether it has the appropriate information. If so, it sends it back. We could imagine separate *data paths* from the central processor to each node, but a more economical arrangement is a *bus,* which is a data path shared by all of the elements, each one being able to read whatever is put onto the line by the central processor. The difference between these organizations is like the difference between sending a set of packages out by taxis, one going to every household, versus sending them out on a bus which goes along a route, stopping at every house along the way to let the owner look at the packages and see which is his. Figure 7.7 illustrates a simple bus arrangement for a content-addressable memory.

Response

Once the cue has been broadcast, the individual elements must respond in some way. There, are several different models of what this response might

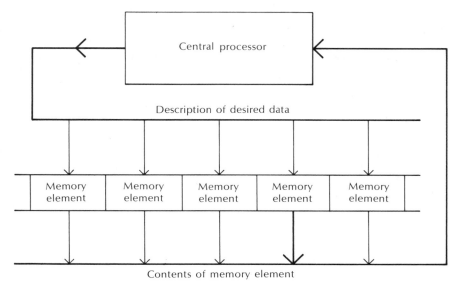

Figure 7.7
Content-addressable memory with bus organization.

be. We will call these the *polling* model, the *return-address* model, the *contents* model, and the *actor* model.

Polling. In the polling model, there is a limited set of responses that can be sent back to the central processor, essentially corresponding to some kind of "vote" by the elements. For uses in which the main concern is whether a particular item is present in the memory or not, all that is necessary is a single shared return wire along which any element can return a "yes" response. In a simple recognition task, if one or more elements responds, the system knows the item is present.

Return address. In most cases, though, we are interested in knowing more than just whether the probe triggers a response. There is an association between the probe and a larger piece of memory (such as a proposition), and the purpose of sending out the request is to get back that additional information. In this case, we can mix the active response device with an addressable one. When an element recognizes its cue, it sends back an address that enables the central processor to access the desired chunk of memory directly. This allows an arbitrarily large amount of information to be associated with a probe, but at the cost of including a rigid addressing scheme in which to store the data.

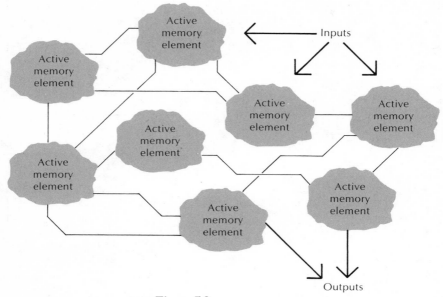

Figure 7.8
A distributed actor model.

Contents. In order to avoid addressing, we can simply have the activated element return its contents through the communication channel to the central processor. This necessitates a data path that can carry messages of a larger complexity, and raises questions as to just what the message should look like for complicated cases where there is a large amount of information stored in a single element.

Actor. Many recent models (for example, see the chapters by Schank and by Norman and Bobrow in this volume, or the studies in Bobrow and Collins, 1975), reject the conception of memory that represents cognitive processes in terms of simple elements which can store retrievable contents. Rather, they base their operations on larger active elements or *schemata* that can activate independent processing. In these models, the general distinction between central processor and memory elements is blurred, and the computation is much more distributed. Figure 7.8 illustrates a distributed, actor-like system. This idea is also being explored in computer systems[3] but is still in such an early stage of development that it is difficult to cull out the essential ideas and see what their implications are.

---

[3]See for example, Hewitt and Smith, 1975.

The Problem of Conflict and Control

Neither the return-address model nor the return-message mechanism can handle multiple answers satisfactorily. For many uses of associative hardware in current computer systems this is not a problem, since the computer memory is designed in such a way that no two elements can respond to the same probe. But this solution is not valid for simulations of interesting tasks related to human memory. People have many different memories involving the same object, different definitions of the same word, etc. If their central processor is expecting a message back, then it must have a way to handle several messages simultaneously.

There is an obvious solution: provide each computer element with its own data path back to the central processor to avoid confusion of what message is coming from where. But this leaves the processor with the task of deciding what to do with a whole set of incoming messages and involves an extremely large number of interconnections since every element must have its own connection. If we use a bus organization, the memory elements can share a common return data path like sharing the bus coming from the central processor, but there is a conflict if two elements try to return messages (either addresses or contents) at the same time. In a system where the time required to transmit a message is much less than the average time between messages, and in which garbled messages can be recognized as garbled, there is a clever way to get around this problem. In the *Aloha* model,[4] each element with a message to return simply shouts it out along the common bus. If two elements respond at the same time, the resulting message will be a mishmash. On receiving a good message, the central processor sends back an *acknowledgement* (via the bus) with some indication of which message it has received. If a memory element does not get back an acknowledgement, it waits some specified amount of time (chosen by some random method) and tries again. Since two conflicting elements will wait different amounts of time, both messages are likely to get through separately on the second or further tries.

In the actor model, the situation is more complex, since several schemata may all be activated at once and have conflicting goals for what the system as a whole should do. This *control problem* is one of the fundamental issues researchers are exploring under headings such as "distributed computing," "parallel processing," and "multiprocess systems."

The Problem of Partial Match

Most of the schemes described above depend on the ability of a memory element to recognize that a signal sent out is intended for it. In the content-

---

[4]See Abramson, 1973.

addressable memory built into computers, this is usually done by a simple network like the address decoding network shown in Figure 7.5. This structure makes it easy for an element to recognize that a signal is *exactly* correct, but does not provide any mechanism for recognizing a signal that is a close match. In general, the problem of finding the closest match to a signal is extremely complex, since the notion of "closeness" depends on interactions between both the uses and the meanings of symbols. The goal is to get the most flexible matching possible while keeping the complexity of computations done by the individual elements to a minimum, which makes it reasonable to build a large number of elements into a memory system.

3. Recall Using Simple Memory Organization

Many of the ideas that have been put forward to explain human memory seem to be based on concepts of active message processing. Since most of the physical devices used in computer memories are much more suitable for constructing passive models of memory, computer scientists have explored a number of techniques for achieving association-like results without using specialized memory devices.[5] In this section, I would like to present one of the rather surprising results of this exploration to give some idea of the variety and complexity of the issues that arise in the search for a computational understanding of memory. As a simple example, we will take the paradigm of associative recall and try to implement it using an addressable, random-access memory (described in Section 2).

Let us assume that each item to be remembered has a well-defined set of cues. There are many problems involved in deciding just what kind of element should be an atomic "object" in the memory system, but, for the moment, we will simply assume that some set of objects is present, and concern ourselves with the process of linking them to larger propositional structures. In the case of simple propositions (like those in Anderson and Bower, 1973) we may establish the link by focusing on the people and places involved or the type of action performed. In list learning, we may use the word itself as the cue, and remember a proposition of the form "this word occurred in the experimental list." To implement our paradigm, we will think of the cues as English words and of the association as a set of propositions, for example, a set of definitions or facts about the lists in which they appear.

If we were able to assign an address to every possible combination of letters our job would be done. Each address would correspond exactly to a specific word, and recall would be accomplished by simply probing the memory location at the address corresponding to the cue and seeing what came out. This

---

[5]See Knuth, 1973, for a compendium of the techniques that have been developed.

is not a very realistic system, since even if we restrict ourselves to words of a limited length, the number of possible combinations of letters would be extremely large and the proportion actually used would be extremely small. The system would be far too wasteful of memory elements. We need some way to store our associations using a number of memory elements much closer to the number of actual items stored. We could design a system in which the memory is organized as a sequence of "slots," with each slot containing enough elements to hold the definition of a word; these slots would have individual names, indicated by the integers *1, 2, . . .* To implement such a model, we must decide how to allocate words to these slots in order to make our recall have the properties we desire.

Linear Memory Organization

The simplest form of encoding for our word-slot model would be to go through the slots in order, putting one word and its associated data in each. We could describe such a system as follows.

Organization of the Memory
> Assign a contiguous set of slots to hold the items, with at least as many slots as there will be separate items.

Learning
> Each time a new item is presented, put the name, followed by the data into the next empty slot, beginning with the first.

Recall
> When a cue is presented, scan down the list, beginning at the first slot.
> If you encounter the cue as the first item in any slot, recall the contents of that slot.
> If you reach an empty slot, stop without recalling anything.

If the list *tiger, elephant, rabbit, bear, dog, giraffe, flea, gerbil* were presented, the contents of memory would be as shown in Figure 7.9. If each check of a memory slot takes one time unit, then the response to various probes, with the corresponding retrieval times, would be as shown in the first column of Table 7.1.

Of course the behavior of this program is very different from the behavior of humans during list learning. The amount of time it takes for the computer to retrieve an item depends directly on how far along in the list the item appears; there is no forgetting; the amount of time to say "no" grows linearly with the length of the list; and so on for a number of measurements that do not at all correspond to experimental evidence on human recall. However, equally simple algorithms, with slightly different ways of ending the search,

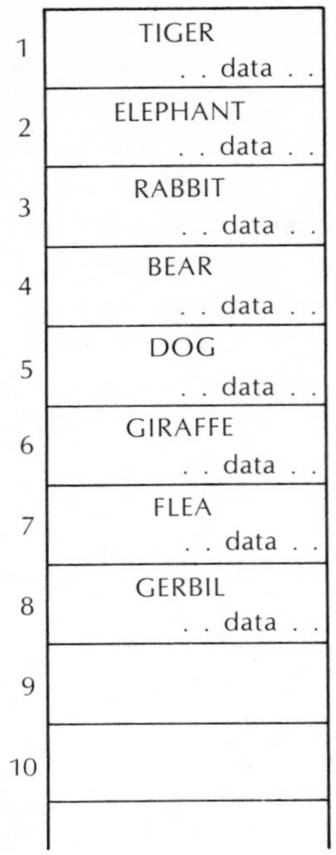

Figure 7.9
Linear memory organization.

can be used to explain an interesting range of experimental data on the recognition of items in short-term memory.[6]

Ordered Memory Organization

A more efficient scheme of encoding would make use of some sort of ordering to enable the system to do a much faster *logarithmic search*. For purposes of illustration, we can use standard alphabetical ordering, recognizing of course that it is not a plausible psychological model.

Organization of the Memory
　　Assign a contiguous set of slots to hold the items, with at least as many slots as there will be separate items.

Learning
　　Each time a new item is presented, start at the first slot and search (see under RECALL) for the place in the ordering where it

---
[6]See Sternberg, 1969.

Table 7.1 Recall time for different memory schemes

Probe	Response	Time Between Probe and Response		
In the example:		linear	ordered	hash-coded
TIGER	yes	1	4	1
BEAR	yes	4	3	2
FLEA	yes	7	1	1
COW	no	9	4	1
CAT	no	9	4	7
For list of length n:				
Average	yes	$n/2$	$\log n$	2
Average	no	n	$\log n$	2
First of list	yes	1	$\log n$	1
Middle of list	yes	$n/2$	1	avg. 2
Last of list	yes	n	$\log n$	avg. 2

should appear. Move everything appearing below that location in the list forward one slot, leaving one empty slot in which to insert the new item.

Recall

When the cue is presented, look halfway down the list and see if the item there is before or after the cue in the ordering. Choose the appropriate half of the list and repeat the midpoint check.

If at any stage you encounter the cue, recall the contents of the slot.

If you reduce the size of the list being scanned to one item, and that item does not match the cue, stop without recalling anything.

The list *tiger, elephant, rabbit, bear, dog, giraffe, flea, gerbil* would result in the memory contents of Figure 7.10 regardless of the order in which it was presented. If each check of a memory slot takes one time unit, then the response to various probes, with the corresponding retrieval times, would be as in the second column of Table 7.1.

This ordered organization of memory makes retrieval time much less dependent on the size of the memory. The maximum time for a probe is the logarithm (base 2) of the number of items, and there is only a small difference in the averages for the negative and positive cases. However, adding a new item means completely reshuffling all of the memory items below the point in the list where the new item is to be added, an operation which takes an amount of time proportional to the amount already learned. This feature seems highly improbable for human memory organization, as does the notion that things would be stored away based on a rigid ordering like alphabetical order.

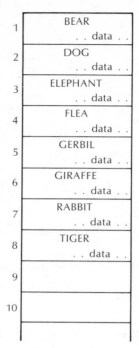

Figure 7.10
Ordered memory organization.

Hash-coded Memory Organization

Our first tendency might be to view the peculiarities of behavior of these two standard memory retrieval algorithms as showing that computers must function very differently from people. But one basic point we have learned from experience in designing memory organizations for computer systems is that the same underlying mechanism can be programmed to yield very different types of behavior. As a simple example, I will describe the notion of *hash coding*, which is used extensively in computer programming to provide a memory with certain associative characteristics. I do not claim that this explains in any direct way the organization of human memory, but I do want to demonstrate that straightforward "coding tricks" can drastically change the characteristics of a memory system.

The hash-coded scheme depends on having some standard arbitrary function for assigning a new item to one of a small number of classes. Preferably this function should be designed so that for a typical range of inputs, each class would have about the same number of members. In general, there is no attempt to use meaningful classifications; rather, an attempt is made to select classifications that make "hash" of the clustering found in typical data (hence the name *hash coding*); otherwise some categories would contain many more elements than others. The hash-coded scheme is organized as follows.

Organization of the Memory

Assign a set of contiguous memory locations with enough room to hold more items (say twice as many) as the expected list will contain.

Create a *hashing function* that divides the set of possible input items into classes, so that the number of distinct classes is the same as the number of locations in the table.

Assign a *primary location* in the table to each class.

Learning

Every time a new item is received, compute its class and look into the primary location for that class. If that slot is empty, insert the item, including both the symbol and the associated data.

If that slot is not empty, scan the table sequentially for the next open slot, and put the new item there.

Recall

Compute the class for the probe item, and look in the primary location assigned to that class.

If the slot contains the probe item, recall the contents of the slot.

If the slot is empty, stop without recalling anything.

Otherwise, scan forward in the table until you either run across the probe item or find an empty space; then, answer as above.

To implement the list-of-animals example given above, let us begin with a hash table containing 16 slots and a hashing function that divides all animals into 16 classes (see Figure 7.11). Remember that the way of dividing things up is not critical to the scheme. All that matters is that every potential item can be assigned uniquely to one class or another. If the computer now "learns" the list of animals cited above, the memory mechanism will go through the sequence of states shown in Figures 7.12 through 7.14.

The initial item, *tiger* is in Class 16, so the association with it is put into slot 16 in the hash table. Similarly, *elephant* goes into Slot 15 and *rabbit* into Slot 2. If at this point we probe with any of these three cues, the retrieval algorithm would simply look in the appropriate slot and find the item in a single access. The next item, though is in the same category as one of the previously learned ones. *Bear* cannot get into the slot with *rabbit*, since it is occupied. Therefore, it is moved forward one place into the slot normally used for Class 3, resulting in the situation shown in Figure 7.13.

Categories
for 16-slot hash table

Hash table
for learning 8-item list

1. DOG, ANTELOPE, . . .
2. BEAR, RABBIT, . . .
3. MOOSE, LION, . . .
4. GERBIL, GIRAFFE, . . .
. . .
. . .
. . .
10. FLEA, SEA OTTER, . . .
. . .
. . .
14. COW, ZEBRA, . . .
15. ELEPHANT, CAT, . . .
16. HORSE, TIGER, . . .

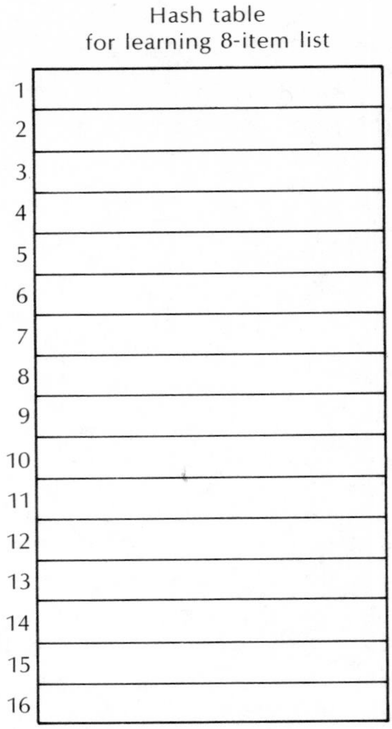

Figure 7.11
Arbitrary categories for hash coding.

Learning List: "TIGER, ELEPHANT, RABBIT, . . ."

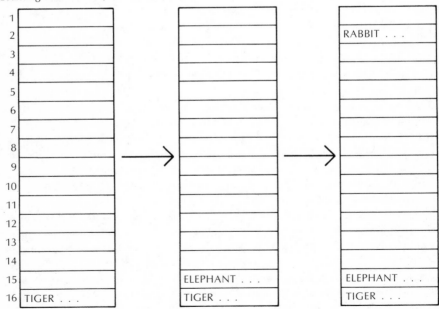

Figure 7.12
Progression of hash table contents.

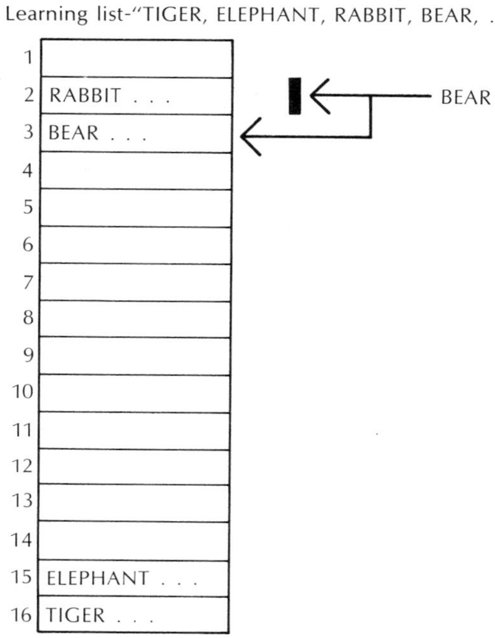
Learning list-"TIGER, ELEPHANT, RABBIT, BEAR, . . ."
1
2 RABBIT . . .
3 BEAR . . .
4
5
6
7
8
9
10
11
12
13
14
15 ELEPHANT . . .
16 TIGER . . .
BEAR

Figure 7.13
Hash table conflict resolution.

If at some later point, we present the system with another class-2 or class-3 item to learn, the system will forward the item to Slot 4, and so on. After the computer has learned the entire list, its memory contents will be as shown in Figure 7.14. If we now make probes of the list shown in Table 7.1, the retrieval times will be as indicated in the last column of the table.

The characteristics of this new algorithm are very different from those for linear and ordered memory organizations. We can analyze the behavior of a hash-coded system for the general case in which the table is of size S, and the number of items in it at any time is N. If our hashing function assigns things in an evenly distributed way, then when a new item is entered, the probability that its primary location will be filled is N/S, which we can guarantee to be less than a fixed proportion (say $\frac{1}{2}$) by making sure that the table is that much larger than the maximum number of items to be learned. If the slot is empty (more than half the time), the item will go into the primary slot, and any probe for the item will discover it by looking at only one place in the memory. If the primary location for the new item is already filled, then the probability that the location following it is also filled is the same as the probability describing the likelihood that the primary location will be filled—N/S. If that subsequent location is empty, the item will be placed in it, and on a probe, two locations (the primary location for the item, and the one following the

Learning list: TIGER, ELEPHANT, RABBIT, BEAR,
DOG, GIRAFFE, FLEA, GERBIL

1	DOG . . .
2	RABBIT . . .
3	BEAR . . .
4	GIRAFFE . . .
5	GERBIL . . .
6	
7	
8	
9	
10	FLEA . . .
11	
12	
13	
14	
15	ELEPHANT . . .
16	TIGER . . .

Figure 7.14
Final contents of hash table.

primary location, where it actually resides) will be accessed. Similarly, we can calculate the probability of needing to scan forward 3, 4, or more slots. If we consider the words put in at the end of the list, when the table is approximately half full, then we can calculate the average access time as follows:

in $\frac{1}{2}$ of the cases it will be found with 1 access;
in $\frac{1}{2}$ of the remaining $\frac{1}{2}$ it will be found with 2 accesses;
in $\frac{1}{2}$ of the remaining $\frac{1}{4}$ it will be found with 3 accesses, etc.

the average is $\frac{1}{2} + \frac{2}{4} + \frac{3}{8} + \frac{4}{16} + \ldots + n/2^n + \ldots$, which sums to exactly 2. The computation for the amount of time for the negative case is similar—given a probe for an item that is not in the list, we compute its class and have a $\frac{1}{2}$ probability of finding the primary location empty, in which case we answer "no" immediately. Otherwise, there is a $\frac{1}{2}$ chance that the next location is empty, etc., leading to an average of 2 accesses as well.

This model does not match human behavior either, but in very different ways from the other two models. The amount of time required for retrieval does not depend strongly on the number of items in the list; in our example, by keeping the number of learned items to half of the memory capacity, we were able to keep the average access time down to 2. Items learned later in the list will take slightly longer (since they have more probability of running into conflicts and being pushed along), but not much longer. Negatives take the same amount of time as positives, regardless of the length of the list. Of course, there is also the consideration of how much time it takes to classify each object. If this time is not a constant, then other characteristics of timing will result from the program.

There are variations on this scheme which produce still different behavior. For example, instead of having a single slot for each class, we can have a list, and instead of pushing items along to successive slots, we can simply put all items from a single class into the list for that class. This causes a kind of interference phenomenon between "similar" items (those that fall into the same class), while keeping the relative insensitivity of recall time to the exact number of items in the memory.

The point of all this detail is not to imply that the mind is organized using this particular trick. Hash coding has some characteristics that are by nature ideally suited to a machine capable of fast arithmetic operations. Rather, the example indicates the ease with which a special mechanism can be used to alter radically some of the behavior parameters of a system that uses a single underlying memory mechanism. In trying to account for the behavior of a complex system like human memory, we must be very sensitive to questions of how much each level of structuring contributes to external behavior and how the various levels interact.

4. Memory Hierarchies

In Section 3 we explored the consequences of different memory organizations by measuring the amount of time needed for recall in each system. We assumed that we could measure retrieval times in terms of a standard unit indicating *access time*, that is, the time required by the system to look at the contents of a single memory element. In reality, most computer systems use a hierarchy of memory elements with different timing characteristics. These multileveled models are somewhat analogous to the current theories of human cognitive processing that separate memory into at least two levels, labelled *short term* and *long term*, and often make a number of distinctions within these categories. However, the differences between the properties of the computer memory levels are not as great as those separating the levels of the human memory organization—the former tend to be differences in speed characteristics rather than in what sorts of things will be remembered. But computer scientists are now working to develop systems with structures that are more varied in their styles of recall and their ability to hold detail of varying types.

Table 7.2 Sizes and speeds of operation of typical computer memory devices

Type of Device	Typical Size of Memory (in no. of bits)	Seek Time (seconds)	Stream
Registers	10^2	10^{-8}	o o o
Cache	10^3	10^{-7}	o o o
Main Memory	10^7	10^{-6}	o o o
Magnetic Disc	10^8–10^{10}	10^{-5}	10^{-7}–10^{-6}
Magnetic Tape	10^8–10^{10}	1–100	10^{-7}–10^{-6}
Laser Stores	10^{12}	1–10	10^{-6}
For Comparison:			
Human Brain	$\sim 10^{10}$ (neurons)		
Library of Congress	$\sim 10^{15}$ (bits)		

Table 7.2 lists some of the main types of computer memory, giving their relative speeds of operation and their typical sizes as measured by the number of bits in a large computer system. The specific numbers are not very revealing, but it is interesting to note that the speed and size of memory for a given cost has doubled every 3 years since the first electronic computer was built 20 years ago, and that a projection of this growth over the next few years yields systems that have as many separate elements as the human nervous system, which contains approximately 10^{10} separate neurons. (Although we can estimate the number of neurons in the nervous system and can calculate the number of bits in a computer system, we do not yet know what relation exists between a neuron and a bit of information: is one neuron a conglomeration containing many bits—as some researchers propose, or does it take a whole set of neurons to provide reliable storage for a single bit— as others assert?)

It is more interesting to look at the memory organizations that have been invented to take advantage of the characteristics of the different sorts of memory. In particular, many current systems can be described as 4-level hierarchies, containing *registers*, a *cache*, a *main memory*, and a *secondary store*.

Register Memory

A typical computer contains from 1 to 16 *registers* made up of extremely fast logic circuitry, each capable of holding a single computer word (roughly equivalent in size to a natural-language word). The operations of the computer are designed to store and retrieve items from these registers whenever possible, rather than using the slower memories.

Cache Memory

The cache is a content-addressable memory built with physical devices (usually semiconductor circuits) that are slower and cheaper than the register logic, but expensive enough to make it impractical to use them as components of a very large memory. The memory system is organized to keep only the items currently being worked on in the cache memory, and there is a special addressing system that enables programs to place items in the cache without making an explicit decision about each one.

Main Memory

The main memory (often called *core memory*) is reasonably fast, is usually built with slower, cheaper semiconductor technologies or magnetic cores, and is randomly accessible. This means that the contents of any memory location can be retrieved in a single *cycle* (the basic timing unit of the memory) without regard to its address in the memory.

Secondary Store

The secondary store is very large, at the price of being slow and having limited access. It is organized sequentially, and it is often a physical device (like a magnetic tape or disk) that must move to a particular position in order to find the memory contents. The organization of the data (for example, where along the reel of tape an item appears) is critical to the amount of time it takes to access it. Often, there is a large difference between *seek time* (the amount of time it takes to get to the right place) and *stream* or *transfer rate* (the speed at which successive locations in the memory can be accessed once the device is at the right place.)

A computer system with these different memory levels will contain strategies for getting the optimal use out of them. In general, those pieces of program and data that are currently in use will be stored in the cache and can therefore be manipulated with very little retrieval effort. If a piece of data (corresponding to a single English word in our earlier example) is needed but is not in the cache, the system finds it in one of the other memories and enters it into the cache so that it will be there for further accesses. Of course, this involves throwing some other item out of the cache to make room, and there must be a way for the system to decide what to throw out. A commonly used algorithm is *LRU* (Least Recently Used), which involves keeping track of when items in the cache are actually accessed and getting rid of the one that has been sitting around unused the longest.

The main memory is used for a much larger *working set* of programs and data that are being used on a current time scale of several seconds, but are not actively running at the moment. If the body of material needed to run a given program is too large to fit into the main memory all at once, an LRU strategy is used to bring *pages* (units involving tens or hundreds of memory words) into memory from the secondary store, and move them out to make room if they aren't being used.

Finally the secondary store is the permanent memory. It is usually the only part of the memory hierarchy to remain after a particular computing session is over, holding programs and data that will be used at other times to compute other things. Much effort goes into organizing it so that it will be able to seek desired data efficiently, and much of this organization is based on similarity clustering: items likely to be used together are placed together in the memory so that they can be brought into the main memory in a single chunk, rather than having to be retrieved one by one with expensive seeks.

The parallel between 4-level computer memory hierarchies and human memory organization is inexact but obvious. The registers and cache form a short-term memory, which includes only the items of immediate attention and from which items fade not by being explicitly deleted but by being pushed out by newer elements. There is a long-term memory, which is organized in a way that makes it easy to bring in whole contexts rather than a single item at a time. It may be very slow at finding a particular stored item, but once the system "remembers" and moves the corresponding page into active memory, a number of related items become much more quickly accessible.

Conclusions

It would be a naive oversimplification to look for exact analogs in the human brain for all of the computer elements described in this chapter. The brain has no "core memories" or alphabetic lists, and no hash functions assigning items to be learned to simple numerical classes. However, the metaphors are applicable at a higher level. Concepts of coding strategy, of passive and active elements with data paths of various sorts, and of multiple memory levels are all part of the stock of ideas we use in building psychological models and testing their properties. As we strive to build more comprehensive models of human memory, the basic notions of the computational metaphor will become increasingly important tools in our investigation of the principles of human intelligence.

REFERENCES

Abramson, N. The aloha system. In N. Abramson and F. Kuo, (Eds.), *Computer communication networks.* Englewood Cliffs, N.J.: Prentice Hall, 1973.

Anderson, J., and Bower, G. *Human associative memory.* Washington, D.C.: Winston, 1973.

Bobrow, D., and Collins, A. (Eds.), *Representation and understanding: Studies in cognitive science.* New York: Academic Press, 1975.

Hewitt, C., and Smith, B. Towards a programming apprentice. *IEEE Transactions on Software Engineering,* March 1975, *SE-1*(1).

Knuth, D. *The art of computer programming* (Vols. 1–3). Reading, Mass.: Addison Wesley, 1968–1973.

Lin, S. *Introduction to error-correcting codes.* Englewood Cliffs, N.J.: Prentice Hall, 1970.

Norman, D., and Bobrow, D. Chapter 6 in this book.

Norman, D., Rumelhart, D., and the LNR Research Group. *Explorations in Cognition.* San Francisco: W. H. Freeman and Company, 1975.

Sammet, J. *Programming languages: History and fundamentals.* Englewood Cliffs, N.J.: Prentice Hall, 1969.

Schank, R. C. Chapter 8 in this book.

Schank, R. C., and Colby, K. (Eds.), *Computer models of thought and language.* San Francisco: W. H. Freeman and Company, 1973.

Sternberg, S. Memory-scanning: Mental processes revealed by reaction time experiments. *Acta Psychologica,* 1969, *30.*

Winograd, T. *Understanding natural language.* New York: Academic Press, 1972.

Winograd, T. Frame representations and the procedural-declarative controversy. In D. Bobrow and D. Collins (Eds.), *Representation and understanding: Studies in cognitive science.* New York: Academic Press, 1975.

8

The Role of Memory in Language Processing

Roger C. Schank

Introduction

How can we get a computer to act like a human being? In attempting to set out just what processes and abilities an "intelligent" computer must have, we face the fact that no machine can seem very humanlike unless we can talk to it. Furthermore such a machine should be able to talk back.

The problem of getting a machine to understand human language is extremely complex. A machine that has stored the information that "Shakespeare was the author of *Hamlet*" will not be able to answer the question "Who wrote Hamlet?" without fairly sophisticated knowledge about what actions these words really refer to. In addition, processes must be present that relate the answer to the question such that the relevant fact can actually be found in memory when it is needed.

Understanding means being able to associate knowledge of the world with linguistic inputs so as to make sense of a sentence like "John kissed Mary when she threw Bill out of the house." To understand this sentence, a person must know about the relationships and motivations of the people involved. The problem of getting machines to understand and talk is largely one of ascertaining what knowledge people have and finding out how they recall it at the appropriate time. It is from this computer-modelling point of view that I will discuss the issue of human memory.

Most researchers in this area have avoided the problems of memory and knowledge. They have treated language processing as being divided into the problems of *parsing* and *generating*. Initially, parsing meant the assigning of a syntactic structure (typically a phrase-structure tree diagram) to an input sentence. Generating was defined as the random generation of sentences, which was accomplished by constructing syntax trees using phrase-structure rules and the substitution of words at the terminal nodes.

Techniques and attitudes from the field of artificial intelligence have significantly altered this view of natural language processing in the last five years or so. The desire to have programs that can converse with the user in natural English has forced researchers to redefine the problem of parsing as the problem of language comprehension. Basically this redefinition means that the output of parsing an input sentence should not be a syntactic tree; rather, the output should express the meaning of the input sentence. Researchers have adopted two general approaches to reach this goal. One (exemplified by the work of Simmons, 1973; Winograd, 1972; Woods, 1970; and others) is to build semantic routines that receive the output of syntactic parses as input. The other (exemplified by the work of Riesbeck, 1975; Schank, 1973; Wilks, 1973) stresses that syntactic processing is secondary to the analysis of meaning and should thus be necessary only if resolution of ambiguity by meaning analysis fails.

Similarly, generating has been redefined as the task of putting the information the machine wants to express into reasonable English. Here too syntax is used as a processing tool only after meaning has been determined.

All of the researchers mentioned above have realized that a very important consequence of this restructuring of the natural-language-processing paradigm is that the *inference* and *knowledge* processes must be included in any model of understanding. A person cannot understand a sentence without some knowledge of what is being talked about. Most human communication and understanding seem to be based on the inferences made from an input sentence rather than on the input sentence itself.

Consider a simple conversation:

A: John hit Mary yesterday.
B: Oh, that's awful.

This sequence makes sense only if you know why hitting somebody can be a bad thing. Now in fact there are many reasons why the fact that "John hit Mary" could be bad. There are also many reasons (perhaps less likely out of context) why "John hit Mary" could be good (from the point of view of the speaker). A system that understands that hitting people can hurt them and that being hurt is unpleasant can apply rules of belief that determine why this event could have been awful. Without rules and knowledge of this type, understanding cannot be achieved. In other words, memory, the repository for knowledge and rules of inference, is crucial to the process of understanding natural language. Moreover, the problems of parsing into meaning structures and generation from meaning structures, once seemingly separable problems, simply cannot be solved in the absence of a memory that contains knowledge of the world and rules of inference.

In the next section of this Chapter I shall discuss why parsing and generating are inseparable from memory. In later sections I shall discuss the nature of the contents of memory, and I shall speculate on how the processes in memory are organized and what their responsibilities within an understanding system are.

Parsing and Generating with Memory

Consider the problem of analyzing the meaning of the sentence:

I am going to the store for mother.

(This example and the insights drawn from it are taken from Hemphill, 1975.) The task of parsing this sentence by dividing it into its syntactic components presents no problem. But this sentence has at least two different meanings and we could thus generate two different meaning structures as the correct output. The problem of disambiguating sentences such as this can often be handled by referring to some of the semantic features of the individual words contained in the sentence so as to obtain their preferred combination. For example, consider:

The old man's glasses were filled with sherry.

When an ambiguity results from the fact that one word can refer to two distinct concepts, these concepts must be checked to see whether one of the features that distinguishes them is connected to another concept contained in the sentence. In our example, the action underlying the verb *fill* requires that the object of that action have a "containment" feature (i.e., the memory must know that it can contain things). The "spectacles" sense of *glasses* does not satisfy that requirement as well as the "drinking glasses" sense of *glasses*. The discovery of this fact helps us to select the correct sense of the ambiguous word and to complete the analysis of the sentence.

The process outlined above requires that what is known about the words in the sentence be obtained from memory. This fact would seem to show the need for memory even in parsing mundane sentences. But the memory that has been accessed in the resolution of the "glasses" example is a memory for words, commonly referred to as *semantic memory*. Arguments could be and have been made that semantic memory is little more than a dictionary. If our thesis were simply that semantic memory is necessary for parsing, there would be little novelty in it.

The "store" sentence quoted above illustrates the limitations of such an approach. Both senses of the sentence make sense in an appropriate context. Furthermore, neither of the senses is preferred over the other out of context. In a real understanding task, it would be necessary to establish the context. The only way to establish the context is to consult memory. Here we do not mean semantic memory but rather what is referred to as *episodic memory* (e.g., see Tulving, 1972). That is, we must formulate the question "Where is mother?" If we find out that she is at the store then *for* means "in order to pick her up." If she is not at the store, at least as far as the speaker is concerned, then *for* means "to do something on her behalf." In this latter sense, what action was being done on her behalf could be determined by consulting what is known about stores. It would then be determined that the speaker intends to buy something at the store and is doing so to benefit mother in some way.

The process of obtaining an analysis of meaning, then, is inextricably tied up with the problem of finding out what the individual words mean and cannot be separated from the knowledge of the world contained in those words. Moreover, memory for past events sometimes determines the meaning of an input sentence. The analysis process makes extensive use of the parts and processes of memory.

We can draw the same conclusion with respect to the generation of sentences. Goldman (1975) has written a computer program that takes representations of meaning, as formulated in *conceptual dependency theory* (see Schank, 1973, 1975), and maps them into English sentences. These representations of meaning are intended to express the conceptual content of a statement apart from the particular words of the particular language chosen to express that content. In computer programs based on conceptual dependency theory, the generation process consists in mapping well-formed meaning structures that are language-free into a well-formed sentence of a natural language. (This task is different from that posed by Chomsky, 1965 and his followers, which is concerned with deciding whether a syntactic or semantic structure is well-formed. There is no need here to worry about whether the sentence being generated is meaningful since it is what the machine that generated it wanted to say. The problem of deciding what to say is a difficult one that requires motivations, knowledge, and rules of appropriateness as input.)

Consider the task of generating a sentence such as:

John told Mary he would kill her husband.

The conceptual-dependency structures we use to express meaning would pass to the generator a formal structure that unambiguously expresses the explicit and implicit information present in an idea. For our sample sentence, that formal structure is roughly equivalent to:

> John transferred some information to Mary indicating that John intends to perform some unknown action which he expects will result in the death of Mary's husband.

In the process of encoding this structure into English, the first question that must be decided is the choice of the appropriate main verb. All other lexical decisions will depend on that selection.

For the structure presented above, a number of different verbs can describe the event that took place. *Tell* might function well here. However, people usually choose to describe the kind of event under discussion with a more descriptive verb if they have access to additional information about the situation. For example, knowledge of Mary's viewpoint of the consequence of the proposed action can affect the choice of an appropriate verb. Before selecting a verb, our program would pose a question to its memory, inquiring whether Mary feels that her husband's imminent death will have the effect of making her feel better or worse. If it finds that she wants this action to occur, it might decide that the verb *promise* is most appropriate. If it finds that she does not want this event to take place, it might select *threaten* as the most appropriate verb. If nothing is known of Mary's relationship with her husband, the program would probe for more general information about husbands' relationships with their wives, which might also produce *threaten*. (Of course, this might not always be correct.) In a more neutral context, the program might decide that *tell* is best.

We can examine another example of the phenomenon of generation after checking with memory by considering how an observer would attempt to describe a situation where John has just handed a book to Mary. He might want to say, "John gave the book to Mary." However, if it is Mary's birthday and the book is wrapped in pretty paper he might wish to use the verb *presented*. If Mary is a representative of a large library and the book is very valuable, he might wish to use *donated*. If Mary has previously handed the book to John, the observer might choose to say *returned*.

A computer program that attempts to talk must "know" all this information, of course. The only way it can determine what to say in order to describe what it has received as input (in this case the meaning presented to it would be "John transferred a book to the receiver Mary") is to consult its memory. That is, its memory is a repository for information about the world in general and about the people and things that it knows in particular. A knowledgeable generator is really the only kind that can perform the task well. Likewise, a knowledgeable understander is really the only kind there can be. Thus, it is clear that memory is an integral part of the processes of parsing and generation.

Inference

I have claimed in the previous section that memory is needed to solve the trickier problems in parsing and generating and that in any real understanding system, therefore, memory is at the base of the parsing and generating processes. I would like to make an even stronger claim: memory controls and underlies the whole process of understanding. It is simply not possible to make sense of new inputs without some sense of the place of those inputs in the world. People understand new inputs in terms of everything else they know relevant to those new inputs.

The understanding process is basically one of trying to make enough sense out of a new input to know what body of knowledge and what processes to bring into play in order to understand the rest of that input as well as any subsequent inputs likely to be related to it. Thus, we conceive of the process of understanding language as a set of procedures that seek to extract what is explicit in an input and attach it to the body of knowledge associated with that explicit information in a way that will allow the system to formulate questions whose answers will fill in the holes that exist in the final meaning representation of that input. People understand more from a sentence than they have been told explicitly. They understand what they have not been told and what they must infer in order to make sense of what they have been told. Knowing what they don't know allows them to generate the processes that will fill in the empty holes.

What I am saying is that human communication is based largely on what is left out of a discourse. People rarely specify everything they intend to communicate. Rather, they specify enough to lead the hearer to an understanding of what is meant. They leave out anything they assume the hearer can figure out for himself. It is easy to see that the problem of understanding is the problem of recreating what has been left out.

The propositions that have been left out are *inferences*. Simply defined, an inference is anything that is likely to be true about a given input but is not necessarily true. The rule of thumb that can be used to determine what is and what is not an inference is called the *"but"* test. A proposition is a reasonable inference from another proposition (in English) if the negation of that proposition preceded by the word *but* in conjunction with the first sentence yields a sensible sentence. If the result of this "butting" yields a sentence that denies its own premise, then the second proposition is said to be *implicit* within the first. If there is no obvious relation between the clauses in the conjoined sentence, then the second proposition is not an inference from the first. Some examples of different types of inferences are:

> John punched Mary, but his hand didn't touch her.   implicit
>
> John punched Mary, but she didn't cry.   valid inference
>
> John punched Mary, but it didn't rain.   invalid inference

The question of understanding sentences like the last one cited above cannot be dismissed by marking the statement invalid. If somebody said the last sentence, we would want to know why he expected that such a consequence would result. (For the purposes of the test we simply show that raining is not usually to be inferred from punching.)

Inferences, then, are never certain. They come from rules that a hearer learns to apply to various words, concepts, and situations. Inference is the core of the understanding process, and thus inferences lie at the center of human communication. They serve to tie inputs together into a related whole. Often, the inferences themselves are the main point of the message.

If inferences are such a crucial part of understanding, we might wonder why they are left out of spoken language. The answer is simply that people try to conserve space; they try to be as concise as possible by avoiding remarks that are obvious to the hearer. In conversation, this process involves assessing what the hearer knows while talking to him. This assessment is not always accurate and if what has been left out is important and must be inferred on the basis of knowledge different from that assumed by the speaker, a misunderstanding can result. Inferences are also left out because speakers don't want to accept responsibility for having said them. Politicians make use of the inferential capability of hearers all the time.

The process of inference is wholly dependent on an adequate supply of knowledge of the world. Without knowing what can happen in the world, it is impossible to make sense out of what has happened. Small children are capable of witnessing earth-shaking events without making sense of them because of their lack of knowledge about the implications of these events. That is, they don't know what they are seeing.

Rieger (1975) has classified the process of inference into sixteen distinct inference classes. It is his thesis that people subject every input sentence to the mechanisms that are linked to these classes to produce inferences every time a sentence is received. Below are Rieger's classes of inferences.

1. *Specification* What parts of the meaning underlying a sentence are implicit and must be filled in?
2. *Causative* What caused the action or state in the sentence to come about?

3. *Resultative*   What are the likely results of an input action or state in terms of its effect on the world?

4. *Motivational*   Why did the actor perform the action? What did he intend to happen?

5. *Enablement*   What states of the world must have been true for the actor to perform his action?

6. *Function*   What is the value or use of a given object?

7. *Enablement/prediction*   If a person wants a state of the world to exist, what action will it then be possible to perform?

8. *Missing enablement*   If a person can't do what he wants, what state will have to change in order to permit it?

9. *Intervention*   What can an actor do to prevent an undesirable state from occurring?

10. *Action/prediction*   Knowing a person's needs and desires, what actions is he likely to perform?

11. *Knowledge propagation*   Knowing that a person knows certain things, what else is he likely to know?

12. *Normative*   What things that are normal in the world should be assumed in the absence of being told them specifically?

13. *State-duration*   How long will a given state or action last?

14. *Feature*   What can be predicted about an entity when a set of facts is known about it?

15. *Situation*   What other information can be assumed about a given situation?

16. *Utterance-intent*   Why did the speaker say what he said?

It is memory's responsibility to establish the inferences that are likely to be true in a given situation. These inferences are made partially because it is often the inferences themselves that are the point of the input. Inferences are also made because they will result in questions and knowledge that will lead to the understanding of a sequence of sentences as a whole.

The basic mechanism in understanding is the inference process. People understand more than what they have explicitly been told. They do this by tying together what they have heard with what they know about what they have heard. We can illustrate this interaction of knowledge and inference in understanding by considering the sentence:

John saw a large boulder rolling down the mountain towards his house.

followed by each of the sentences listed below as the second sentence in a two-sentence paragraph:

1. He ran inside to get his pet mouse.
2. He started digging a path that led away from his house.
3. He hid under his bed.

4. He picked up the telephone.
5. He started to cry.
6. He ran inside to get a mattress.
7. He yelled for his wife.
8. He called the geological society.
9. He started to write his will.

The process of understanding involves considerably more than just deciding upon the appropriate meaning for a given sentence. The meaning of a paragraph is more than the sum total of the meaning of each individual sentence contained in it. People leave out from a story or sequence of sentences the reasons for each action in the sequence and the way in which the individual items in the sequence relate to each other. These things are left out largely because they are obvious. We could ask a person who has just heard any of the nine sequences listed above why the action communicated in the second sentence occurred and he would probably give answers of the following sort:

1r. Because he wanted to save the mouse's life.
2r. To cause the boulder to veer away from the house.
3r. Because he was frightened and irrational.
4r. He intended to call for help.
5r. He was frightened and gave up hope of saving himself.
6r. Maybe he thought he could cushion the blow of the boulder by putting the mattress in front of the impact point.
7r. He wanted to make his wife aware of the problem so she could leave the house and save herself.
8r. Perhaps he thought the rock was an interesting specimen and he wasn't aware of the danger.
9r. He assumed he was going to die and wanted his possessions dispersed according to his wishes.

These responses indicate an understanding of the situation being discussed apart from and in addition to what has actually been related. Within the process of understanding, memory is responsible for finding the knowledge it contains that is relevant to what it has heard and for using that knowledge to make inferences about the intentions, motivations, and effects of the actions in the sequence it has heard. Here again, memory is at the base of the understanding process.

What is obvious to a person is of course not obvious to a computer. The problem of getting a computer to understand is at least partially the problem of finding out what information is necessary when. In order to understand the two-sentence sequence related above in which Sentence 1 is the second sentence, it is necessary to access the facts that:

A. Large objects moving at a sufficient speed can destroy objects of insufficient rigidity.

B. A boulder rolling down a mountain is an instance of the first part of Fact A and a house is an instance of the second part.

C. Things inside objects about to be destroyed often get destroyed as well.

D. People try to prevent actions that have consequences for them.

E. People value their possessions and dislike losing them.

F. Taking something away from a situation that will destroy it will prevent that destruction.

G. Pets are valued possessions.

A combination of these seven facts will help to process the first two-line sequence. Only Facts A and B are used in all nine sequences. The other eight sequences require facts of their own to make sense out of them. Thus, it is obvious that part of the problem of understanding is organizing the knowledge that one has so that it is possible to find what is needed in a given situation. A model of the understanding process must necessarily be extremely complicated. The basis of any solution must contain a memory for facts that can apply as inferences in a given situation.

The Nature of Memory

We are now ready to consider what the contents of memory look like. I have stated that propositions appear in the form of known facts about the world, as inferences that can be made about new inputs, and as new inputs themselves. It is thus important to consider what a proposition probably looks like inside memory.

The first thing to consider is that a proposition cannot be stored in memory simply in the form of a natural-language sentence. Since it is possible to say the same thing in a number of different ways, it is unreasonable to suppose that people are constantly checking to see whether a proposition they have stored in one way in memory is the same as another proposition they have stored somewhere else in an alternate form. What is far more likely is that people have developed a kind of canonical form for encoding meanings. Every new input is transformed into this canonical form. According to this view, no two propositions in memory can have the same meaning unless they are identically represented.

What would such a canonical form look like? First, a canonical representational scheme could not have natural-language words as its elements. Words can be ambiguous, and such a scheme would have to be unambiguous. Furthermore, words can be synonymous and overlap in meaning. By disallowing synonymous canonical forms for propositions, we have also disallowed the use of words in the representation.

The consequences of this disallowal of words is consistent with what we know about people. In memory experiments people consistently exhibit recognition confusions because they remember the gist of a sentence rather than the words they have actually seen or heard.

The only canonical form proposed for representing propositional information previous to our work is the predicate calculus. Since my work on language processing precluded the possibility that human cognitive processes are organized around procedures designed for proving theorems, I was forced to set out on my own in search of a representational format that could meet the criteria described above and that could be a serious candidate for a model of human memory.

The system I came up with is called *conceptual dependency* and has as its basic tenets all the ideas presented above plus the idea that an *action* is the basis of any proposition that is not descriptive of a static piece of the world.

All propositions that describe events are made up of *conceptualizations*. A conceptualization is composed of an *actor*, an *action*, and a set of *cases* (i.e., certain dependent objects) that are *dependent on that action*.

The main insight of conceptual dependency theory is that there must be a canonical form for representations of meaning. The types of conceptual roles that comprise this canonical form need not correspond to syntactic roles. Rather, words must be broken down into their conceptual parts so that they can be placed in the meaning representation that corresponds to their conceptual roles rather than to the syntactic roles that were chosen for them as a result of some, perhaps random, lexical choices. For example, the concept of danger can be expressed in a nominal form *(danger)*, a verbal form *(endanger)*, an adjectival form *(dangerous)*, and an adverbial form *(dangerously)*. The meaning of the underlying concept of danger is the same no matter what lexical form is selected to realize that concept. Basically, the concept of danger is that something can possibly happen that will have a negative effect on somebody's physical state. In a conceptual-dependency model, danger is represented conceptually as a conceptualization linked to a state description. The elements of the conceptualization are unknown but can be filled in by the words surrounding the concept of danger. The state description is partially known. It says that somebody's physical state may be negatively changed. The link between these entities is called *result causation*.

So we see that *endanger* is no more an action than it is an actor. Rather, *endanger* sets up a partial conceptual structure. The word *endanger* also sets up an expectation that the subject of that verb will contain the item that will fill in the *action* in the empty conceptualization. Thus, in the sentence "The bees endangered Bill," the bees are the actors of a conceptualization that is causally related to a state description of the fact that Bill will undergo a negative change. The action is still unknown, but knowing that it's unknown allows us to try to infer it. When we consult our memory for actions that bees are known to perform that endanger human beings, the simplest explanation is preferred and the best candidate for the action is the verb *sting*. The object of that action is *Bill*.

I said before that words do not appear in conceptualizations. Following that point of view, it is obvious that *sting* cannot really satisfy our needs here. The idea conveyed by *sting* is correct, but it must be broken down into its component parts. For this discussion I define an action as something an actor can do to an object; I define an actor as an animate object, and an object as any concrete physical object. *Sting* still works under these constraints, but couldn't we just as well use the word *bite?* Although the two words have slightly different meanings in their strict interpretations, we are interested here in how people use language rather than how a grammarian or philosopher sees the problem. To the average user, these words are synonyms, and we are left with the problem of describing the concept underlying them in order to satisfy the requirements that we have set out above.

To handle the similarities and overlaps in meaning between words as they are used by the man in the street, I have developed the concept of the *primitive action*. Primitive actions are intended to be the building blocks out of which verbs and abstract and complex nouns are constructed. The primitive actions are not category names but rather elements that can be used in multiple combinations to express the meaning of the concept that underlies a given word.

Conceptual-dependency representations use only eleven primitive acts. These acts were arrived at by noticing structural similarities that existed when sentences were put into an actor-action-object framework. Using this set of acts and a larger set of states, it is possible to express a large amount, if not all, of the meanings expressible in natural language. I will now describe the most important of the eleven primitive acts and briefly mention the others.

ATRANS   The transfer of an abstract relationship such as possession, ownership, or control. ATRANS requires an actor, an object, and a recipient.

Examples:

give   = ATRANS an object from the actor to the recipient.

take   = ATRANS an object from someone to the actor.

buy   = two ATRANS actions, each causing the other. ATRANS of money from the first actor to the second actor; ATRANS of an object from the second to the first.

PTRANS The transfer of physical location of an object. PTRANS requires an actor, an object, and a direction.
Examples:

go   = PTRANS of an actor by an actor to a location.

fly   = PTRANS of an actor to a location. Any act can have another act as its instrument. For *fly*, that instrument is PROPEL.

PROPEL The application of a physical force to an object. If movement takes place as a result of PROPEL, a PTRANS has taken place too if it can be determined that the PROPEL was intended by the actor. PROPEL requires a direction, an object, and an actor.
Examples:

push = PROPEL an object in a direction by an actor.

pull   = PROPEL an object in a direction (toward actor) by an actor.

kick   = PROPEL an object in a direction by an actor using the instrument MOVEd object's foot.

MTRANS The transfer of information between animals or within an animal. For the purpose of dealing with the words people use to discuss memory, we partition memory into three parts: (1) the *CP*, the *conscious processor*, is where an item is located at the moment it is being thought of; (2) the *IM*, the *intermediate memory*, is where current processing goes on and contextually relevant information is stored; (3) the *LTM*, the *long-term memory*, is where information is stored. The various sense organs serve as the originators of an MTRANS, for which a recipient, an object, and an actor are required; mental locations can qualify as recipients in an MTRANS and mental items of information can qualify as possible objects.
Examples:

remember = MTRANS information from LTM to IM.

forget   = MTRANS cannot be accomplished on some information from LTM.

see   = MTRANS information to IM from the eyes.

tell   = an actor MTRANSes information to another actor.

read   = MTRANS information from a book to IM by means of ATTEND-eye-to-the-book.

MBUILD   The construction within an animal of new information from old information. MBUILDing takes place within IM and receives its inputs from the CP and from LTM. It transforms these inputs into a new idea and places that idea in the CP.
Examples:

decide   = MBUILD a future action or a new state.

imagine   = MBUILD a new idea that is hypothetical.

consider   = MBUILD from a mentioned input into an unspecified output.

answer   = MBUILD specific output for an input that has just been received in the CP from some other person.

INGEST   The taking of an object by an animal into the inner working of that animal. INGEST requires an actor, an object, and a direction.
Examples:

eat   = INGEST a solid into the body through the mouth.

breathe   = INGEST air into the body through the mouth and nose.

shoot up   = INGEST a narcotic into the body through a vein by PROPEL-narcotic-through-needle.

smoke   = INGEST smoke from a cigarette into the mouth by INGEST-air-through-the-cigarette.

All conceptualizations require other conceptualizations as instruments of implementation. The remainder of the primitive acts are the acts of instrumental conceptualization.

GRASP	To grasp an object.
ATTEND	To focus a sense organ to an object.
SPEAK	To make a noise.
MOVE	To move a body part.
EXPEL	To push something out of the body.

We have listed above only one sense of each verb that we have chosen to describe as an example. The power of the primitive acts is that they can point up similarities among words (such as the use of ATRANS for *give, take* and *buy*) while also highlighting their differences. In addition, they serve as a vehicle for disambiguating ambiguous words. Thus, the representation for *smoke* as in "The barn is smoking" would not have INGEST in it but would use a state description involving *smoke* and *heat*. Similarly, the representation of *take* as in "take an aspirin" would be INGEST rather than ATRANS. A program that makes these disambiguations and assigns the correct conceptual structure to an input sentence was written by Riesbeck (1975). To make its distinctions, the program uses knowledge about how words fit together in English and some general knowledge about the physical world. Upon encountering *take*, for example, the program asks whether there is an object around that is medication. It also finds out whether the sentential object is really an action, as in "take a beating." If it is, the program assigns neither ATRANS nor INGEST as the representation but rather a causal structure. This series of tests helps to determine the correct conceptual sense for a word.

The primitive acts are useful for organizing the inference process. For example, rather than stating that if we see something then we know it, and if we hear something then we know it, and if we read something then we know it, and so on, we can simply state that whenever an MTRANS exists, a likely inference is that the MTRANSed information is in the mental location LTM (the representation for *know*). Another example: any number of forces and verbs describing those forces can cause different kinds of state changes (due to either damage, or location, or the like). By listing the criteria that must be met for valid inferences of state changes once, under PROPEL, rather than under each individual verb that might call them up, we can organize our knowledge of facts and events in a very useful way.

Organizing the inferences under the primitive acts also serves to define the acts themselves. The theoretical decision for what constitutes a primitive act is based on whether the proposed new act carries with it a set of inferences not already accounted for by an act that is already in use. Similarly, a primitive act is dropped if it can be determined that its inferences are already handled by another act.

While the basic unit of memory is the conceptualization (made up of a primitive act and the concepts and conceptualizations that are dependent on it), each unit does not stand alone unrelated to other conceptualizations in memory. The basic unit of relationship between conceptualizations is the causal link. There are four kinds of causal links in memory:

Result causation: The change of the state of an object along some dimension. Only actions can cause state changes.

Enable causation: The enablement of an action by the existence of a particular state or set of states.

Reason causation: The relationship between an action and the decision to do that action.

Initiation causation: The initiation of a thought after some related visual, aural, or internal input has been received.

Memory for events (or stories about events) consists of conceptualizations causally linked to each other. These causal links are often established because there are words input that have causal links implicit in them. For example, "X prevented Y" means X performed an action that resulted in a state change that ended the conditions enabling Y to occur. (Example: "John prevented Mary from leaving by breaking her leg.") Often, of course, some common causal word such as *because* or *and* will be used and then the particular type of causal link must be inferred.

One of the most important uses of inference techniques, then, is establishing the causal connections among conceptualizations. We view stories as being sequences of result and enable causal linkings. The problem of understanding stories is at least partially the problem of establishing a *causal chain* that connects the story into a related whole. Thus, for the following simple story we could obtain the representation shown below it as output:

> John was throwing darts against a tree when he heard a girl cry out. He looked behind the tree and saw Mary rubbing her leg. He apologized at once.

John MBUILD (John PROPEL darts TO tree)
    result
    (darts LOCATION tree)
  reason
John PROPEL dart TO girl
    result
girl BE hurt
    enable
girl SPEAK cry
    initiate
John MBUILD (who? SPEAK cry)
    initiate

John MBUILD (John PTRANS John TO behind tree)
 result/enable
(John ATTEND eye TO whom?)
 reason
John PTRANS John TO behind tree
 result/enable
John MTRANS (Mary MOVE hand TO leg) TO IM
 initiate
John MBUILD (John PROPEL dart TO leg of Mary)
 result
 reason Mary BE hurt
  initiate
(John BE unhappy)
John MTRANS (John BE sorry) TO Mary

The story representation outlined above makes use of a number of abbreviations that are used only to save space here. Result/enable causation is really two causals with an intermediate state that I have left out. The MBUILDS are considerably more complex than I have shown here and would normally include certain reasoning patterns and belief structures that are necessary for deciding a particular output of an MBUILD.

The main disadvantage of the above representation is that it is very large and unwieldy. Yet, after people hear a story like the one represented, they know all the specific pieces I have shown, and we must assume that they do something quite like the representation. We must also assume that after a small amount of time has elapsed some of the less salient points of a story get forgotten. What is forgotten first are the dead-end causal chains. (These are not shown above but would be generated from inconsequential statements such as "It was a warm day" or "He was holding a brass bell." Such sentences lack meaning unless their existence can be somehow causally related to something else in a story.) Next, people may forget conceptual inferences that can be easily regenerated. Notice that certain inferences are crucial; not only will the hearer remember them, but he is likely to feel that they were included in the original statement of the story. In our sample representation, such an inference is (John PROPEL dart TO leg of Mary)—an inference that is crucial to the whole story but has never been explicitly mentioned.

Thus, people remember inputs to memory as linked chains of conceptualizations made up of the concepts that have been extracted from words of the input sentences.

The Organization of Memory

I have discussed the role of memory in language processing in a general way and have attempted to outline the rules specifying the form that a proposition can take in memory. I still need to discuss the issues of how propositions are organized within memory, how memory is searched for information, and how memory actually functions in the understanding process. After touching on each of these topics, I will briefly describe the state of the computer model of memory currently serving as the basis of experimental work in our laboratory.

Most proposals for memory organization are based on the notion of semantic memory. Briefly, semantic memory is a memory for words that is organized in a hierarchical fashion using class membership for the word as the superset node in a tree structure. According to this model, *canary* is linked to *bird* and *bird* to *animal* in a hierarchical tree.

We can see at once that such an organization will not work for verbs or for nouns that are abstract or for nouns that do not submit easily to standard categories (such as *teletype*). More importantly, such an organization implies that people store propositions in memory by linking them to the words that they contain. According to the conceptual, non-word-oriented system described above, this is not possible. We could breach this difficulty by also organizing concepts in a hierarchical tree, but such a solution would still be in error.

If we ask someone to tell us a color that a car can be, he usually answers with the color of a car he has just seen. Often it is the color of his own car. A hierarchical organization cannot explain such an answer. Under that scheme, we would simply find the node for car, find the possible colors that are listed for cars (many semantic memory systems lack this feature actually and would simply output all colors), and produce an answer. Experimental evidence implies that the procedure people use to answer such a question is much closer to simply visualizing any car that comes to mind and then seeing what color it is.

A view of memory that attempts to handle items in this latter way relies on *episodic memory* as its organizing principle. An episodic memory is organized around propositions linked together by their occurrence in the same event or time span. There are no general nodes for "car" or "trip taking." There are only instances of "my car" and "the trip I took to Colorado last Christmas." These items are there as sequences of propositions describing the events that define that entity for the individual. A trip is stored in memory as a sequence of the conceptualizations that encompassed that trip, that is, as a sequence describing what happened on the trip. Some of the conceptualizations are marked as salient (especially important or interesting), and some make little impression and will be forgotten altogether.

Within this view of memory, nominal concepts (concrete nouns) are defined with a two-part definition. The first and primary part is a functional definition that attempts to generalize over particular episodes the salient events in which the noun has occurred. The complete functional, primary definition of a given noun lists all occurrences of that noun in memory. The second part of the definition contains a physical description of one particular member of the class that is being defined.

For *spoon*, for example, the definition in memory first lists the general usage of a spoon (e.g., it is a thing that you PTRANS into mushy or liquid objects in order to PTRANS that object to your mouth so as to INGEST it). All interesting specific instances of *spoon* are there too (including, for example, "the time I was camping and washed my spoon in the sand"). Lastly there is a physical description of a particular spoon (most likely of the kind you have at home).

The overall organization of memory is a sequence of episodes organized roughly along the time line of one's life. Considering a problem of search in memory helps bear this out.

If we ask a man, "Who was your girlfriend in 1968?" and ask him to report his strategy for the answer, his reply is roughly: "First I thought about where I was and what I was doing in 1968. Then I remembered who I used to go out with then."

In other words, it really isn't possible to answer such a question directly. There really are no slots in memory labeled "past girlfriends." Such lists are constructed over and over again. If they are needed often enough, the lists do become permanent entries in memory, but only after repeated access.

So search occurs through episodes. Past episodes must be found and re-created in order to answer questions about them. Memory is simply a morass of episodes. These episodes are organized in the sequence in which they occurred, more or less. They are accessible by the concepts that make them up. These concepts are stored in a "dictionary" of known concepts whose entries are the addresses of the various episodes in which the concepts occur.

Where do inferences fit into this scheme? Since inferences are stored in memory, they must be basically episodes. They are generalized episodes. That is, when a consequence or reason for a given event occurs often enough it gets set apart from the rest of memory as *world knowledge*. World knowledge is precisely that set of episodes that are not stored with their original occurrences because the propositions comprising those episodes occur so frequently that it is impossible to trace their origins and they are so boring that memory does not especially note them when they occur.

The process of understanding, then, is essentially one of finding the generalized episode (set of world-knowledge inferences) that fits a new input. A particular, new episode is then constructed that includes the original input and the applicable parts that have been inferred from the generalized episode.

Scripts

A generalized episode is called a *script*. A script is a giant causal chain of conceptualizations that have been known to occur in that order many times before. Scripts can be called up from memory by various words in the correct

ROGER C. SCHANK   181

context, by visual inputs, or by expectations generated through inferences. What a script does is to set up expectations about events that are likely to follow in a given situation. These events can be predicted because they have occurred in precisely this fashion before. Scripts are associated, then, with static everyday events such as restaurants, birthday parties, classrooms, bus riding, theater going, and so on. A simple test, called a *reference test,* can be used to determine when a script is helpful. The reference test consists of trying to introduce a new object by use of *the* and seeing whether the text makes sense. Some examples:

> John went to a restaurant.
> He asked the waitress to tell the chef to cook him a hot dog.

> John went to a restaurant.
> He asked the bus driver to talk to the midget.

> John went to a birthday party.
> First Bill opened the presents and then they ate the cake.

> John went to a birthday party.
> He asked the waitress to tell the chef to cook him a hot dog.

Every *the* in the first and third paragraphs makes perfect sense because a script has been introduced and the objects prefaced by *the* have all been implicitly referenced by the script. In English it is usually incorrect to preface an object by *the* unless it has been referred to before. It is all right here because the script effectively "says" that these items were present before they were actually mentioned. When these rules are violated, as they were in the second and fourth paragraphs, it makes the hearer uneasy and he is forced to fill in the missing sentence that introduces these objects. Thus, in the fourth paragraph we are surprised that a waitress and a chef were present at the party, but we can cope with this information by augmenting our birthday-party script into a very-fancy-party script.

I am saying that new inputs are handled by hearers in terms of the old knowledge they have about the words and the participants in a situation. More importantly, I am saying that we would expect this to be the case because of the way in which people interpret what they hear: since a script is called up to interpret new inputs and the script contains "blank events" (events that are expected but not necessarily explicitly mentioned), hearers infer the actual existence of these blank events and often confuse what they have inferred with what they have actually been told. Consider the following two paragraphs:

> John went into a restaurant and ordered a hamburger.
> He enjoyed it and left the waitress a big tip.

> John got on the bus to go to Grant Avenue. The driver wouldn't make change for him but an old lady helped him out.

We would expect people to have no trouble answering the questions "Who served John the hamburger?" and "Did John pay the fare?" Yet neither of these events occurs explicitly in the stories. Rather, they are transmitted implicitly by the scripts attached to those stories. I would claim that scripts take over the understanding task in everyday situations to such a degree as to blur the distinction between what one hears and what one infers.

The general form of a script is a causal chain that connects the expected events of a given situation. A restaurant script might have in it a set of different scenes, each dealing with the kinds of interactions that take place in a restaurant. For example there might be an "enter" scene, followed by a "sit-down" scene, followed by an "order" scene, followed by an "eat" scene, followed by a "pay" scene, and so on. There would be many possible variations that such scenes could have. One possible variety of the order scene might be:

MTRANS desire for a menu to waitress
ATRANS menu to customer
MTRANS read menu
MBUILD decide to order
MTRANS order to waitress

Of course, possible variations must be built into such a scene. The enabling conditions for each act have to be checked and if they are found to be unsatisfied, they will have to be rectified. (For example, if the waitress isn't near you she will have to be signaled in order to MTRANS the order.)

A script is useful because it fills in the blanks in our understanding. (This is similar to the *frames* idea suggested by Minsky, 1975.) If we are told that John sat down, and later we find that he ate, we can assume that the order scene took place. Alternatively, if we hear that John asked the waitress for the menu and then ordered a steak, we would want to assume that he read the menu, that a steak was on it, and that his order was transmitted to the waitress. All of these pieces of information come from the order scene and would be difficult to figure out without such a piece of scriptlike information.

Plans

We might ask where scripts come from. One answer is that scripts are simply *plans* that have been used a lot. Plans are sets of information that are attached to the various goals people have. Some of the goals we can assume people have are to eat, to be warm, to possess certain things, to have self-respect, to have power, to know things, to love, and so on. Attached to each of these goals are methods known to the person to be useful for achieving the goals. These methods are possibly explicit sequences of actions that will acheive these goals together with the conditions necessary for the performance of those actions. Or they may be general, only partly formed action lists that have either unknown or unachievable crucial parts that prevent the implementation of the lists.

However, whether or not a person is capable of achieving a certain goal has little to do with whether or not he can understand sentences that make use of such goal-achieving or planful knowledge. Consider the following sequences:

> John wanted to become chairman of the department. He went and got some arsenic.

> John wanted to be chairman of the department. He invited the Dean over for dinner.

> John was lonely. He thought if he could find a cab the driver might be able to help him out.

People have general knowledge about plans. They know that to achieve the power goal one has several options. Doing favors for people currently in power, getting powerful people to like you, or getting rid of the competition are three (possibly interrelated) options. People use this information to interpret other people's behavior. If they don't have the information that pertains to someone's plan, it is impossible for them to interpret what they perceive. Specialized knowledge about what is being referred to is needed to understand the third paragraph cited above. Without this knowledge (about one type of plan), this paragraph is incomprehensible.

To get a general idea about how plans work, consider an anthropomorphic bear. This bear lives in a bear world but he and the animals he interacts with can talk. Such a bear has some simple goals: to satiate his hunger, his sex drive, and his need for rest, and to preserve his health. Suppose our bear is hungry. He must get some food. Having food in his control will enable the desired INGEST act. The bear uses the plan GET (X) where X is food. GET(X) is a plan that will, he hopes, translate into a sequence of acts that he can perform that will result in the desired state (CONTROL(food)), which enables the INGEST. GET (X) is rewritten into two subplans FIND(X), which will enable TAKE(X). FIND(X) requires knowledge of where X is located, so this is translated into ΔKNOW(LOC(X)). (Here we borrow the change-of-state notation called *deltacts*, used by Abelson, 1975.)

The completion of the change of knowledge will enable a PTRANS to the new location so that

$$FIND\ (LOC(X))\ =\ \Delta KNOW(LOC(X))\ +\ PTRANS\ (TO\ LOC(X))$$

Many possible plans come from ΔKNOW. If someone else might know, the plan called ASK might be used. The ASK plan consists of the act to be done (an MTRANS of the question "Where is the food?") and the preconditions that must be satisfied in order to make that plan have a positive outcome. For example, in order to ask, the locations of the asker and the asked must be the same (in the bear world). In addition, the asked must want to convey the answer. The ASK plan is responsible for telling the user how to overcome any unsatisfied preconditions. If the asked doesn't wish to tell, then the asker may wish to THREATEN. The result of the ASK plan is that the asker now knows where the food is. This enables a PTRANS and now the problem of TAKING the food must be met. This comes under ΔCONTROL(X). Under ΔCONTROL(X) there are many possible plans, one of which is BARGAIN OBJECT. If this plan is successful, then control is gotten and the INGEST can take place.

Planning sequences such as the one just described for the anthropomorphic bear can be used for both telling and understanding stories. Using the structure and choices summarized above, a generated story might be:

> Joe Bear was hungry. He went to Irving Bird and asked him whether he knew of any bees' nests. Irving said he wouldn't tell him, so Joe threatened to bust him in the beak. Irving said there was a nest two trees down. Joe Bear went there and offered the bees a bunch of flowers in exchange for their honey. The bees agreed and Joe sat down and ate.

The planning structures outlined above could be used for understanding sequences such as:

> Joe Bear was hungry.
> He found Irving Bird.

Where it is known that birds are not sources of food for bears, it can be determined that Irving might be a source of information.

Planning structures are an integral part of memory processes. People know how others handle the world and thus can understand pieces of a plan they are told about. The theoretical entities that are part of these plans (such as ASK and THREATEN) are simply names of possible sequences of events that will yield the desired result. (They should not be confused with the conceptual representation of the meaning of these words, which is something apart from the intention of an act and its place within a plan. You needn't use the words *ask* or *threaten* in order to ASK or THREATEN. The conceptual entities underlying these and other words call up the plans that might have been intended.)

If a plan is used often enough it becomes a script. What are scripts for some people are not necessarily scripts for others. What is important here is that language understanding simply cannot take place in the absence of the knowledge contained in memory. Higher-level structures, such as plans and scripts, are just glorified inference techniques. The basis of understanding is the assignment of new inputs to previously stored episodes in memory that will make sense of them. If relevant knowledge is found in memory, understanding can be achieved. Otherwise it cannot be.

Knowledge and Understanding

The process of understanding language, then, has the following components.

1. *Conceptual-dependency assignment:* New inputs are assigned conceptual representations. This is done in conjunction with a lexical memory that gives conceptual meanings to words and an episodic memory that makes the correct choice in ambiguous situations by consulting the context and remembrances of similar contexts.

2. *Knowledge application:* New input conceptualizations are tested against stored patterns to make predictions. If a script or plan is recognized, it is used to generate predictions about future events and to make assumptions about parts of the script or plan that are implicit.

3. *Inference establishment:* New input conceptualizations are subjected to inferencing. Knowledge application may not be possible until certain inferences are established. The first inferences that are established are those that come directly from each primitive act that has been used. Next, inferences about intents and reasons can be established. Lastly belief-pattern inferences are tried; these look for motivations behind actions according to what is known about people. (In the boulder and mouse example, information about possible destruction comes from the act PROPEL; information about possessions emerges from the state POSSESSION; and the belief about preventing the loss of what you value can be used to explain future inputs about the actors' actions. In particular, since a PROPEL is going to be prevented, the enabling conditions for PROPEL, or its consequences—harm, are considered.)

4. *Finding causal chains:* If components 1 and 2 fail to find a causal chain that can represent the meaning of a sequence of sentences, then inferences are attempted that will find a causal chain based only on the results and enabling conditions of acts.

5. *Storage:* Eventually the final causal chain (whether arrived at from a plan, a script, a belief pattern, or just straight inferencing) is stored as an episode in memory. This episode is compared with past episodes in memory to find instances of plans, scripts, belief patterns, and inferences that come from past episodes and might now be applicable.

Computer Model

A word is in order about the capabilities of current computer programs and our future goals. Prior to the winter of 1973, programs were developed at

Stanford University that comprised the MARGIE system (see Schank et al., in press; the people responsible for designing and programming MARGIE were Neil Goldman, Charles Rieger, and Christopher Riesbeck.) The MARGIE system was a paraphrase and inference program that was developed to show the power of the three individual programs it tied together. Work stopped on it in late 1973 so that certain theoretical problems (some described here) could be attacked. In its paraphrase mode, the program would take an input sentence, analyze it into conceptual-dependency representation, and send that representation to a generator that would then read it back into English in many different possible ways. Some examples are:

Input: John killed Mary by choking Mary.
Output: John strangled Mary.
         John choked Mary and she died because she was unable to breathe.
         Mary died because she was unable to inhale some air and she was unable to inhale some air because John grabbed her neck.

Input: John prevented Bill from giving a banana to Mary by selling a banana to Rita.
Output: Bill was unable to give a banana to Mary because Rita traded John some money for a banana.
         Mary could not get a banana from Bill because Rita bought a banana from John.

In its inference mode, the program would make all the inferences that it could find on individual sentences. The program was the most goal-directed in its inference making when it dealt with short short stories:

Input: Bill took Mary's book from Mary.
         Mary kissed John because he hit Bill.
Output: John hit Bill.
         Bill became hurt.
         Mary became pleased because she felt a negative emotion toward Bill.
         Mary became pleased because John hit Bill.
         Mary liked John because John hit Bill.
         Mary kissed John because she liked John.

Input: John went to the drugstore.
Output: What did he want to buy?
Input: He wanted some aspirin.
Output: Is he sick?
Input: No, his wife is sick.
Output: John is single. You must mean John Smith, not John Jones.

The MARGIE program had a wide range of understanding but a very small vocabulary. Although it had a lot of knowledge that enabled it to make inferences, its organization of knowledge and realization of when to use what knowledge was incomplete.

Our current projects at Yale include remedying these failures. In particular we are working on adding more understanding of context to the analysis process and on devising ways to apply scripts, plans, and other knowledge structures to facilitate the understanding of complex stories. In other words, we are working on putting more knowledge and more knowledge processes into the understanding process.

Making use of the ideas about knowledge structures and language processing discussed above, we now have a new system running at Yale called SAM. (SAM was designed and programmed by Richard Cullingford, Gerald De Jong, Wendy Lehnert, Christopher Riesbeck, and Walter Stutzman.) SAM (Script Applier Mechanism) processes short texts (rather than unrelated sentences) by the use of scripts. Below is an example of SAM's input and output in a combined paraphrase-inference model.

Input:

John went to New York by bus. On the bus he talked to an old lady. When he left the bus, he thanked the driver. He took the subway to Leone's. On the subway his pocket was picked. He got off the train and entered Leone's. He had some lasagna. When the check came, he discovered he couldn't pay. The management told him he would have to wash dishes. When he left, he caught a bus to New Haven.

Long paraphrase:

John went to a bus stop. He waited at it a few minutes. He entered a bus. The driver got the ticket from John. He went to a seat. He sat down in it. While John was on the bus an old lady and John talked. The driver took John to New York. He went to the driver. When getting off the bus John thanked the driver. John got off it.

He entered a station. He put a token into the turnstile. He went to the platform. He waited at it a few minutes. He entered a subway car. A thief went to John. The thief picked John's pocket. He went. John went to the seat. He sat down in it. The driver took John to Leone's. He left the subway car. He left the station.

He entered Leone's. He looked around inside it. He saw he could go to a table. He went to it. He sat down in the seat. He ordered some lasagna. The waiter indicated to the chef John would like him to prepare something. The chef prepared the lasagna. The waiter got it from the chef. The waiter went to the table. He served the lasagna to John. He ate it. He became full.

He asked the waiter for the check. John got it from the waiter. John read the check. John discovered he was unable to pay the check. He indicated to the waiter he was unable to pay the check. The management told John he would have had to wash dishes. He entered the kitchen. He washed dishes. He left Leone's.

He went to the bus stop. He waited at it a few minutes. He entered the bus. The driver got the ticket from John. He went to the seat. He sat down in it. The driver took John to New Haven. He got off the bus.

[Paragraphing has been added to the computer output for ease of reading.]

SAM also serves as a translation system. We can translate an input text about which we have knowledge into any language that has been coded into the generator.

As an example, we show SAM's translation of the above story into Mandarin Chinese (transcribed in Harvard Romanization).

John tzuoh charng tu chi che daw neou iue chiuh le. Ta tzuoh dih shiah tiee luh daw Leone's chiuh de shyh how, tzeir tou le chyan. John sheang daw ta bu kee yi fu le chyan. Suoo yii ta shi bei tz le. Ta tzuoh charng tu chi che daw shin gang chiuh le.

In addition, SAM can answer questions about stories it has read. Below are some examples of input questions concerning the above story and the answers produced by SAM.

Q1: Why did John go to New York?
A1: Because John wanted to go to Leone's.

Q2: Why did John go to Leone's?
A2: Because John wanted to eat some lasagna.

Q3: How did John get to Leone's?
A3: John took a bus to New York and then he took the subway to Leone's.

Q4: Did anything unusual happen to John on the subway?
A4: A thief picked John's pocket.

Q5: Why did John have to wash dishes?
A5: Because John did not have any money.

Q6: Why didn't John have any money?
A6: Because a thief picked John's pocket.

Q7: How could John take a bus to New Haven?
A7: John probably had a return ticket.

Q8: What did John eat?
A8: John ate lasagna.

Q9: Did John leave the waiter a tip?
A9: No, John did not have any money.

The role of memory in language processing as we see it is to direct it, control it, and provide the solution for it; therefore, the solution to the problem of memory is the solution to the problem of language processing and possibly vice versa.

REFERENCES

Abelson, R. P. Concepts for representing mundane reality in plans. In D. Bobrow and A. Collins (Eds.), *Representation and understanding: Studies in cognitive science.* New York: Academic Press, 1975.
Chomsky, N. *Aspects of the theory of syntax.* Cambridge, Mass.: MIT Press, 1965.
Goldman, N. Conceptual generation. In R. C. Schank (Ed.), *Conceptual information processing.* Amsterdam: North-Holland, 1975.
Hemphill, L. The relationship of language and belief: With special emphasis on English "for" constructions. Unpublished doctoral thesis, Stanford University, Stanford, Calif., 1975.
Minsky, M. A framework for representing knowledge. In P. H. Winston (Ed.), *The psychology of computer vision.* New York: McGraw-Hill, 1975.
Rieger, C. Conceptual memory. In R. C. Schank (Ed.), *Conceptual information processing.* Amsterdam: North-Holland, 1975.
Riesbeck, C. Conceptual analysis. In R. C. Schank (Ed.), *Conceptual information processing.* Amsterdam: North-Holland, 1975.
Schank, R. C. Identification of conceptualizations underlying natural language. In R. C. Schank and K. M. Colby (Eds.), *Computer models of thought and language.* San Francisco: W. H. Freeman and Company, 1973.
Schank, R. C. (Ed.), *Conceptual information processing.* Amsterdam: North-Holland, 1975.
Schank, R. C., and Colby, K. M. (Eds.), *Computer models of thought and language.* San Francisco: W. H. Freeman and Company, 1973.
Schank, R. C., Goldman, N., Rieger, C., and Riesbeck, C. Inference and paraphrase by computer. *Journal of the Association for Computing Machinery,* 1975, 22 (no. 3), pp. 309–328.
Simmons, R. Semantic networks: Their computation and use for understanding English sentences. In R. C. Schank and K. M. Colby (Eds.), *Computer models of thought and language.* San Francisco: W. H. Freeman and Company, 1973.
Tulving, E. Episodic and semantic memory. In E. Tulving and W. Donaldson (Eds.), *Organization of memory.* New York: Academic Press, 1972.
Wilks, Y. An artificial intelligence approach to machine translation. In R. C. Schank and K. M. Colby (Eds.), *Computer models of thought and language.* San Francisco: W. H. Freeman and Company, 1973.
Winograd, T. *Understanding natural language.* New York: Academic Press, 1972.
Woods, W. Transition network grammars for natural language analysis. *Communications of the Association for Computing Machinery,* 1970, 13(10).

9

Constructive Processes and the Structure of Human Memory

Charles N. Cofer, Donna L. Chmielewski, and John P. Brockway

In this chapter, we present evidence concerning the knowledge that people have which is engaged by reading a short prose passage. As we consider this evidence, it should become clear that while a passage may activate a portion of a person's knowledge, the consequences of that activation will depend strongly upon what the individual sees his task to be. If the task is to reproduce the input, there will be one outcome, but if the task requires extensions beyond the input, the result will (or may) be different. One thing we wish to show is how the assigned task affects what one finds in a study involving memory. But we also wish to argue that the processes underlying *reproductive* and *productive* memory have a lot in common. However, even if we assume this commonality to be true, the fact that outcomes in a study of memory are to some extent task dependent causes us to question the utility of the concept of a static structure of memory, as proposed, for example, in chapters two and three of this book.

Preparation of this paper was supported by NSF Grant GB 30111 (first author), by Public Health Service Training Grant HD 00151 from the National Institute of Child Health and Human Development (second author), and by a Graduate Fellowship from the Graduate School, The Pennsylvania State University (third author).

We can develop the general problem with which we have been concerned in our research as follows. Two general findings have emerged from studies of immediate recall of prose. One is that people have fairly accurate recall for the substance of the material presented to them, but their ability to recall extends only so far. When a passage exceeds a certain length their recalls are incomplete, that is, they do not include all of the items contained in the original passage. This finding has been reported by Cofer (1941) and Gomulicki (1956) in the older literature, and it is corroborated in the recent reports of such investigators as Spencer (1973), B. Meyer (1974) and Kintsch (1974), to name only a few. The observed tendency for accurate but limited renditions of a passage in recall was so striking as to lead Gomulicki (1956) and Zangwill (1972) to construe recall as an abstract of the passage. B. Meyer (1974; see, also, B. Meyer and McConkie, 1973) and Kintsch (in his presentation in this book) among others, have had some success in differentiating the components of a passage that are recalled from those that are not. B. Meyer distinguishes the two types of components in terms of their location in the hierarchical structure of the passage; Kintsch distinguishes them in terms of the level on which a proposition functions in the text base.

The second general finding contrasts with the one just described, and this contrast provides the problem that has interested us. The finding is epitomized by Bartlett's (1932) observation that recall is seldom exact; rather, he said, it is constructed or reconstructed from a few remembered details combined with an impression left by the original. Recallers think the result is actually a reproduction of what they have retained, whereas, in fact, it has been built up from fragments. In the last several years, this *constructive* view of memory has received a great deal of support from a variety of research; the investigators who have reported this support include Bransford, Barclay and Franks (1972), Johnson, Bransford, and Solomon (1973), Bock and Brewer (1974), Pompi and Lachman (1967), Sulin and Dooling (1974), and Hewett (1974), to name only a few of the pertinent references.

In Chapter 5 of this volume, Kintsch provides a striking illustration of the contrast that interests us. He describes an experiment in which he gave subjects a passage to read about a familiar topic, such as the Biblical story of Joseph and his brothers. Immediate recall seems to have been accurate but with omissions; however recall occurring 24 hours after a reading was not accurate. The delayed recalls, Kintsch says, showed "an almost complete lack of differentiation . . . between the contents of the paragraph read a day ago and the subjects' general knowledge of the story."

The contrast between accurate recognition and accurate if incomplete recall, on the one hand, and highly inaccurate recall and inaccurate recognition, on the other hand, provides the problem with which we have concerned ourselves. This problem is complex. In our earlier publication (Brockway, Chmielewski, and Cofer, 1974), we outlined the various facets of the problem as we saw them. Among those facets is the knowledge that the subject possesses with which the passage he or she reads makes contact. That knowledge is presumably the source of the "inaccuracy" that occurs during the recall, and among the tasks we have set for ourselves is the description of that knowledge. Whether that knowledge enters into memorial performance in such a way as to make recall or recognition inaccurate is a function of numerous conditions about which we are slowly learning. The retention interval is one such condition, as already suggested by Kintsch's results with the Joseph story and by investigations such as those reported by Sachs (1967) and by Jarvella (1971). Indeed, one can argue that we can never really tell whether recall is reproductive or not; apparent replicas in recall of sentences of a passage may be constructed in the same way as those sentences that were not in the passage are constructed. Through recall experiments using the Bransford and Franks (1971) idea sets, Cofer (1973) and Griggs (1974) have shown that subjects produce two types of sentences during recall: exact replicas of the sentences that were presented, and original sentences that were not presented but are nevertheless members of the total idea sets. There is no way to tell from the data whether the recalled, presented sentences were reproduced or constructed. The difference between the processes that produce these sentences and the processes that produce the sentences appearing for the first time in recall may be only that the experimenter knows which ones were presented and which ones were not presented.

But let us turn to the problem of the subject's knowledge. In 1971 we collected data in the following way. We asked our subjects to read a short prose passage without telling them specifically what they would be asked to do after they had finished reading it. In fact, we asked them to do three tasks, and over the group of subjects participating in the experiment, we presented these tasks in every possible order. We asked for a *free recall* of the sentences, for the performance of a *recognition test,* and for *generated statements.* We hoped that in the last of these three tasks people would display for us at least some of the stored, general knowledge that was engaged by the passage. In the instructions for this generated-statements task, we asked each subject to produce from his or her memory of the passage 10 statements pertinent or germane to the passage. We said that the statements could be "logical extensions or conclusions, or ideas compatible with the paragraph, or associations of any type." However, we prohibited statements that were repetitions or close paraphrases of sentences contained in the passage.

We can make two general observations about the generated statements we analyzed. The first is that our subjects had no apparent difficulty in complying with our instructions. Most of them produced 10 statements and, as you will see later, most of these statements deviate from the wording of the passage while remaining within the general framework or schema of the passage. However, we obtained an occasional protocol in which some of the statements deviate so far from this framework that it is impossible to identify them as relevant to the framework (see Table 9.3). In the context of individual protocols, however, it is not difficult to determine the logic that produced such deviant statements from the passage content.

A second observation is that in the case of many of the statements, we think our subjects outdid Bartlett's subjects in deviating from the content of the passage (examples are provided again in Table 9.3). Perhaps most of the statements of our subjects reflect transformations of content that are somewhat less bizarre than those reported by Bartlett, but the passage we presented was not as strange as "The War of the Ghosts" passage that Bartlett used. Remember that our subjects were working from memory as they produced their generated statements. If we did not know the special instructions that preceded their productions, we might make sweeping generalizations about the inaccuracy of memory. Let us be clear: we think the statements indicate that people have a potential for generating highly inaccurate statements when responding to a passage which engages a rich lode in their particular store of knowledge. We might even say that an important question is why memorial performances are as accurate as they are, given the potential of prior knowledge to interact with a passage in such a way as to lead the reader "from anything to almost anything" (to use a phrase from Thomas Hobbes). The conditions which constrain recall performance so that it approximates input assume the utmost importance in this regard.

We now describe our data pool and some of the procedures we followed in analyzing that pool. We have so far concerned ourselves with only one of the two passages we used in collecting our data, and we have limited our analyses to samples of the generated statements and the recalls produced by our subjects. One subgroup of the original experiment, which produced generated statements as the first of their three tasks, provided 93 generated statements. For the sorting procedure to be discussed in a moment, we added to these 93 statements the 7 original passage sentences, making 100 sentences in all.

We also worked with 100 free-recalled sentences. Ninety-five of these were produced by the subgroups that performed the recall task as the first of their three assignments; of the five sentences that we added to make 100, three were from recalls produced by another subgroup and two were sentences from the passage that had not been recalled verbatim.

Our initial inspection of the generated statements indicated that, while they were diverse, they seemed to fall into clusters of thematically related items. Hence, we decided to have one new group of subjects sort the 100 generated statements into categories according to meaning and another new group sort the 100 free recalls similarly. Our subjects seemed to have no difficulty with this sorting task. We then applied a clustering procedure to the data obtained from each of these "sorts." As a result, the generated statements were divided into 11 clusters and the free recalls into 12 clusters. In the discussion that follows we describe the kinds of items contained in some of these clusters. But first, we present the short prose passage we used in our experiments; it is a descriptive paragraph about the Ekawas, written to contain an inference structure in accordance with the procedures described by Frase (1969). It contains 7 sentences and 58 words.

> The Ekawas are horsemen in Southwestern Ruganda. It is the custom in this country to be skilled in horsemanship. The horsemen are plainspeople. The plainspeople of Southwestern Ruganda are nomads. The grasslands provide excellent ground for hunting. The nomads of this area are warlike, which is reflected in their artwork. There are nine tribes in this area.

The first three sentences of the passage deal with horses or horsemanship. Four of the clusters of generated statements and four of the clusters of recalls seem to be concerned with these topics, and if one wished to make much of the hierarchical organization of the clusters occurring in recall or generated statements, each of these groups of four clusters would be bracketed together under a superordinate node. As examples of what our data are like, we will review one cluster of generated statements and one cluster of recalls, both of which refer to the same passage sentence, and a cluster of each type of statement in which no passage sentence is represented.

The first sentence of the passage, "The Ekawas are horsemen in Southwestern Ruganda," is included in both of the clusters shown in Table 9.1. It is fairly obvious that the recalled sentences deviate very little from the passage sentence itself. Yet only one of the recalled sentences shown is verbatim repetition of the passage sentence itself (other verbatim repetitions did occasionally occur). The high degree of accuracy in this case is unusual in our recall data, and it may arise from the fact that the passage sentence is short and has the advantage of primacy. (The last sentence of the passage also occurs verbatim in a number of recalls.)

The seven generated statements clustered with the first sentence from the passage are also shown in Table 9.1. It is obvious that these sentences deviate from the passage sentence with which they are clustered as well as from the corresponding recalls. Some of the generated statements represent a positive evaluation of the Ekawas' horsemanship, others integrate horsemanship with hunting, even though the passage mentions hunting grounds, not hunters. Horsemanship is said to be an art and an achievement looked up to in the society; it is a skill, whose mastery requires training beginning at an early age. It is clear that the processes involved in generating these statements are complex. (Later we will present in some detail our analysis of how people generate sentences; however, we did not use the statements in this cluster as the basis of our analysis.)

The next pair of clusters (shown in Table 9.2) does not include an exact replica of a sentence from the passage. In the case of the recalls the last sen-

Table 9.1 Clusters of Generated Statements and Sentences from Free Recall
That Refer to the Same Sentence of the Passage

Recalls	Generated Statements
1. The Ekawas are horsemen from the Southwest part of Ruganda.	9. Skill in hunting is mastered only after they (the Ekawas) have developed skill in horseback riding.
72. The Ekawas are horsemen in Southern Ruganda.	38. Children are taught to ride at young ages.
33. The Ekawas are horsemen from Northern Ruganda.	79. The Ekawas use horses to hunt.
90. The Ekawas are the horsemen of Ruganda.	°94. The Ekawas are horsemen in Southwestern Ruganda.
54. The Ekawas of Southwestern Ruganda are horsemen.	28. Excellent horsemanship is an achievement that is looked up to in this society.
42. The Ekawas are horsemen in Southwest Ruganda.	90. The men of Southwestern Ruganda are excellent horsemen.
49. Ekawas are horsemen in Southwestern Ruganda.	84. Each Ekawa child, especially the boys, is taught horsemanship.
85. The Ekawas are horsemen of Southwestern Ruganda.	91. Horsemanship is an art.
°13. The Ekawas are horsemen in Southwestern Ruganda.	
36. Ekawas are horsemen of Southwest Ruganda.	

°Passage Sentence No. 1.

tence (59) deletes the locative of the first passage sentence; the other four do one or both of two things: they integrate skill in horsemanship with the assertion that some people are horsemen, making the horsemanship excellent, and they tend to predicate horsemanship of a nominal (the Ruganda people, for example), which is a transformation of the locative or of the nominal plainspeople (which the passage has said the horsemen are). One could not say that these recalls are accurate. Yet they transform and relate concepts contained in the passage. As such, they do not deviate very far, if at all, from the overall gist (meaning) of the passage.

The cluster of generated statements shown in Table 9.2 may or may not be appropriately juxtaposed with the cluster of recalls. Neither cluster, it may be remembered, contains an exact replica of a passage sentence. However, the generated statements deviate from the passage to a much greater extent than do the recalls. These kinds of sentences, which include items not contained in the passage (American Indians, Afghanistans), seldom occur in

Table 9.2 Clusters of Generated Statements and Sentences from free Recall not Including an Exact Repetition of a Passage Sentence

Recalls	Generated Statements
12. The people of Ruganda are excellent horsemen.	29. Afghanistan also produces horsemen.
21. The Ruganda are excellent horsemen.	32. Many tribes of American Indians are also horsemen.
27. They (Ruganda people) are excellent horsemen.	37. Afghanistans take pride in their horsemen.
25. The plainspeople have to be excellent horsemen.	
59. The Ekawas are horsemen.	

recall. Further, when generated statements are rated according to how closely their meaning matches the meaning of the original passage (Brockway et al., 1974), these kinds of sentences received the lowest ratings, that is, ratings of most distant. (However, not all statements receiving this rating are of this kind.) We propose that this kind of generated statement arises from a generative operation called *listing*. It is as if the subject, remembering the concept of horsemen from the passage, consults his knowledge for other pertinent things he knows about the concept. In this case, American Indians and Afghanistans are produced. The subject may well have other information about horsemen, such as that there are jockeys who ride race horses or that there are horsemen who ride to hounds. Presumably, display of this information in generated statements is constrained by the general "primitivity" character of the passage. That Afghanistanis are said to take pride in their horsemanship reflects an interpretive process initiated in the passage through reference to the custom of being skilled horsemen.

Listing is one process of generation revealed in the data under review; we can see it in relation to other topics of the passage, such as nomads, in connection with which we have statements like "Nomads are found in many Middle Eastern Countries" and "Many tribes of American Indians were also nomads."

We now summarize and interpret our findings for recall. The recalls essentially restate the concepts and the relations of the passage. Although the number of sentences recalled verbatim is small, the recalls show little deviation from the passage. What usually occurs is either the partial representation of a passage sentence, the paraphrase or restatement in different words of a sentence or a part of a sentence from the passage, the combination of sentences or of parts of sentences, or the representation of set inclusionary relations, many of which are provided for in the structure of the passage but are not asserted there directly for the particular concepts involved (e.g., a sentence in recall like "The horsemen are warlike").

Processing that reduces original sentences by deletion, combines sentences or parts of sentences of the original, paraphrases sentences or parts of sentences, or provides set inclusionary relations not directly stated in the passage indicates that recall is not a passive activity. Nevertheless, the recalls do remain within the limits of the information contained in the passage itself; when they go beyond particular sentences, they integrate the concepts in two or more sentences, often through elaborating on the relation expressed by the verb in one of the sentences.

The recalls, then, go beyond the information in the passage when that information is rather strictly specified. However, they do not go very far beyond this strictly specified information, remaining in general within paraphrastic and combinatorial alterations of the passage content. The limits of content are so well respected in our recall data as to lead us to suggest that our recalls proceed largely from an immediate memory of the passage. By *immediate memory* we mean that relatively little processing of the input has occurred. Much of the passage content—its concepts, relations, and central theme—is immediately available. Nevertheless, the presence of paraphrases and combinations indicates that some processing does occur. Furthermore, some subjects may remember not only the gist of a passage but also its style. If a person remembers the concepts communicated in a text and how they are related as well as some stylistic features of the passage (like the fact that most of the sentences are simple, active, affirmative, and declarative in form), it would not be difficult for him or her to produce in recall a number of sentences which look as if they have been taken verbatim from the passage but which in fact have been constructed from knowledge of the gist of the passage in the same way as those recalled sentences whose structures deviate from the style and form of the input.

So much for recall. We now take a generated statement that we have found interesting and speculate as to how it might have been generated. The interaction of the passage with the subject's knowledge and with the operations he or she performs on that knowledge should be suggested by this example; however, the operations will not be specified very clearly.

The statement in question is, "The Ekawas do not live in a real dry area." There is little in the passage we presented that would directly forecast a statement like this one, and it stands alone among the other statements the subjects (a male) produced. Thus we can proceed without either the benefit or the disadvantage of knowing what context the subject had in mind in producing the statement. We can be entirely speculative.

In this analysis, we postulate a level of processing that integrates the concepts and relations of the passage with the knowledge the subject already possesses. At this level, in contrast to the listing of specific instantiations of a concept (a process of generation we have already discussed), the subject identifies *definitional characteristics of the concept*. For example, in producing the above statement, our subject may have had his concept of "plains" activated by the word *plainspeople* in the passage. This concept includes knowledge that the Great Plains of the United States are a subset of plains and also that the Great Plains have certain defining attributes (for example, according to the dictionary, they are semiarid and flat). If a subject's depth of processing is limited to listing, he or she can do no more than provide other instantiations, leading to the production of a statement like "Africa has plains, too." If, however, the subject goes beyond listing, the identification of defining attributes may provide extensive generative potential.

The generative potential of defining attributes is illustrated by the sentence in question. Let us assume that the subject has identified plains as a concept and has produced an instance, the Great Plains. He knows that the Great Plains have as one defining attribute their semiaridity. The subject could stop here and produce a version of this attribute as a generated statement, for example, he could say that "the Ekawas live in a dry area." Perhaps this sentence occurs to him (it did to other subjects) but before he produces it he remembers the information that the location mentioned in the passage is called a grasslands. His knowledge of this concept includes the requirement that for good grass there must be rainfall. This requirement conflicts with the previously activated attribute of dryness. The subject must resolve this conflict, and he does so by denying that the Ekawas live in a *real* dry area. To put this another way, since the content of the passage activates conflicting elements in the subject's knowledge (i.e., one of the attributes of plains conflicts with one of the conditions for the growth of grass), he must reduce the discrepancy by compromising the aridity of the plains.

The operations, or processes, that we think are involved in producing generated statements at the depth of processing illustrated by this example may be numerous. We are not yet sure just how many there are. However, we believe we can identify several operations. All of them are brought to bear on the knowledge engaged by a passage, and that knowledge includes all the presuppositions, assumptions, and conventions that are embedded in the concepts comprising the passage. Beyond listing, these operations are: drawing implications, presuming causality, and evaluation—both judgmental and affective.

Drawing implications in the form of set inclusion is provided for in many prose passages, so its appearance in recall and generation is not surprising. As to presuming causality, we think it allows for integration of knowledge with the concepts presented in a passage. Thus, the knowledge a subject has about nomads includes the definitional attribute that they are highly mobile, or are wanderers. The structure of the passage we used related the Ekawas to both nomads and horsemanship. If a subject's knowledge includes the fact that horsemanship involves the equestrian skill of horsemen and that by definition, horsemen ride and care for horses, the subject will construct a causal framework for the Ekawas' horsemanship through the knowledge he or she has of nomads. This operation produces the causal inference, "These people are good at horsemanship because that is their mode of transportation," a statement actually included in one of the horsemen clusters.

Evaluation entails judgments of or emotional reactions to the qualities and characteristics of people, actions, and the location of those people and those actions. Bartlett, of course, spoke of the affective and attitudinal aspects of the schemata he proposed. From our passage on the Ekawas, a subject could obtain an evaluative orientation through the sentence "The grasslands provide excellent grounds for hunting." The word *excellent*, let us say, primes the evaluative operations. A search of knowledge with regard to the concepts of "grasslands" and "grounds for hunting" is made, and information is retrieved both about the defining attributes of grasslands—they have much grass and are flat, and about the defining attribute of excellent hunting grounds—they contain abundant game. The combination of these judgmental evaluations (as distinct from affective evaluations) results in the statement, "The grass of the plains makes good food for animals," which is a generated statement. To produce this statement, the subject had to assume that if there is abundant game there must be abundant food, and, of course, for many animals grass is a prime food.

Affective evaluation may also occur; in fact, we think this type of evaluation caused one of our subjects to produce the generated statement, "The Ekawas are headhunters, why not?" We hypothesize that the subject had knowledge about African tribes who are or were headhunters. This knowledge produced, through listing, the major assertion of the statement, but headhunting may have been an emotionally charged concept for the subject. This affective evaluation rendered the generated assertion discrepant with the bland emotional tone of the paragraph and compelled the subject to judge his statement as emotionally inappropriate for the assigned task; as a result, he added the tag question, "Why not?"

Our analysis of generated statements in terms of the operations of drawing implications, presuming causality, and evaluation is highly speculative. One of the difficult problems in this line of research is to provide tests for these postulated operations. Another problem is to devise procedures that can reveal operations other than those displayed by our data on the Ekawas paragraph, which we compiled through the specific procedures outlined above. The ground here is largely uncharted, but we do have one investigation under way. Brockway has designed a procedure in which an investigator asks a subject to read one of several passages, with or without knowledge of what he or she will be asked to do. In either case, the investigator then asks the subject to provide a background for the paragraph, *or* to describe what follows from the paragraph. The purpose of these instructions is to get at the presuppositions, in the first case, or the causal consequences, in the second case, that the subject's knowledge will provide for the paragraph. This investigation is in its preliminary stages, but the evidence so far suggests that we do get different information as a function of these instructions. We think other, more specific, kinds of probes can be used to tell us about the various types of operations and their effects on the productions we obtain in this general experimental paradigm.

In conclusion, it seems to us that our data suggest the following notions. Immediate recall may not require much processing, although, as we have indicated, it is not easy to tell from a protocol whether an accurately stated sentence was reproduced or constructed. In any case, immediate recalls remain close to the content of the passage, perhaps as a consequence of an editorial function which monitors potential outputs against a fairly strict model of passage content and style.

It is interesting to observe that our "sorting" subjects had no difficulty with their assigned task: despite their lack of knowledge of the passage itself and despite the unsystematic order in which we provided them with the items, they were able, with considerable agreement, to sort generated statements into clusters that make good sense to us. We think they must have been able to provide contexts for the items that approximated but did not match the contexts in which the items were generated. These contexts of generation, (including even listing) probably require deeper processing than does immediate recall. Yet, if the views that we have advanced in this chapter have merit, we might predict that if a subject cannot retrieve from memory the specific content of a passage after, say, a substantial time interval, and if the subject is nevertheless willing to produce a substantial recall protocol, such a protocol might be indistinguishable in content from the protocols of the generated statements obtained in our experiment. It would be reasonable to say that if the knowledge accessed by a passage like the one on the Ekawas were worked upon by the kinds of operations we have suggested, such knowledge could underlie the production of an indefinitely large number of pertinent generated statements.

What do the data we have discussed indicate with respect to the structure of human memory? The answer to this question must remain uncertain, but a possible direction the search for that answer could take would be as follows. Fundamentally, the problem anyone faces in a task situation is to figure out what must be done to satisfy the demands of that situation. Our subjects in experiments calling for recall, generated statements, and sorting (not to mention recognition as described by Brockway et al., 1974) showed substantial adaptability to task demands, that is, they did what we asked and what they did varied as a function of what we asked. Perhaps the best way to show the variation is to display and analyze a recall and generated-statements protocol obtained from the same subject—a female (see Table 9.3).

Table 9.3   A generated-statements and a free-recall protocol from the same
subject°

Generated Statements	Free Recall
Horsemen are nomads.	The Ekawas are horsemen in Southwestern Ruganda.
Since this work is passed on, the people don't have a choice of the life they would like to live.	The horsemen who live in Southwestern Ruganda are nomads.
Maybe the passing on of a way of life makes them the warlike people they are.	The horsemen are plainspeople. The plainspeople are nomads.
These people may not be able to follow the ideas of life they might have.	The horseman trade is passed on through tradition. Nomads are warlike.
Forcing a person to do something they don't want to do can ruin their personality.	They are good hunters The horsemen do primitive artwork.
A ruined personality can hinder a person's way of associating with others.	
Associating with others is very important to the development of a person.	
The warlike actions of these people probably would not be done if they could think and do what they would like to do.	
People restricted in their actions aren't "real" people.	
A person must have a free will and should be given the chance to use his own free will in deciding his way of life.	

°For this subject, generated statements was the first and recall was the third of the three tasks required. A recognition test intervened.

We can see that although the recalls deviate from the passage, it is possible to find a relatively specific source in the passage for every recalled sentence. Even in the case of the fifth sentence, which is fairly deviant, one can see a possible origin in the second sentence of the passage. The last recalled sentence seems to be a summary evaluation of the people as primitive, which is probably supported by several aspects of the passage—horsemen, nomads, tribes, etc.

Reading from top to bottom of Table 9.3, the generated statements begin with an inference from the passage and move in chain-like fashion away from the passage to general concerns expressed almost as a theory of personality or as a theory of aggression (a theme set in the passage). There is little reason to doubt that our subject could have produced a set of generated statements like those shown in Tables 9.1 and 9.2. And, in fact, this subject's performances on the recognition test for the Ekawas passage and on all the tasks, including generated statements, for the other passage presented in our experiments were not at all unusual.

When a subject shows this kind of deviation from a more standard pattern, one must wonder whether the standard patterns are a consequence of memorial structure or whether, alternatively, they may be forced or prejudiced by our ordinary instructions, procedures, and tasks. One could contrive a structural view of memory by examining the two clusters of generated statements shown in Tables 9.1 and 9.2 (see also Chmielewski, Brockway, and Cofer, in preparation). But it is possible that these and other relatively coherent clusters arose only because we asked our subjects to produce statements *germane* to the passage. Perhaps it was this constraint that the subject of Table 9.3 violated. Had other subjects violated this constraint, we would have obtained clusters that looked very different from the ones presented in Tables 9.1 and 9.2 (cf. Jenkins, 1974).

The point of all this discussion is to warn against an irreversible decision opting for a conception of human memory that contains fixed structural arrangements. Knowledge may be arranged somewhere in our heads somewhat as it is in dictionaries, encyclopedias, and libraries (as come views imply), but the operations we perform on knowledge, in the light of the tasks we are asked to perform, suggest to us that those arrangements can be highly flexible.

REFERENCES

Bartlett, F. C. *Remembering.* Cambridge: Cambridge University Press, 1932.
Bock, J. K., and Brewer, W. F. Reconstructive recall in sentences with alternative surface structures. *Journal of Experimental Psychology,* 1974, *103,* 837–843.
Bransford, J. D., Barclay, J. R., and Franks, J. J. Sentence memory: A constructive versus interpretive approach. *Cognitive Psychology,* 1972, *3,* 193–208.
Bransford, J. D., and Franks, J. J. The abstraction of linguistic ideas. *Cognitive Psychology,* 1971, *2,* 331–350.
Brockway, J., Chmielewski, D., and Cofer, C. N. Remembering prose: Productivity and accuracy constraints in recognition memory. *Journal of Verbal Learning and Verbal Behavior,* 1974, *13,* 194–208.
Chmielewski, D., Brockway, J., and Cofer, C. N. Knowledge and memory (in preparation).
Cofer, C. N. A comparison of logical and verbatim learning of prose passages of different lengths. *American Journal of Psychology,* 1941, *54,* 1–20.
Cofer, C.N. Constructive processes in memory. *American Scientist,* 1973, *61,* 537–543.

Frase, L. Structural analysis of the knowledge that results from thinking about text. *Journal of Educational Psychology Monograph*, 1969, *60*(Suppl. No. 6).

Gomulicki, B. R. Recall as an abstractive process. *Acta Psychologica*, 1956, *12*, 77–94.

Griggs, R. A. The recall of linguistic ideas. *Journal of Experimental Psychology*, 1974, *103*, 807–809.

Hewett, T. T. The role of presuppositions in creating and understanding sentences. Unpublished doctoral dissertation, University of Illinois, Urbana-Champaign, 1974.

Jarvella, R. J. Syntactic processing of connected speech. *Journal of Verbal Learning and Verbal Behavior*, 1971, *10*, 409–416.

Jenkins, J. J. Remember that old theory of memory? Well, forget it! *American Psychologist*, 1974, *29*, 785–795.

Johnson, M. K., Bransford, J., and Solomon, S. Memory for tacit implications of sentences. *Journal of Experimental Psychology*, 1973, *98*, 203–205.

Kintsch, W. *The representation of meaning in memory*. Hillsdale, N.J.: Erlbaum, 1974.

Meyer, B. J. F. *The organization of prose and its effect on recall*. Research Report No. 1, Reading and Learning Series, Ithaca, N.Y.: Department of Education, Cornell University, 1974.

Meyer, B. J. F., and McConkie, G. W. What is recalled after hearing a passage? *Journal of Educational Psychology*, 1973, *65*, 109–117.

Pompi, K. F., and Lachman, R. Surrogate processes in the short-term retention of connected discourse. *Journal of Experimental Psychology*, 1967, *75*, 143–150.

Sachs, J. S. Recognition memory for syntactic and semantic aspects of connected discourse. *Perception and Psychophysics*, 1967, *2*, 437–442.

Spencer, N. J. *Changes in representation and memory of prose*. Unpublished doctoral dissertation, The Pennsylvania State University, 1973.

Sulin, R. A., and Dooling, D. J. Intrusion of a thematic idea in retention of prose. *Journal of Experimental Psychology*, 1974, *103*, 255–262.

Zangwill, O. L. Remembering revisited. *Quarterly Journal of Experimental Psychology*, 1972, *24*, 123–138.

Postscript

This book contains the papers presented at a symposium on *The Structure of Human Memory*, held under the joint sponsorship of the Section on Psychology (J) and the Section on Information and Communication (T) on January 29, 1975 at the Annual Meeting of the American Association for the Advancement of Science. The papers as published here have been revised by their authors since their oral presentation at the symposium.

In 1962, Arthur W. Melton, then the retiring chairman of the Section on Psychology, arranged a symposium on *Short-term Memory*, and, in 1967, Leo Postman, also as retiring chairman, organized one on *The Interference Theory of Forgetting*. As retiring chairman, it seemed to me to be appropriate that I also arrange a symposium on some aspect of memory, and the result is shown in this book. In each of the preceding symposia new developments in the study of memory were brought forward. The present book indicates that changes in the study of memory continue at a rapid rate, perhaps exponentially.

In arranging this symposium, I consulted with my successor as chairman of Section J, Richard C. Atkinson, about topics and speakers. We established the list of persons to be invited, and all but three of them were willing and able to participate. Dr. Atkinson was to serve as discussant of the symposium, but he found that he would not be able to do so shortly before the symposium took place. I then prepared a paper for presentation in order to fill out the program.

The first chapter of this book was not presented at the symposium. I prepared it as an introduction in order to place the remaining chapters in the context of the study of memory and to indicate at least some of the interrelations among the chapters. However, my introductory summaries of the other contributions to this volume are no substitute for the full contributions.

C. N. C.

Index of Names

Topical Index